The Definitive Refe
on Fifties *EASY-POP* Music

Remembering 1950s *EASY-POP* Songs and Singers

One hundred quintessential singers,
five hundred classic songs, and
fifty all-but-forgotten, should-have-been-hits

by Daniel Niemeyer, Ph.D.

December 31, 2008

FIFTIES BOOK PUBLISHERS

Published in the United States of America
by Fifties Book Publishers
1390 Oak Court, Boulder, Colorado 80304

www.50sMusic.com

Library of Congress Control Number

ISBN# 978-0-615-25245-2

Manufactured in the United States of America

Big Band music dominated the first half
of the twentieth century...

Rock 'n' Roll ruled the second half...

but between the two there was the decade of
fun and infectious EASY-POP music and captivating vocalists

For my family
Rita, Jerry, Stacy, Robert, Teri, Daniel, and Emily

Neither popular music, nor we, will ever be the same because of Top 40, 1950s music at 45 rpm.

James F. Harris in *Philosophy at 33 $^1/_3$ rpm* (1993)

Contents

List of Charts

Like pop music itself, this book is not intended as a work of art, but at the very least it should prove helpful in settling arguments that often arise in pop circles...and at the same time I sincerely hope it will do what pop music itself sets out to do—entertain.

Ken Barnes, introduction to his book *Twenty Years of Pop* (1973)

Preface

I have been a great fan of popular music as long as I can remember. I was eleven-years-old and living with my parents and sister in Breese, Illinois, when the decade of the fifties began. When I was very young, I would enjoy listening to the wind-up Victrola at my grandmother's home in Carlyle, Illinois. I grew up listening to the radio and pretending that I was a disc jockey spinning platters.

I remember listening to 78s at home and I'll never forget how badly I felt the first time I broke a section out of a record. For me, the new, less expensive, 45s were great and I can still picture my first RCA automatic record changing player. I could listen to the same records over and over. Often when my mother would go shopping in Saint Louis, she would bring home a 45 for me.

As a teenager, I remember going by myself to the department stores in Saint Louis, where, at the time, the clerks would permit you to choose a record for possible purchase and let you take it into a small cubicle where you could listen to it before you decided to purchase it. Having little money, I would listen to many records and purchase very few. It was not unusual for one of the clerks to display limited patience for a teenager without a charge-a-plate.

In high school we would ride around in the car for hours listening to popular music on the radio, when we would take a break at the Hi-Way Café, we would listen to popular music on their jukebox. In college the walls of my room were decorated with the album covers of my favorite girl singers.

I never quite left the music of the fifties. When my wife and I had children, we traded-in the convertible for a coupe and I didn't hear fifties music as often. But when my sons were a little older, possibly to recapture the feelings of my teenage years, we purchased a new 1983 Ford Mustang convertible. The car was outfitted with a cassette tape player and it just seemed right to play 50s music while riding with the top down. It still does.

In the spring of 2004, with the purchase of a new laptop computer and the construction of a new outdoor deck, I began putting down on paper some of the ideas for this book. Four years later this final draft was completed on Doris Day's birthday, April 3, 2008.

I still believe in the future of love songs. After all, nobody has yet written a hit song about hate.

Richard Rodgers, quoted in *ASCAP Toda,y* (March 1971)

Acknowledgements

I owe a huge debt of gratitude to Rita Berndsen Niemeyer, who made time to listen to innumerable songs from the fifties—many titles more than once—and she doesn't share my obsessive fascination with every one of them. She was willing to help me think through dozens of issues and questions throughout the four-year ordeal of eight revisions.

I am also grateful to Stacy Gardner Niemeyer who reviewed the manuscript for clarity and consistency, offered valuable perspective, and added and subtracted dozens of commas while helping edit the book.

To my sister, Diane Kay Niemeyer, for listening to these songs with me during the last fifty years, I am truly appreciative.

Perhaps, more than anyone, my classmates and friends at St. Dominic's Grade School and Breese High School provided the inspiration for this book. They created my memories of the 1950s and they shared my enthusiasm for fifties *EASY-POP* songs and singers.

I also owe thanks to the helpful staff at the Boulder Public Library in Boulder, Colorado, the Breese Municipal Library in Breese, Illinois, the Coe Library at the University of Wyoming in Laramie, and the Music Library at the University of Colorado at Boulder.

x

Popular music has not received much notice from sociologists, who spend more time assessing the impact of television, despite the fact that many people from the ages of ten to twenty-five are more heavily exposed to radio and records. For many people in this age group, popular music provides a sense of change...that enriches feelings, extends the sense of love or despair, and feeds fantasies or fires some real relationship.

Charlie Gillett in *The Sound of the City* (1970)

Chapter 1

EASY-POP: Between Big Band and Hard Rock

Music historians divide the twentieth century into two eras: the big band craze that dominated the first half of the century and rock 'n' roll that ruled the last half, with the transition in the fifties. In 1950, Guy Lombardo's *Third Man Theme* was the last big band recording to become a number-one-seller and in 1954, the Crew-Cuts' *Sh-Boom*, often cited as the first rock 'n' roll record, rose to #1 on the charts. But in that narrow window between big band and rock there was the carefree musical decade of easy-to-listen-to singers, infectious arrangements, and sing-along lyrics. It was the decade of 50s EASY-POP.

The big band sound is easy to recognize with its melodic reed sound and lush orchestrations featuring trombone, saxophone, cornet, clarinet, and trumpet. It is also easy to detect rock 'n' roll with its strident, pulsating emphasis on guitar, keyboard, bass, and drums. The transitional EASY-POP music has defining elements too: the singer is enthusiastic; the lyrics are youthful and idealistic; there is a melody you can hum; and the beat is finger snapping. This lively concinnity of elements creates the memorable sound of quintessential 50s EASY-POP. Bing Crosby may have initiated it in the early 1940s and Frank Sinatra certainly advanced it in the late 1940s, but in the fifties it flourished.

1

Popular Music in the first half of the 20th Century – The Big Band Era

World famous orchestra leaders, swing music, and dance bands will always be associated with the first half of the twentieth century (see chart 1.1). Big bands crisscrossed the country playing one-night stands in hundreds of ballrooms coast-to-coast. Dance marathons, the jitterbug, and bebop were all the rage. The recording industry, with 78rpm recordings of swing bands, saw sales soar in the thirties. Commercial radio broadcasts began transmitting news, drama, and comedy programs in 1922 and in the thirties and forties listeners were introduced to live radio broadcasts from dance ballrooms all across the nation. Audiences heard the orchestras play the new swing music and the big band sound took the country by storm.

The first great radio singer was Rudy Vallee. He brought a gracious sex appeal into pop music with his wavy and plaintive voice. By the 1930s he was a national institution. Kate Smith, the 'Song Bird of the South,' joined him as the first great queen of the airways. While Rudy Vallee could convey the gentleman lover, Smith was the comfy mother. She was a down-to-earth, homey, football loving, all-American. Her voice seemed honest and, even though she was singing to 60 million people, she conveyed to her listener that she was singing only to one.

The end of the 1940s began a transition in popular music. The demand for sheet music was collapsing. Creamy big band music and the swing sounds of Sammy Kaye, Glenn Miller, Benny Goodman, and Tommy Dorsey passed their peak. The big band vocalists, Tex Beneke, Bob Eberly, and Helen O'Connell were no longer as popular and the songwriters, George Gershwin, Irving Berlin, and Cole Porter were aging. The recording industry changed popular music too, dictating that songs be only three minutes long, and introducing records to a younger public anxious to purchase. The fall of the big bands, the rise of the solo singer, the sales of records, and the developing teen frenzy, revolutionized popular music as the halfway point of the century approached.

Popular Big Bands of the 1920s, 1930s, and 1940s

Les Brown & his Orchestra   1939-1953
(Featured Vocalists included: Doris Day)
Sentimental Journey; Day by Day; I've Got My Love to Keep Me Warm

Jimmy Dorsey & his Orchestra   1935-1950
(Featured Vocalists included: Bob Eberly, Helen O'Connell, and Kitty Kallen)
Is It True What They Say about Dixie; Amapola; Green Eyes; Tangerine

Tommy Dorsey & his Orchestra   1935-1949
(Featured Vocalists included: Frank Sinatra)
Marie; I'll Never Smile Again; Boogie Woogie; Music, Maestro, Please

Duke Ellington & his Orchestra   1927-1953
Mood Indigo; It Don't Mean a Thing (If It Ain't Got That Swing); Take the 'A' Train

Benny Goodman & his Orchestra   1931-1950
(Vocalists included: Helen Forrest, Peggy Lee, Martha Tilton, Helen Ward, and Eve Young)
And the Angels Sing; Darn That Dream; Jersey Bounce; Sing, Sing, Sing

Harry James & his Orchestra   1938-1953
(Featured Vocalists included: Helen Forrest, Dick Haymes, and Frank Sinatra)
I've Heard that Song Before; All or Nothing at All; I'll Get By

Sammy Kaye & his Orchestra   1937-1952
(Featured Vocalists included: Don Cornell, Billy Williams, and the Three Kaydets)
Rosalie; Love Walked In; Chickery Chick; The Old Lamplighter

Kay Kyser & his Orchestra   1935-1948
(Featured Vocalists included: Harry Babbitt and Ginny Simms)
Jingle, Jangle, Jingle; Praise the Lord, Pass the Ammunition; Ole Buttermilk Sky

Guy Lombardo & his Royal Canadians   1927-1950
Charmaine; Goodnight, Sweetheart; Stars Fell on Alabama; Easter Parade

Glenn Miller & his Orchestra   1935-1944
(Featured Vocalists included: Tex Beneke, Ray Eberle, Marion Hutton, and the Modernaires)
In the Mood; Blueberry Hill; Chattanooga Choo Choo; Kalamazoo

Fred Waring's Pennsylvanians   1923-1944
Little White Lies; I Found a Million-Dollar Baby (in a Five-&-Ten-Cent Store)

Ted Weems & his Orchestra   1922-1947
(Featured Vocalists included: Perry Como)
Somebody Stole My Gal; Peg O' My Heart; I Wonder Who's Kissing Her Now

Paul Whiteman & his Orchestra   1920-1943
(Featured Vocalists included: Bing Crosby and Jack Fulton)
Three O'clock in the Morning; Linger Awhile; Whispering; My Blue Heaven

Chart 1.1.   Popular Big Bands, Years on the Charts, and Hit Songs

Setting the Stage for the Solo Singer

The solo singer gained popularity in the forties. Bandleaders competed with one another by featuring their increasingly famous singers. The strategy backfired and the featured soloists gradually replaced the band-leaders themselves. While Glenn Miller's reputation always exceeded that of his singer Tex Beneke, Frank Sinatra began to attract more attention than his bandleaders Tommy Dorsey and Harry James.

Martha Tilton, Peggy Lee, and Helen Ward rose to stardom as featured vocalists with the 'King of Swing' Benny Goodman. Bob Eberly and Helen O'Connell were featured with the Jimmy Dorsey orchestra and created hit records including *Green Eyes, Amapola, Tangerine, Maria Elena*, and *Yours*. As the fifties approached, the vocalists began their rise to fame (see chart 1.2).

Perry Como, featured singer with Ted Weems' Orchestra, following in Frank Sinatra's footsteps, struck out on his own to become the most popular singer in the fifties. (Schicke, 1974, p.113) Doris Day began as a featured singer with Les Brown's Orchestra and Dinah Shore first sang with Xavier Cugat and his band.

All of these vocalists were influenced by the creator of the modern ballad style, Bing Crosby, a light tenor with vocal warmth and gentle humor. To be heard above the orchestra, he learned the technique of singing with a megaphone that formed the basis of the 'crooning' style. (Gillett, 1970, p.11)

Radio Moves from Live Programming to Recorded Music

Radio stations in the 1940s sustained high listener ratings and huge advertising revenue by broadcasting popular live network shows but in the middle of the century, television replaced radio as the source for live entertainment. By the 1950s, the live dramatic programs, the morning soap operas, and the hugely popular radio comedies were moving to television. The mercurial rise of television prompted major sponsors to divert their advertising dollars from radio to television. It was not long before all of the network shows, even those featuring Bob Hope, Bing Crosby, Jack Benny, and George Burns and Gracie Allen disappeared from radio.

Popular Vocalists during the 1940s

Andrews Sisters *Boogie Woogie Bugle Boy; (I'll Be With You) In Apple Blossom Time; Pennsylvania Polka; Rum and Coca-Cola*

Harry Babbitt *Who Wouldn't Love You; Jingle, Jangle, Jingle*

Tex Beneke *Chattanooga Choo Choo* w/Modernaires and Paula Kelly; *Don't Sit Under the Apple Tree (With Anyone Else But Me)* w/Modernaires and Marion Hutton

Buddy Clark *Linda; Peg O' My Heart; Love Somebody* w/ Doris Day

Perry Como *Till the End of Time; Prisoner of Love; Surrender; Chi-Baba, Chi-Baba, 'A' You're Adorable* w/ Fontane Sisters; *Some Enchanted Evening*

Bing Crosby *White Christmas; Moonlight Becomes You; Sunday, Monday, or Always; Swinging on a Star; Now is the Hour*

Doris Day *Sentimental Journey; Love Somebody* w/Buddy Clark; *It's Magic*

Ray Eberle *Imagination; Fools Rush In; Blueberry Hill*

Bob Eberly & Helen O'Connell *Amaopla; Green Eyes; Tangerine*

Helen Forrest *I've Heard That Song Before; Time Waits for No One; Long Ago (and Far Away)* w/Dick Haymes

Dick Haymes *It Can't Be Wrong; You'll Never Know; Laura; Little White Lies; The Old Master Painter*

Ink Spots *Into Each Life Some Rain Must Fall; Gypsy; To Each His Own*

Peggy Lee *It's A Good Day; Manana (Is Soon Enough for Me)*

Johnny Mercer *Ac-cent-chu-ate the Positive; Candy* w/Jo Stafford & the Pied Pipers; *On the Atchison, Topeka and the Santa Fe*

Merry Macs *Mairzy Doats; Praise the Lord and Pass the Ammunition*

Mills Brothers *Paper Doll; You Always Hurt the One You Love; Glow-Worm*

Vaughn Monroe *There! I've Said It Again; Ballerina; Riders in the Sky*

Dinah Shore *I'll Walk Alone; The Gypsy; Buttons and Bows; Dear Hearts and Gentle People*

Frank Sinatra *All or Nothing At All; Oh! What It Seemed To Be; Five Minutes More; Mam'selle; Let's Take An Old-Fashioned Walk* w/Doris Day

Chart 1.2.   Popular Vocalists of the 1940s and some of their Hit Songs

Deprived of national network programming, individual radio stations had neither the expertise nor the financing to produce their own programs. This predicament led radio broadcasters to turn to a new, and even more lucrative, source of program material—recorded music—and audiences couldn't get enough. In the 1950s virtually every radio station in the country began devoting most of its broadcast day to recorded music. (Schicke, 1974, p.13) The development of the transistor made radios smaller and batteries made them portable so that the young music-buying public could take their radios and their music with them. At the same time car radios mushroomed. The coincidence of technology and timing provided just the avenue that the singers needed to reach larger audiences and national fame.

Popular Music in the middle of the 20th Century – 50s EASY-POP

Singers that are easy to like and songs that are easy to sing-along-with characterize 50s EASY-POP music. The sounds of the fifties are inter-twined with the images of the song stylists—the unforgettable 'girl singers': Doris Day and Patti Page; and the even more popular 'guy singers': Nat King Cole, Perry Como, Eddie Fisher, and Frank Sinatra.

The popular recording artists of the fifties comprise a widely varied group. Pop music researcher Joel Whitburn developed a point system for ranking the popularity of recording artists:
> (1) Each artist's records are awarded points based on their highest po-sition on Billboard magazine's weekly Top 100 Pop Singles Chart; (2) bonus points are awarded to each record based on its highest charted position; (3) the total weeks that the record is on the top 100 chart are added in; and (4) the total weeks an artist held the #1 position are added. (Whitburn, 1986, p.624)

The twelve most popular recording artists of the 1950's, based on Whit-burn's point system, are identified in chart 1.3.

For singers in the fifties, style was as important as music in the effective-ness and success of a song. Frank Sinatra, in many ways, set the stan-dards for popular music in the fifties. British musicologist Charlie Gillett calls his style 'involved.' Frank Sinatra often improvised his own timing of phrases by stretching some syllables and cutting others. The effect was a personal style involving the audience in his singing—and in him

Most Popular* Recording Artists of the Fifties 1950-59
and a partial list of their biggest fifties hit songs

#1.   Perry Como   7392 points*   pop recording career: 1943 - 1974
Don't Let the Stars Get in Your Eyes; Wanted; Round and Round; Magic Moments; Catch a Falling Star; Hot Diggity (Dog Ziggity Boom)

#2.   Nat King Cole   6365 points*   pop recording career: 1943 - 1964
Mona Lisa; Too Young; (I Love You) For Sentimental Reasons; Nature Boy; Answer Me My Love; The Christmas Song; Ballerina; Non Dimenticar

#3.   Patti Page   6024 points*   pop recording career: 1948 - 1981
The Tennessee Waltz; The Doggie in the Window; I Went to Your Wedding; Changing Partners; With My Eyes Wide Open I'm Dreaming; Old Cape Cod

#4.   Frank Sinatra   5031 points*   pop recording career: 1942 - 1994
Five Minutes More; Young at Heart; Saturday Night (is the Loneliest Night of the Week); Love and Marriage; Chicago; Hey! Jealous Lover; All the Way

#5.   Elvis Presley   4331 points*   pop recording career: 1956 - 1977
Heartbreak Hotel; Don't Be Cruel; Hound Dog; Love Me Tender; Loving You; Too Much; All Shook Up; Teddy Bear; It's Now or Never

#6.   Eddie Fisher   4225 points*   pop recording career: 1950 - 1967
Any Time; Wish You Were Here; I'm Walking Behind You; I Need You Now; Turn Back the Hands of Time; Dungaree Doll; Cindy, Oh Cindy

#7.   Frankie Laine   4208 points*   pop recording career: 1947 - 1997
Jezebel; Rose, Rose, I Love You; Jealousy; Sugarbush; High Noon (Do Not Forsake Me); The Kid's Last Fight; Moonlight Gambler

#8.   Pat Boone   4114 points*   pop recording career: 1955 - 1966
Ain't That a Shame; Long Tall Sally; Friendly Persuasion (Thee I Love); Don't Forbid Me; Love Letters in the Sand; April Love

#9.   Jo Stafford   3397 points*   pop recording career: 1944 - 1957
Jambalaya; You Belong to Me; No Other Love; Shrimp Boats (is a Commin')

#10.   Bing Crosby   3380 points*   pop recording career: 1931 - 1976
In the Cool, Cool, Cool of the Evening; White Christmas; True Love

#11.   Kay Starr   2797 points*   pop recording career: 1948 - 1975
Hoop-Dee-Doo; Bonaparte's Retreat; Wheel of Fortune; Half a Photograph; If You Love Me (Really Love Me); Rock and Roll Waltz

#12.   Doris Day   2636 points*   pop recording career: 1947 - 1967
A Guy is a Guy; When I Fall In Love; Mister Tap Toe; Secret Love; If I Give My Heart to You; Everybody Loves a Lover; Que Sera, Sera (Whatever Will Be, Will Be)

*Ranking and points determined by Joel Whitburn Record Research

Chart 1.3.   Most Popular Singers of the 50s and some of their Hit Songs

—as no previous singer had done. It stimulated devotion comparable to that previously aroused only by film stars. The audience willingly confused Sinatra's image with his private self, amplifying the character promoted by the singer's public relations staff and the press. (Gillett, 1970, p.12)

Television

Two television programs had a huge impact on popular music in the fifties—'Your Hit Parade,' that reflected musical tastes and 'American Bandstand,' that shaped them. During the first half of the decade the television series 'Your Hit Parade' aired every Saturday night with a stable of singers performing the most popular seven songs of the week. 'American Bandstand' began as a local program in Philadelphia in 1952. Squeaky-clean Dick Clark, then a disc jockey on a Philadelphia radio station, took over as host in 1956. The ninety-minute show, telecast every weekday afternoon from the studios of WFIL-TV in Philadelphia, helped form popular music tastes. In addition to these two series, many popular singers had hit television programs in the fifties. Dinah Shore, Eddie Fisher, Nat King Cole, Patti Page, and Perry Como were major television stars. For a complete list of popular singers and fifties television programs see charts 7.3, 7.4, 7.5, 7.6, and 7.7 in Chapter 7.

45rpm Records & Hi-Fi

The fifties marked the beginning of teenage dominance in record buying. The smaller, lighter, and cheaper 45rpm records represented a significant technological advance over the large, fragile 78rpm records of the early part of the century and the sale of 45s soared. By 1954, the improved sound technology of high-fidelity was so pervasive that it became difficult to sell records not clearly labeled 'high fidelity.' The record player was called a 'hi-fi' just as earlier generations called any kind of playback machine a Victrola. In addition, the hi-fi was easy to operate. Teenagers could take the self-contained units and their collection of 45s anywhere—to a sockhop or a sleep-over—at anytime. This was casual music and a format made for bobby-sox and bluejeans. Since producing hit songs and distributing 45rpm records became the financial driving force for the recording industry, these three-minute 'singles' contained the kinds of musical compositions that characterized the hits of the 1950s—short, foot-tapping songs that could fit on a 45 and secure AM radio play time. For a complete historical look at the evolution of the 45rpm record see chapter 10.

The Juke Box

The nickelodeon re-appeared in the mid twentieth century as a stream-lined super entertainer with a jivey moniker. Taking its name from the slang expression for southern joints frequented by blacks, the Juke Box provided another avenue for teens to listen to recorded music. It attracted a young audience who loved to spend a 'jukebox Saturday night' loafing at the corner drugstore sipping at a soda, while other guys fed coins into the machine. (Whitcomb, 1972, p.101)

The Radio DJ

In the 1950s, the announcers who played records on the radio began to be called 'disc jockeys' or 'deejays'. The DJ would select the best, or at least the most commercial, of the current record releases for the audi-ence. If fans liked what they heard they would set their radio dial to their favorite DJ and chances are they would buy some of the records they heard. So the DJ was, in effect, something of a shop window for the record industry. As a result, record promoters were constantly pressuring popular DJs to include their songs on a radio station's playlist. Suddenly the DJs became kingmakers in the eyes of music publishers. Gifts given to DJs for promoting songs became known in the business as 'payola.' This type of bribery was never as rampant as it was in the mid-fifties. For a complete examination of the 'payola' issue see chapter 11.

The Music Business: Recording Companies

The music publishing fraternity quickly realized that the record business had acquired new economic influence. Not only did the record compa-nies control the music on records, they also provided the music pro-grammed on radio. Six major recording companies dominated the popular music market in the middle of the century. Of the one hundred and sixty three records that sold over a million copies from 1946 to 1952 all but five were recorded by one of the six major companies. (Gillett, 1970, p.14)

The most successful recording company was Columbia Records with Tony Bennett, Rosemary Clooney, Doris Day, Frankie Laine, Johnny Mathis, Guy Mitchell, Johnnie Ray, and Jo Stafford chasing each other up the charts. The other record pioneer, RCA Victor, had contracts with the Ames Brothers, Perry Como, Eddie Fisher, Eartha Kitt, Jaye P. Morgan, Elvis Presley, Kay Starr, and June Valli. Decca Records, established in England in the 1930s, snagged Bing Crosby, the Four Aces and the Mills Brothers. Hollywood-based Capitol's classy galaxy of vocalists included Nat King Cole, Judy Garland, Dean Martin, and Frank Sinatra, while MGM had Tommy Edwards and Joni James. Chicago's Mercury Records had big hits with the Crew-Cuts, Patti Page, and Sarah Vaughan. For a complete list of record companies and their recording vocalists see chart 11.1 in chapter 11.

All of these popular singers were contractually obligated to be adaptable and record any song their recording company selected for them. The sounds, styles, and arrangements for 50s songs were usually created by record producers. The successful producer, or 'artist and repertoire' man decided what songs to record, who should record them, and how each song was to be treated. The A&R man at the recording company was a powerful force in creating the fifties musical sound.

Popular Music in the last half of the 20th Century – The Rock Era

The middle of the 20th century witnessed the birth of rock-and-roll music. In 1952, Cleveland disc jockey Alan Freed coined the term rock 'n' roll for his radio program. In 1955, the seminal rock 'n' roll hit song, *Rock Around the Clock,* recorded by Bill Haley and his Comets, was featured in the dramatic movie 'Blackboard Jungle.' The film was set in an urban high school and the song became an anthem for edgy teenagers. Interestingly the lyrics for *Rock Around the Clock* were written by sixty-three-year-old Max Freedman whose previous songs included *Sioux City Sue, Liebestraum,* and the *Blue Danube Waltz.* (Whitcomb, 1972, p.225)

While there is a popular belief that rock 'n' roll records dominated the music popularity charts in the fifties, in fact there was not one rock 'n' roll song in the top ten records of the decade. Chart 1.4 describes the top ten hits between 1950 and 1959.

Top Ten Hit Records of the 1950s

Computed by calculating the length of time that each recording stayed in
Billboard Magazine's Top Ten list between 1950 and 1959 (Whitcomb, 1974, p.212)

1. ***Mack the Knife***   Bobby Darin   1959
    Written in 1929 for the German play 'The Threepenny Opera'

2. ***Vaya Con Dios***   Les Paul & Mary Ford   1953
    Multi-track guitar and vocal recording of *May God be with You*

3. ***Because of You***   Tony Bennett   1951
    Published in 1940 and first recorded by Larry Clinton in 1941

4. ***Unchained Melody***   Al Hibbler   1955
    Oscar-nominated song from the obscure 1955 prison film 'Unchained'

5. ***Melody of Love***   Billy Vaughn   1955
    Instrumental hit originally composed in 1903 by Hans Engelmann

6. ***You, You, You***   the Ames Brothers   1953
    Last #1 hit record from this popular singing quartet

7. ***Battle of New Orleans***   Johnny Horton   1959
    Original melody was written to celebrate the last battle of 1812 War

8. ***Singin' the Blues***   Guy Mitchell   1956
    Country song that became a cross-over hit on the popular charts

9. ***Love Me Tender***   Elvis Presley   1956
    Civil War song that was originally called *Aura Lee*

10. ***Love Letters in the Sand***   Pat Boone   1957
    Recorded by Ted Black in 1931, based on 1881 song *The Spanish Cavalier*

Chart 1.4. Most Popular Songs 1950-1959, Artist, and Background

In many respects, the sounds of rock 'n' roll contradicted those of 50s
EASY-POP. The vocal style was harsh, the songs were explicit, and the
dominant instruments—guitar, bass, saxophone, keyboard, and drums—
were played loudly and with an emphatic dance rhythm. (Gillett, 1970, p.19)

Musicologist Peter Gammond calls rock 'n' roll an amalgam of white
American country music, boogie-woogie, and black rhythm 'n' blues
that became the trademark of popular music in the 1960s and thereafter.
(Gammond, 1991, p.495) The driving beat was a fundamental attraction—often
the overriding element. The hard driving tempo and the pulsating rhythm
provided the obvious sexual tension that gave it its appeal. (Harris, 1993, p.2)

According to rock music analyst James Harris, rock 'n' roll used the twelve-bar phrase structure of black rhythm and blues (4 + 4 + 2 + 2) with the very simple chord progressions of blues music (simple, three-chord melodies). There is no development of the chords towards a big ending for the song as was characteristic of Tin Pan Alley. The same three chords are repeated over and over again. And, most importantly, the rhythm of rock 'n' roll accented the second and fourth beats, the off beats—pa-BOOM! pa-BOOM! This gave rock 'n' roll its pulsating beat and made it impossible for young people to sit still while listening to it. And the tempo was fast—much faster than anything typical of earlier Tin Pan Alley songs. The repetition of the same three chords, the emphasis on the off-beat, and the fast tempo provided early rock 'n' roll music with its sense of urgency and energy. (Harris, 1993, p.3)

Rock 'n' roll traces its roots to the early fifties, and in a sense even further back than that to early black rhythm and blues. Elvis Presley, the King of Rock 'n' Roll, first recorded for Sun records in 1954 and signed with RCA Victor records in 1955. His recordings and television appearances were phenomenally successful. His unprecedented style, his swiveling hips, his sensual demeanor, and his rhythm-and-blues sound took the musical world by storm. His contemporaries, Fats Domino, Buddy Holly, Jerry Lee Lewis, Little Richard, and Ricky Nelson all began recording rock 'n' roll hits as the decade ended.

Along with Elvis Presley, Ray Charles, Chubby Checker, Roy Orbison, and Del Shannon continued recording rock 'n' roll hits into the 60s. Then came the British invasion of the Beatles. The tidal wave of 'Beatlemania' engulfed the world when the Liverpool, mop-haired quartet appeared on stage. By the end of 1963, the Beatles were legendary figures and forced the world market wide-open for British artists and writers including the Animals, the Dave Clark Five, and the Rolling Stones. Chart 1.5 lists popular and influential rock 'n' roll performers during the second half of the twentieth century.

In addition to Big Band, EASY-POP and Rock 'n' Roll, the twentieth century included jazz, folk, and country; thirty years of doo wop; the Motown sound; a decade of disco; as well as rap, hip-hop, heavy metal, alternative, blues, funk, reggae, honky tonk, bluegrass, salsa, R&B, and ever-enduring classical music.

Popular Rock Artists of the 1950s and 1960s

Elvis Presley ('King of Rock & Roll')　　　　　　　　1956 - 1977
Heartbreak Hotel; All Shook Up; Jailhouse Rock; Can't Help Falling in Love; Return to Sender; In the Ghetto; Suspicious Minds

Rolling Stones (London all-time great rock and roll band)　　1964 -
(I Can't Get No) Satisfaction; Ruby Tuesday; Honky Tonk Women; Angie; Miss You; Start Me Up

Beatles (Liverpool, England #1 rock group)　　　　　1962 - 1970
I Want to Hold Your Hand; Can't Buy Me Love; A Hard Day's Night; We Can Work It Out; Penny Lane; All You Need is Love; Hey Jude; Let It Be

The Grateful Dead (Legendary San Francisco rock group)　　1965 -
Dark Star; Casey Jones; Touch of Grey; West L.A. Fadeaway; Black Muddy River

Popular Rock Artists of the 1970s and 1980s

AC/DC (Australia hard-rock group)　　　　　　　　1978 -
You Shook Me All Night Long; For Those About to Rock; Back in Black; Money Talks

Fleetwood Mac (English pop-rock group)　　　　　　1970 -
Dreams; Don't Stop; You Make Loving Fun; Tusk; Sara; Hold Me; Big Love; Little Lies

Jefferson Airplane/Starship (San Francisco pop-rock group)　1967 - 1992
Somebody to Love; White Rabbit; Miracles; We Built This City; Sara; Nothing's Gonna Stop Us Now

Led Zeppelin (English hard-rock group)　　　　　　1969 - 1979
Whole Lotta Love; Immigrant Song; Black Dog; Stairway to Heaven

Queen (English pop-rock group)　　　　　　　　　1975 - 1991
Bohemian Rhapsody; We Will Rock You/We Are the Champions; Crazy Little Thing Called Love; Another One Bites the Dust

Bob Seger (Michigan rock singer/songwriter)　　　　1970 -
Night Moves; Still the Same; Fire Lake; Against the Wind; Shame on the Moon; Shakedown

Van Halen (California hard-rock group)　　　　　　1978 -
Jump; Why Can't This Be Love; When It's Love; I'll Wait; Panama; Finish What Ya Started

Popular Rock Artists of the 1980s and 1990s

Bon Jovi (Sayreville, New Jersey rock group)　　　　1984 -
You Give Love a Bad Name; Livin' On a Prayer; Bad Medicine; Blaze of Glory; I'll Be There for You

Genesis (English pop rock group)　　　　　　　　1977 -
Invisible Touch; Tonight, Tonight, Tonight; In Too Deep; I Can't Dance

REO Speedwagon (Champaign, Illinois rock group)　　1980 - 1988
Keep on Loving You; Take It On the Run; Can't Fight This Feeling

U-2 (Irish rock group)　　　　　　　　　　　　1983 -
With or Without You; I Still Haven't Found What I'm Looking For; Desire; Pride (In the Name of Love); Where the Streets Have No Name, Discotheque

Chart 1.5.　Popular Rock Artists, Years on the Charts, and Hit Songs

New Recording Formats

Along with musical styles, technology was changing. Hi-fi records had scarcely reached their peak when stereo records were introduced in 1958. By the sixties the record player was called a 'Stereo' instead of the, oh-so-fifties, 'Hi-Fi.' Quadraphonic 4-track and 8-track audio tape players seemed ready to become a standard in the 1970s, but instead cassette tapes proved more adaptable and less expensive. Abruptly, in the 1980s, digital technology and Compact Discs (CDs) were introduced and by the end of the century, the CDs had eclipsed them all. For a complete historical look at the evolution of recording formats see chapter 10.

The 50s Transition between Big Band and Rock

The middle of the twentieth century was a transitional period in history. The first half of the century was plagued by World War I (1914–1918) and World War II (1939–1944). The end of the Korean Conflict (1950–1953) marked a transitional period in American history before Viet Nam (1965–1973) shook the last half of the century. Transitional periods in history produce inclusive times. 50s EASY-POP incorporated big band ingredients and introduced seminal elements for rock 'n' roll. There is not always consensus on exactly what defines the sound of 50s EASY-POP music and chapter 2 investigates that question.

References from Chapter 1:

Gammond, Peter. *The Oxford Companion to Popular Music*. New York: Oxford University Press, 1991.

Gillett, Charlie. *The Sound of the City – The Rise of Rock 'n' Roll*. New York: Dell Publishing, 1970.

Harris, James F. *Philosophy at 33 $^1/_3$ rpm – Themes of Classic Rock Music*. Chicago: Open Court Publishing, 1993.

Schicke, C.A., *Revolution in Sound – A Biography of the Recording Industry*. Boston: Little, Brown and Company, 1974.

Whitburn, Joel. *Billboard Book of Top 40 Hits*. 7th Edition. NY: Billboard Books, 2000.

Whitburn, Joel. *Top Pop Singles 1955-1986*. New York: Billboard Books, 1987.

Whitcomb, Ian. *After the Ball*. London: Allen Lane the Penguin Press, 1972.

Beauty of style and harmony and grace and good rhythm depend on simplicity.

Plato

Chapter 2

What is a Fifties EASY-POP Song?

The cultural impact of rock 'n' roll was so dramatic that it completely eclipsed the under-appreciated EASY-POP music of the fifties. Appearing as early as 1948 and still being recorded late into the century, quintessential EASY-POP recordings peaked in the nineteen-fifties. But during this single decade there was an astonishing variety of sparkling singers, infectious arrangements, and catchy lyrics that produced recordings much more innovative than the sum of their parts.

No single recording typifies the decade. To capture the gist of the 50s EASY-POP genre you need to synthesize the unique sound by listening to a selection of quintessential recordings. Twenty-five archetypical songs and singers that epitomize the fifties are identified in chart 2.1.

The concinnity of singers, arrangements, and lyrics create a memorable sound—quintessential 50s EASY-POP. The harmonious relationship between vocalist and lyric is epitomized in the recording of *Tenderly*. Jack Lawrence and Walter Gross provide the memorable lyric, "I can't forget how two hearts met breathlessly" and Rosemary Clooney, with her husky delivery, conveys a perfect earthiness in the word 'breathlessly.'

Archetypical EASY-POP Songs and Singers of the Fifties

| *Mona Lisa* | Nat King Cole | 1950 |

There were 6 top-twenty versions of this Academy Award winning song, but popular, expressive vocalist Nat King Cole with Nelson Riddle's arrangement had the #1 hit record.

| *My Heart Cries For You* | Dinah Shore | 1950 |

Guy Mitchell, Vic Damone, and Dinah Shore all had top-five hits with *My Heart Cries For You,* one of dozens of country-flavored EASY-POP hits like Tony Bennett's *Cold, Cold Heart*, Patti Page's *Detour* and *Tennessee Waltz*, Joni James' *Your Cheatin' Heart*, Sonny James' *Young Love*, and Guy Mitchell's *Heartaches by the Number*.

| *My Truly, Truly Fair* | Guy Mitchell | 1951 |

This early fifties recording features an infectious melody, a buoyant Mitch Miller arrangement, and a spirited, likable singer. It exemplifies the popular male baritones including Frankie Laine, Don Cherry, Steve Lawrence, and Don Cornell.

| *Mockin' Bird Hill* | Les Paul & Mary Ford | 1951 |

One of a dozen multi-layered top-ten hits for guitarist Les Paul and vocalist Mary Ford.

| *I Went to Your Wedding* | Patti Page | 1952 |

Patti Page released this seminal, plaintive lost-love song and it begat her 1953 *Changing Partners*, June Valli's *Crying in the Chapel*, Teresa Brewer's *A Tear Fell*, Caterina Valente's *The Breeze and I*, Toni Arden's *Padre*, and Joan Weber's *Let Me Go Lover*.

| *Don't Let the Stars Get in Your Eyes* | Perry Como | 1952 |

Dozens of these exhilarating, bouncy hits including his *Catch a Falling Star, Tina Marie*, and *Hot Diggity* were recorded by the decade's most popular singer.

| *That's Amore* | Dean Martin | 1953 |

This fifties classic is one of scores of popular Italian songs from singers like Al Martino, Tony Martin, Jerry Vale, Vic Damone, Julius LaRosa, and the Gaylords.

| *Ricochet* | Teresa Brewer | 1953 |

A typical, fast-paced recording with an offbeat lyric. Arrangements were often tailored for the unusual vocal-styles of unique talents like Teresa Brewer, Jaye P. Morgan, Pearl Bailey, Gale Storm, Della Reese, Julie London, and Eartha Kitt.

| *Rags to Riches* | Tony Bennett | 1953 |

With a swinging vocal treatment, Tony Bennett epitomizes the unique phrasing, voicing, and intonation also personified by Frank Sinatra, Andy Williams, and Bing Crosby.

| *Have You Heard* | Joni James | 1953 |

Winsome female singers like Joni James, Connie Francis, Cathy Carr, Debbie Reynolds, and Karen Chandler reflected the feelings of fifties teenage girls.

| *I Need You Now* | Eddie Fisher | 1954 |

Flamboyant bobby sox idols, like Eddie Fisher who had 21 hits in a row, belted out powerful ballads in young, zesty, big-voiced, bravura styles.

| *Little Things Mean a Lot* | Kitty Kallen | 1954 |

Kitty Kallen had a #1 hit with this memorable fifties ballad. Joni James reprised it in 1959.

Chart 2.1. Archetypical EASY-POP Songs and Singers of the Fifties

(Chart continues on the next page)

Archetypical EASY-POP Songs and Singers of the Fifties (continued)

This Ole House   Rosemary Clooney   1954
50s novelty songs also included her *Come-On-A-My House*, Patti Page's *Doggie in the Window*, Perry Como's *Delaware*, and the Ames Brothers' *Naughty Lady of Shady Lane*.

The Man Upstairs   Kay Starr   1954
One of many gospel-flavored hits like Patti Page's *Cross Over the Bridge*, Laurie London's *He's Got the Whole World*, and Pat Boone's *Wonderful Time Up There*.

Sincerely   McGuire Sisters   1955
Like the Andrews Sisters, the prototypical sister group, the McGuire sisters had a string of hits: *Sugartime*, *Muskrat Ramble*, *Something's Gotta Give*, and *May You Always*.

Learnin' the Blues   Frank Sinatra   1955
One of a dozen classy Frank Sinatra hits, this lightly, bluesy song is in the same vain as Dinah Shore's *Blues in Advance*, and Ella Mae Morse's *Blacksmith Blues*.

No, Not Much   Four Lads   1956
This is a typical, stylish, catchy, easy-to-sing-along-with classic fifties hit. Quartet harmony was also heard in recordings from the Four Aces, the Four Preps, the Four Coins, the Crew-Cuts, and the Ames Brothers.

Wayward Wind   Gogi Grant   1956
This haunting, philosophical 50s lyrical ballad was a beguiling anthem for the restless.

(Let Me Be Your) Teddy Bear   Elvis Presley   1957
Elvis Presley, Ricky Nelson, Buddy Holly, and other rock idols, scored with mainstream EASY-POP songs in addition to their rock 'n' roll hits.

Chances Are   Johnny Mathis   1957
Johnny Mathis typifies the skillful, silky, gentle, and tender side of the fifties sound.

Lollipop   Chordettes   1958
The penultimate girl group, the Chordettes, had a #1 hit with *Mr. Sandman* in 1954 and then recorded this classic 'lolly lolly lollypop' hit. The Fontane Sisters had a similar 'do do wah, do do wah' hit with *Hearts of Stone*.

Oh! Oh! I'm Falling in Love Again   Jimmie Rodgers   1958
Jimmie Rodgers, along with the Weavers and the Everly Brothers embody a folk touch in several fifties songs while Harry Belafonte brought calypso to the scene.

26 Miles (Santa Catalina)   Four Preps   1958
The youthful image of summertime fun on the beach was captured by the Four Preps in *26 Miles*, by Jerry Kellor in *Here Comes Summer*, and by the Jamies in *Summertime*.

Everybody Loves a Lover   Doris Day   1958
This recording utilizes the double-track voice overdub technique frequently heard in the 50s. Doris Day, Jo Stafford, Patti Page, Dinah Shore, Margaret Whiting, Peggy Lee, Sarah Vaughan, Georgia Gibbs, and others recorded these lively, upbeat, girlish hits.

Dream Lover   Bobby Darin   1959
Bobby Darin, Paul Anka, Pat Boone, Sam Cooke, and Frankie Avalon were pop idols late in the decade.

Chart 2.1. Archetypical EASY-POP Songs and Singers of the Fifties

In *I Went to Your Wedding*, Jessie Mae Robinson wrote "You came down the aisle, wearing a smile, a vision of loveliness" and Patti Page's slight Oklahoma accent was delightful for the word 'loveliness' in this perfect marriage of vocalist and lyric. Nat King Cole's smoky delivery in his recording of Ray Evans and Jack Livingston's *Mona Lisa* was remarkable—combined with Les Baxter conducting Nelson Riddle's lush arrangement—it is unforgettable. The McGuire Sisters bring their perfect harmony to the words *Sincerely oh yes Sincerely* in their extraordinary recording of the hit song written by Harvey Fuqua and rock 'n' roll disc jockey Allen Freed. And who can imagine a more ideal choice to record *That's Amore* than handsome, Italian singer Dean Martin.

While fifties EASY-POP recordings encompass a wide variety of influences—swing, country, show tunes, rhythm & blues, jazz, gospel, folk, calypso, ragtime, and international sounds—they are recognized in four ways: (1) the singer is the preeminent element of the recording; (2) the infectious musical accompaniment supports the vocalist, often using unusual instruments, back-up singers, and unique recording tricks; (3) the catchy lyrics reflect a youthful idealistic view of love and the world; and (4) there is a melody you can hum—set to a finger-snapping beat.

In the early fifties mass media was truly mainstream popular entertainment. Most markets in the United States were served by only three television networks. Radio programs were designed to appeal to general audiences and EASY-POP songs crossed many musical landscapes. Hit song *Hoop-Dee-Doo* was a polka, *Que Sera* was a lullaby, *Banana Boat* was a calypso song, and *Conquest* was a samba. Radio stations had not yet splintered into narrowcasting to segment adult rock, alternative, urban, Christian, and jazz audiences. Adults and teens listened to the same recordings, the singers appealed to urban and rural audiences, and the hit songs were popular with a wide variety of ethnic groups.

A geographic supermarket of songs was evident in 50s EASY-POP. From Paris came Eartha Kitt's 1953 hit *C'est Si Bon*, from Hawaii came Margaret Whiting's *Now is the Hour*, and from Israel came the Weavers' 1950 hit *Tzena, Tzena, Tzena*. *Skokiaan* was a South African song named for a Zulu tribal drink. Domenico Modugno's *Nel Blu Dipinto di Blu (Volare)* is decidedly Italian. Georgia Gibb's #1 hit *Kiss of Fire* was adapted from the Argentine tango *El Choclo*. (Whitcomb, 1972, p.205) Jimmie Rodgers' *Waltzing Matilda* was Australian and Vic Damone's *April in Portugal* was a Portuguese East African song originally titled *Coimbra*.

Often considered a restrictive decade, the 1950s actually welcomed all forms of popular music—much more so, in fact, than the rockin' decade to follow. Rather than isolate certain musical styles as 'out of the mainstream,' the decade of the 50s seemed open to anything—including the zither featured in *The Third Man Theme*! The pop standards of the fifties evolved from the musical styles of the big bands that preceded them and foreshadowed the tempo of the up-and-coming rock 'n' roll sounds.

The Sparkling Singers

In the early part of the twentieth century, a hit song was associated with the orchestra and the bandleader who made it popular. In the fifties hit songs were associated with the singers who recorded them—the attractive girl singers—Teresa Brewer, Rosemary Clooney, Doris Day, Joni James, Patti Page, Della Reese, Dinah Shore, Jo Stafford, Kay Starr, Sarah Vaughan—the handsome crooners—Paul Anka, Tony Bennett, Pat Boone, Nat King Cole, Perry Como, Vic Damone, Bobby Darin, Tommy Edwards, Eddie Fisher, Frankie Laine, Dean Martin, Al Martino, Johnny Mathis, Guy Mitchell, Johnnie Ray, Frank Sinatra—and the harmonizing groups—the Ames Brothers, the Chordettes, the Everly Brothers, the Fontane Sisters, the Four Aces, the Four Lads, the Four Preps and the McGuire Sisters. The women had natural, clear delivery and beautiful smiles while the men had good looks and confident, hearty voices. (Brief biographies of female singers are presented in chapter 4, male singers in chapter 5, and groups in chapter 6).

Popular recording artists in the fifties were extraordinarily versatile and expected to embrace many types of material. Perry Como's hits ranged from the polka duet *Hoop-Dee-Do* with the Fontane Sisters, to the novelty *Hot Diggity (Dog Ziggity, Boom),* to a moving rendition of composer Richard Rogers' *No Other Love* from the World War II documentary 'Victory at Sea.' Rosemary Clooney scored with the novelty Italian *Botch-A-Me* and the very melodic and breathy *Tenderly.* Eddie Fisher had huge hits with the traditional *Lady of Spain,* the Swiss *Oh My Pa-pa,* and Broadway's rousing *(You Gotta Have) Heart.* Patti Page went from the old fashioned *Tennessee Waltz,* to the exciting flamenco *Conquest,* to the pseudo-gospel *Cross Over the Bridge,* to the country *Detour,* to the classic novelty *Doggie in the Window* (arf, arf), even to the pulsing *All My Love* based on Ravel's *Bolero.* Tony Bennett recorded the swinging *Rags to Riches* and the more classical *Stranger in Paradise* based on music from the *Polovtsian Dances* originally composed by 19th century Russian, Aleksandr Borodin. Doris Day's hits included the plaintive *Secret Love*, the unforgettable lullaby *Que Sera, Sera (Whatever Will Be, Will Be)*, and the novelty song *Choo Choo Train (Ch-Ch-Foo)* adapted from the popular French song *Le Petit Train*.

The asexual nature of the lyrics meant that songs could be, and often were, recorded by several male and female singers as well as trios and quartets. *Hold Me, Thrill Me, Kiss Me* was a hit for Karen Chandler and later for Mel Carter. *There Goes My Heart* was recorded by both Joni James and by Nat King Cole. *Am I That Easy To Forget* was recorded by Debbie Reynolds and by Engelbert Humperdinck.

The vocalists took pride in enunciation and breath control. The lyrics in fifties songs were always clear and easy to understand. The carefree performers portrayed a sanguine lifestyle—youthful, open, and inclusive. The singer's voices were tied to their personalities and it became increasingly important that the performers themselves were personable, casual, and attractive. The style of their singing was fun and effortless with the words flowing from the singer—unlike later rock music where the singing seemed exceedingly difficult and the lyric needed to be expelled as gutturally as possible.

Some pop singers remained exclusively with EASY-POP music, lyrics, and arrangements while others incorporated guitar and drum elements of rock into their recordings. Peggy King's *Learnin' to Love,* Johnnie Ray's *Yes Tonight Josephine*, Gale Storm's *I Hear You Knocking*, Don Cornell's *Teenage Meeting*, and Jaye P. Morgan's *Pepperhot Baby* can certainly be considered lightly rock 'n' roll. At the same time, new teen idols like Elvis Presley, Buddy Holly, and Ricky Nelson recorded EASY-POP songs in addition to their trademark rock 'n' roll material.

Elvis Presley, the personification of rock 'n' roll, actually had several mainstream 50s EASY-POP hits: *Love Me Tender, (Let Me Be Your) Teddy Bear, It's Now or Never*, and *Loving You.* Buddy Holly's 50s EASY-POP song *Everyday* featured Norman Petty on the celeste. Ricky Nelson's music frequently crossed between 50s EASY-POP, rockabilly, and rock 'n' roll: *A Teenager's Romance, Be-Bop Baby, Poor Little Fool, Lonesome Town*, and *Never Be Anyone Else But You*.

Usually 50s songs were happy, but lost love could cause winsome Joni James to lament *Why Don't You Believe Me* and melodramatic Frankie Laine to be a saddened *Moonlight Gambler*. But these were the exceptions. Light, peppy, and cheerful were the typical approaches to singing. Voices ranged from pure to vibrato-laden. Vibrato is that quivering, rapid variation in pitch, that is apparent in the voice of Whitney Houston, exaggerated in Kathryn Grayson, steady in Al Hibbler, very natural in Judy Garland, and subtle in Frank Sinatra. Doris Day displays a tightly spinning vibrato, while Jo Stafford's clear voice is almost vibrato-less.

The Infectious Arrangements

Often a 50s EASY-POP recording can be identified in the first instant as the musical arrangement establishes a unique sound and sets the stage for the singer. Recordings had to contain a 'hook' to catch the listener's ear and stand out from the very first groove. The arrangements often included an unexpected fillip—a finger snap, a slight prod, or a stinging stimulant. There were no introductory verses, as there had been in big band compositions, nor lengthy instrumental introductions. The beat was established and the lyric refrain began in the first few seconds.

In the fifties, the A&R man was often the creative force of a recording company. The title 'Director of Popular Artists and Repertory' indicated a job that was as important as it sounded. They decided what songs artists would record and they demanded creative orchestral accompaniments. The A&R men were producing records for their own sake and this was new. In the past, bands and singers reproduced in the studio what they'd been performing nightly at public appearances. For the first time, musical compositions were created not as live performance pieces but as records for a radio audience with an unprecedented appetite for variety. Musical arrangers were in charge and they created sounds that were different, exciting, and fresh (see chart 2.2).

The prominence of the vocalist did require innovative accompaniment that provided essential support for the singer. A swing band, a jump trio, or a full-blown orchestra backed nearly every recording artist. Doris Day's musical arrangements often included 8 brass players, 5 woodwinds, 10 strings, a rhythm section, and 8 background singers.

There was never a recording decade with more variety in musical accompaniment than the fifties. Maybe the instrumental diversity was driven by the restrictions of the three-minute 45rpm record format, the demands of the audience around the new jukeboxes, or a response to the constantly quickened tempo. But whatever the reason, there was an unprecedented assortment of sounds.

EASY-POP Music Arrangers of the 1950*s*

Ray Anthony
This strong, direct arranger was successful at keeping the big band sound alive in the fifties and scored with television themes from *Dragnet* and *Peter Gunn.*

Les Baxter
At Capitol Records he arranged the music for Nat King Cole's biggest hits *Mona Lisa* and *Too Young.* With his own orchestra he recorded dozens of instrumental LPs, movie themes, and hit singles including *The High and the Mighty, Ruby, The Poor People of Paris,* and *Unchained Melody.*

David Carroll
This arranger and conductor for the Crew-Cuts and Vic Damone at Mercury Records had his own instrumental hits with *Melody of Love, In a Little Spanish Town, It's Almost Tomorrow,* and *The Ship That Never Sailed.*

Don Costa
ABC Paramount Records had this popular arranger work with Paul Anka, Frankie Avalon, Steve Lawrence, and Eydie Gorme.

Frank DeVol
This conductor/arranger at Capitol and Columbia Records brought a distinctive touch to string-laden balladry and a frisky playfulness to his arrangements for Tony Bennett and Doris Day.

Percy Faith
As the arranger at Columbia Records he was responsible for Tony Bennett's *Rags to Riches* and *Stranger in Paradise* as well as his own recordings of *Moulin Rouge (Where is Your Heart)* and *Theme for A Summer Place.*

Gordon Jenkins
As staff conductor at Decca he composed his 'Manhattan Tower' suite and at Capitol he created his signature repeated descending minor-second arrangements for Louis Armstrong, Peggy Lee, Nat King Cole, and Frank Sinatra.

Stan Kenton
This arranger was one of the first to include strings in his arrangements—blurring the definition line between a band and an orchestra. In 1951, he recorded the title song from the 1945 film *Laura.*

Ralph Marterie
A native of Italy and an arranger at Mercury Records, with his orchestra he recorded hits *Caravan* and *Skokiaan.*

Billy May
He was the composer, arranger, and conductor at Capitol for Peggy Lee.

Chart 2.2. Music Arrangers of the 1950s and some of their Hit Songs
(Chart continues on the next page)

EASY-POP Music Arrangers of the 1950s

(continued)

Mitch Miller

Originality was this arranger's hallmark at Columbia Records backing Guy Mitchell and Doris Day. He had a penchant for offbeat material and diverse musical textures. He opened the field to out-of-the-norm instrumentation and orchestration. In 1955, he recorded his own hit single *Yellow Rose of Texas* with his 'Sing along with Mitch' choral group.

Robert Mersey

This arranger at Columbia Records worked with Andy Williams' *Can't Get Used to Losing You, Hopeless*, and *Almost There*.

Jack Pleis

At Coral Records he was the conductor for Karen Chandler's *Hold Me, Thrill Me, Kiss Me* and then at Decca for Toni Fisher's *The Big Hurt*. He composed and recorded the theme from the movie blockbuster 'Giant.'

Joe Reisman

In the early fifties, he was the arranger at Mercury Records for Patty Page's *Conquest* and *You Belong to Me* and later at RCA Victor Records for Perry Como's *Catch a Falling Star* and *Magic Moments*.

Henri Rene

At RCA Records he arranged Eartha Kitt's *C'est Si Bon* and *Santa Baby*.

Nelson Riddle

This popular orchestra leader at Capitol Records collaborated on the original Frank Sinatra 'concept' albums and he created classic arrangements for Ella Fitzgerald, Judy Garland, Rosemary Clooney, and Dinah Shore.

Billy Vaughn

As musical director for Dot Records he oversaw 'cover' recordings by Pat Boone and Gale Storm and his own 1954 violin-laden hit version of *Melody of Love*.

Paul Westin

His sensitive arrangements at Capitol and Columbia lent eloquent support to several female singers including Doris Day, Ella Fitzgerald, Rosemary Clooney, Margaret Whiting, as well as his wife, Jo Stafford.

Hugo Winterhalter

As the musical director and arranger at RCA Records, he brought instrumental flourishes to the recordings of Eddie Fisher and the Ames Brothers.

Chart 2.2. Music Arrangers of the 1950s and some of their Hit Songs

Columbia records was the most successful EASY-POP recording company, thanks in part to its 'Artists and Repertoire' chief Mitch Miller and an important part of his magic was the musical accompaniment— unusual combinations of refreshing sounds that opened up the field to out-of-the-norm instrumentation and orchestrations. He put a harpsichord with Rosemary Clooney on *Come On-A My House*, whiplashes on Frankie Laine's *Mule Train*, and he backed Guy Mitchell with French horns. On Johnny Ray's recordings of *Cry, Please Mr. Sun* and *The Little White Cloud That Cried* he added a singing group, the then unknown Four Lads, to provide vocal background. (Whitcomb, 1972, p.215)

Background singers are another recognizable element in fifties recordings. The familiar "doo doo wah, doo doo wah," "ba ba ba bum," and "la la la" appeared in dozens of recordings. In Doris Day's *Anyway the Wind Blows* the chorus provided "by up up up ah" and it was the background singers that provided the distinctive "ka kunk ka chew" that opens Jane Morgan's recording of *With Open Arms* and chant "mush" in Johnny Horton's *North to Alaska*. Sometimes these 'background singers' provided critical lyric elements. In the recording of *I Dreamed,* the background singers, not the primary vocalist Betty Johnson, sang the phrase 'knights in armor, princes, kings, buccaneers and wedding rings.' In the Margaret Whiting/ Jimmy Wakely duet *A Bushel and a Peck* it was the chorus in the background who sang the phrase 'a thousand chickens goin' to the dickens.'

The unusual arrangements and unique musical instruments were full of surprises and delights. There were snare drums in Patti Page's *Left, Right, Out of Your Heart*; bongo drums in the Four Lads' *Only One of You*; a celeste in Buddy Holly's *Everyday*; a concertina in the polka *Hoop-Dee-Doo*; an organ in Doris Day's *Love Me in the Daytime*; a harp in Joni James' *Among My Souvenirs;* and castanets in Patti Page's *All My Love.*

A&R directors often found rich material in country and western songs that were close to the melodramatic or sentimental modes of conventional popular songs. Country songs were recorded by popular singers in a style that was halfway between country and pop. As pure C&W the songs might not get noticed, but when Columbia's Mitch Miller got Tony Bennett to do *Cold, Cold Heart*, Jo Stafford to do *Jambalaya* and Rosemary Clooney to do *This Ole House* the results were hit records.

In a controversial move, A&R directors, like Billy Vaughn at Dot Records, had their stable of media-friendly vocalists release versions of songs that were 'covers' of original recordings by less well-known performers. This technique used established singers to produce more socially acceptable 'covers' of early rhythm 'n' blues or rock 'n' roll songs. The reconstituted arrangements often incorporated lots of violins (and no drums) to soften the beat. The Crew-Cuts hit pay dirt with their cover recording of the Chord's *Sh-Boom* in 1954 and again with their cover of the Penguin's *Earth Angel* in 1955. Pat Boone had hit recordings with his covers of Little Richard's *Tutti-Frutti* and *Long Tall Sally* in 1956. For a complete examination of 'cover' recordings see chapter 11.

The Catchy Lyrics

A fifties EASY-POP song was usually lilting and playful with an adolescent teen idealism—not intended to be a realistic depiction of the way the listeners were but an optimistic vision of the way they wanted to be. The lyrics were always easy-to-sing-along-with and incorporated catchy phrases, unique meters, and unexpected rhymes. While the songs were neither erudite nor deep, they were often clever and inventive narrative poems consisting of simple stanzas and a recurrent refrain. According to historian James Harris "50s POP is important music, but it is not serious music. The lyrics were simple, straightforward, and upbeat, not cynical like many of the songs near the end of the twentieth century." (Harris, 1993, p.8)

The lyrics in 50s EASY-POP songs capture and validate natural, youthful feelings and sentiments—they say that feelings are important and that they are OK. The songs are personal and intimate, often about emotions, dating, affection, and first love. They support the belief that love can last forever and that being in love is being happy. But the love described in these lyrics is heartfelt, idealistic love, not physical sex—it reflects the clean and simple, optimistic outlook portrayed in 50s EASY-POP music:

> Every treasure that Tony Bennett is hopin' for is in the open arms of his girl friend (from *Rags to Riches* written by Richard Adler and Jerry Ross).

> As she waits by the river, Jane Morgan's life does not begin until her fisherman/boyfriend returns (from *With Open Arms* written by Hal David and Burt Bacharach).

> Doris Day claims that 'when she gives her heart, it will be forever' (from *When I Fall in Love,* written by Victor Young and Edward Heyman).

The universal 'first love' experience was a frequent source of material for pop song lyricists. Finding love and falling in love were the most popular themes for 50s POP recordings:

Teens were promised that their first love would be filled with true devotion and deep emotion (from *Young Love*, recorded by Sonny James and then covered by Tab Hunter, written by Carole Joyner & Ric Cartey).

In *Oh, Oh, I'm Falling in Love Again,* Jimmie Rodgers couldn't run from love even if he wanted to (from *Oh, Oh, I'm Falling in Love Again*, written by Al Hoffman & Dick Manning).

One of the most consistent themes of POP music in the fifties—the belief that love would last forever—was continuously reinforced. Listeners knew that everlasting love and a happy marriage was in their future:

Patti Page waited all her life to give him all her love (from *All My Love*, music by Ravel, adapted by Paul Durand, lyric by Mitchell Parish).

Dean Martin acknowledged 'one man, one wife, one love through life' (from: *Memories are Made of This*, written by Burt Bacharach & Hal David).

The Teddy Bears' life was made worthwhile just seeing him smile (from *To Know, Know, Know Him is to Love, Love, Love Him* written by Phil Spector).

Frank Sinatra's hit recording made it clear that love and marriage go together (from: *Love and Marriage*, written by James Van Heusen & Sammy Cahn).

While fifties lyrics tended to reinforce traditional gender traits, there were insights into role reversal possibilities:

Donald O'Conner, on film, and Eddie Fisher, on record, admit that *A Man Chases a Girl* until she catches him (from *A Man Chases a Girl*, written by Irving Berlin).

Patti Page, in *Conquest,* tells a story where she, the hunted, becomes the huntress and he, the hunter, becomes the prey. The morale of her story is that she led him down the aisle and finally she made the conquest (*Conquest* written by Corky Robbins).

Of course, even in the 50s, girl singers did not always find 'Mr. Right' and guys could easily be tempted by inappropriate girls. Lyricists commiserated with these innocents who fell in love with the wrong person:

Gogi Grant believes that her boyfriend, who was born the 'next of kin' to the *Wayward Wind,* became a slave to his restless ways and left her alone with a broken heart (from *Wayward Wind*, written by Herb Newman & Stan Lebowsky).

Guy Mitchell fell in love with a nice and proper girl whose hair hung down in ringlets but she had a roving eye (from *Roving Kind* written by Jessie Cavanaugh & Arnold Stanton).

Even in the 1950s, heart-wrenching lost-love songs could generate tear-jerking emotional misery:

When her boyfriend told her that the flame in his heart died Teresa Brewer cried (from *A Tear Fell*, written by Dorian Burton & Eugene Randolph).

Eddie Fisher attended his girlfriend's wedding and wanted her to know that if things went wrong he was walking behind (From *I'm Walking Behind You*, written by Billy Reid).

At her boyfriend's wedding, Patti Page uttered a sigh and whispered goodbye to her happiness (from *I Went to Your Wedding*, written by Jessie Mae Robinson).

Musicologist Charlie Gillett observes that although the majority of popular fifties songs are nominally about love, rarely do they attempt to confront emotional or the physical realities of love relationships. 'Charms' was the universal descriptive term, which simultaneously invoked the loved one's physical attractiveness as well as his or her personality: (Gillett, 1970, p.5)

When the night is warm, Debbie Reynolds longs for her boyfriend's 'charms' (from *Tammy*, written by Jay Livingston & Ray Evans).

Steve Lawrence wanted to be the only guy that would know his girlfriends 'charms' (from *A Room Without Windows*, written by Ervin Drake).

Doris Day wanted her boyfriend to thrill her with 'his charms' (from *Hold Me in Your Arms*, written by Ray Heindorf, Charles Henderson, and Don Pippin).

Perry Como warned his best friend that there was danger in 'her charms' (from *Wanted*, written by Fulton & Steele).

By 1950, fewer songs were written in publishing offices in New York. A Tennessean, Pee Wee King wrote *The Tennessee Waltz* that turned into a smash hit for Patti Page. Hillbilly, Hank Williams wrote *Jambalaya*, a #1 hit recorded by Jo Stafford. A desert-living, sandaled, Eden Ahbez wrote *Nature Boy*, Nat King Cole's hit. An ex-murderer named Huddie Ledbetter was composer/lyricist of *Goodnight Irene* that was recorded by the Weavers. A watchman at a dry-cleaning company in Pittsburgh, Kohlman Churchill, wrote Johnny Ray's *Cry*. Polio victim Melvyn Endsley who was confined to a wheelchair wrote Guy Mitchell's *Singing the Blues*. (Whitcomb, 1972, p.205) Alan Freed whose fame as a rock-and-roll disc jockey obscured the fact that he was the songwriter of the gentle and sentimental hit record *Sincerely* for the McGuire Sisters. The original tin-whistle version of *Skokiaan* was recorded in what is now Zimbabwe. Stuart Hamblen wrote *This Ole House* as a gospel song.

The songwriting team of Bob Allen and Al Stillman created several big hits songs during the fifties including: The Four Lad's *Moments to Remember* and *No Not Much*; Johnny Mathis' *Chances Are* and *It's Not For Me To Say*; and Perry Como's Christmas classic *Home for the Holidays*. They are often considered the most talented collaboration to never write a Broadway musical. While 50s EASY-POP songs and singers are easy to recall, the writers are often forgotten. Chart 2.3 identifies some of the more prolific composers and lyricists of 50s EASY-POP songs.

Songwriters were composing lyrics that suggested a fondness for far away places. *April in Paris, Mona Lisa, Arrivederci Roma, Three Coins in the Fountain, Domani, Mambo Italiano, The Last Time I Saw Paris*, and *April in Portugal* lent a universal approach to 50s EASY POP. *Magic Moments* evoked nostalgia for the recent past, with an array of images from the fifties:

> The clutch and floorboard of the car…tying up the telephone line for hours…hayrides…Halloween hops (from *Magic Moments*, recorded by Perry Como, written by Burt Bacharach & Hal David).

Unique 50s slang was reflected in popular songs. Phrases like 'going steady,' 'slippin' around,' and a 'double-dare' often appeared in popular songs. Eddie Fisher had his 'dungaree' doll and Dean Martin called the moon a 'pizza pie.' The Four Lads called Martha 'the most.' Teresa Brewer was 'jilted' in one recording and in another her boyfriend began to 'ricochet' just like a rifle bullet. (Coral records felt that the word 'ricochet' was so unusual that the title should be spelled phonetically *RICK-O-SHAY* in parentheses on the record label so the buyer would recognize it as the song they heard on the radio.)

Fifties lyrics identify names that were popular. Perry Como was taken with *Tina Marie*; in *Mostly Martha*, the Four Lads loved Martha more than Jane, Trudy, Grace, or Jean; and Ricky Nelson loved *Mary Lou*. In *Left, Right Out of Your Heart* Patti Page was mistakenly called Susie by her soldier boy when her name was actually Cindy Lou, Eddie Fisher also longed for *Cindy, Oh Cindy*, and Buddy Holly's biggest hit song was originally called *Cindy Lou*, before it was changed to *Peggy Sue* because that was the name of the Crickets' drummer Jerry Allison's girl friend at the time.

Songwriters of the 50s *and singers who recorded some of their hit songs*

Richard Adler & Jerry Ross
Tony Bennett's *Rags to Riches*; Rosemary Clooney's *Hey There* from Broadway's 'Pajama Game'; Eddie Fisher's *Heart* from 'Damn Yankees'; and Doris Day's *Everybody Loves a Lover* (with music by Robert Allen).

Robert Allen & Al Stillman
Perry Como's Christmas classic *Home for the Holidays*; Johnny Mathis' *Chances Are* and *It's Not For Me To Say*; and the Four Lads' *Moments to Remember, No Not Much*, and *There's Only One of You*.

Bennie Benjamin, composer & George David Weiss, lyricist
Kay Starr's *Wheel of Fortune* and Patti Page's *Cross Over the Bridge*.

Irving Berlin, composer & lyricist
Eddie Fisher's *Count Your Blessings*; Bing Crosby's *White Christmas*; Kate Smith's *God Bless America*; Ethel Merman's *There's No Business Like Show Business*; and Judy Garland's *Easter Parade*.

Jerry Bock, composer & George David Weiss, lyricist
Peggy Lee's and Sarah Vaughan's versions of *Mr. Wonderful*; Eydie Gorme's *Too Close for Comfort* both from Broadway's 'Mr. Wonderful'; and Bobby Darin's *Artificial Flowers* (words by Sheldon Harnick) from Broadway's 'Tenderloin.'

Johnny Burke, composer & lyricist (also composed under the pseudonym K. C. Rogan)
Perry Como's *Wild Horses*; Johnny Mathis' *Misty*; the Skyliners' *Pennies from Heaven*; and Patti Page's *Now That I'm in Love*.

Sammy Cahn, lyricist (often collaborated with Jule Styne and Jimmy Van Heusen)
Doris Day's *It's Magic* and *I'll Never Stop Loving You*; the Four Aces' *Three Coins in the Fountain*; Dinah Shore's *I'll Walk Alone*; Mario Lanza's *Be My Love*; the Ames Brothers' *Forever Darling*; Frank Sinatra's *Love and Marriage, Same Old Saturday Night, Hey Jealous Lover, All the Way*, and *High Hopes*; and the Christmas holiday classic *Let It Snow! Let It Snow! Let It Snow!*

Joe Darion, lyricist
Teresa Brewer's *Ricochet*; Patti Page's *Changing Partners*; and Jack Jones' *The Impossible Dream* from Broadway's 'Man of La Mancha.'

Hal David, lyricist (often collaborated with composer Burt Bacharach)
Perry Como's *Magic Moments*; Teresa Brewer's *Bell Bottom Blues*; Carl Dobkins' *My Heart is an Open Book;* and Sarah Vaughan's *Broken-Hearted Melody*.

Ray Evans, composer & Jay Livingston, lyricist
The Christmas classic *Silver Bells;* Debbie Reynolds' *Tammy*; Nat King Cole's *Mona Lisa*; Dinah Shore's *Buttons & Bows*; and Doris Day's *Que Sera, Sera*.

Sammy Fain, composer (often collaborated with lyricist Paul Francis Webster)
Dinah Shore's *Dear Hearts and Gentle People*; Doris Day's *Secret Love*; the Ames Brothers' *Love Is a Many-Splendored Thing*; Johnny Nash's *A Very Precious Love*; and Pat Boone's *April Love*.

Chart 2.3.   Songwriters of the 50s and some of their Hit Songs

(Chart continues on the next page)

Songwriters of the 50s (continued)

Terry Gilkyson, composer and lyricist
Frankie Laine's *Cry of the Wild Goose*; Doris Day's *Mister Tap Toe*; and Dean Martin's *Memories Are Made of This*.

Norman Gimbel, lyricist
Teresa Brewer's *Ricochet* (with Joe Darion and Larry Coleman); Dean Martin's *Sway*; Andy Williams' *Canadian Sunset*; and Little Peggy March's *I Will Follow Him*.

Al Hoffman, composer/lyricist (often collaborated with Dick Manning and Bob Merrill)
Mairzy Doats; *I'm Gonna Live Till I Die*; Eileen Barton's *If I Knew You Were Coming I'd've Baked a Cake*; Pearl Bailey's *Takes Two to Tango*; Perry Como's *Papa Loves Mambo* and *Hot Diggity Dog*; and the words and music for Walt Disney's 'Cinderella.'

Jack Lawrence, composer and lyricist
Rosemary Clooney's *Tenderly* (with Walter Gross); Bobby Darin's *Beyond the Sea* (with Charles Trenet); Don Cornell's *Hold My Hand*; and Les Baxter's *Poor People of Paris*.

Jerry Leiber & Mike Stoller, composer and lyricist
Elvis Presley's *Jailhouse Rock, Don't, Treat Me Nice* and *She's Not You*; Gale Storm's *Lucky Lips*; and the Drifters' *On Broadway*.

Carolyn Leigh, lyricist
Frank Sinatra's *Witchcraft, Young at Heart*, and *(How Little It Matters) How Little We Know*; Peggy Lee's *Pass Me By*; and Lucille Ball's *Hey Look Me Over*.

Dick Manning, composer/lyricist (often collaborated with composer/lyricist Al Hoffman)
Pearl Bailey's *Takes Two to Tango*; Teresa Brewer's *Jilted*; Tommy Edwards' *Morningside of the Mountain*; Jimmie Rodgers *Secretly*; and Perry Como's *Papa Loves Mambo* and *Hot Diggity Dog*.

Bob Merrill, composer/lyricist (often collaborated with composer/lyricist Al Hoffman)
Patty Page's classic *How Much is that Doggie in the Window?*; Jimmie Rodgers' *Honeycomb*; Rosemary Clooney's *Mambo Italiano*; Eileen Barton's *If I Knew You Were Coming I'd've Baked a Cake*; Perry Como's *Tina Marie*; Guy Mitchell's *My Truly, Truly Fair*; and Sarah Vaughan's *Make Yourself Comfortable*.

Lee Pockress, composer and lyricist
Perry Como's *Catch a Falling Star*; the PlayMates' *What Is Love*; Johnny Tillotson's *Jimmy's Girl*; Anita Bryant's *In My Little Corner of the World*; Shelley Fabares' *Johnny Angel*; and Carl Dobkins' *My Heart is an Open Book*.

Harry Warren, composer
Doris Day's *Lullaby of Broadway*; Vic Damone's *Affair To Remember*; Jill Corey's *I Love My Baby (My Baby Loves Me)*; Judy Garland's *On the Atchison Topeka and the Santa Fe*; and Dean Martin's *That's Amore* and *Inamorata*.

Paul Francis Webster, lyricist (often collaborated with composer Sammy Fain)
Mario Lanza's *Loveliest Night of the Year*; Doris Day's *Secret Love*; the Four Aces' *Love is a Many-Splendored Thing*; Pat Boone's *Friendly Persuasion*; and the Ames Brothers' *A Very Precious Love*.

Chart 2.3. Songwriters of the 50s and some of their Hit Songs

Lyrics were innocent in the fifties—gay meant happy, bawling meant crying, and Doris Day's title song from the film *Tunnel of Love* was understood as a reference to the amusement park ride rather than the sexual connotation it might suggest today. In the recording of *One Boy,* Joannie Sommers having 'coke' with her boyfriend meant a soft drink not an illegal substance.

Rock, R&B, and jazz historians sometimes criticize the lyrics of 50s EASY-POP songs as being 'sappy' and 'gushy.' Fifties POP songs were hopeful and enthusiastic. They were never afraid to show naïve feelings and virtue in simple, straightforward words. The lyrics were neither as trite nor banal as critics claim and while they were not provocative or stimulating, they were imaginative and colorful.

The Beat and Structure

In the fifties, the music needed a beat to tap your foot to, snap your fingers to, and dance to. The beat is the regularly accented part of a bar of music. There are a set number of beats in each bar—two in 2/4 time, three in 3/4 time, four in 4/4 time. A characteristic pulse is created by playing on, before, or after the beat and getting the beat right was a crucial element to a successful recording.

In the 1940s, the structure of the songs tended to follow the VERSE–CHORUS format. The composition would begin with a verse that would sketch out a situation or vignette and then be followed by several stanzas of the more lyrical chorus. Many 'standards' written in the forties are remembered today only by their chorus—the verse is often forgotten.

The structure of fifties EASY-POP songs eliminates a verse altogether and contains several stanzas of the chorus. The Four Lad's *No, Not Much* is a popular example of this STANZA #1 – STANZA #2 – instrumental bridge – repeat STANZA #2 structure. In time, variations on this simple format began to arise adding a catchy refrain between stanzas of the chorus. The structure of Tony Bennett's recording of *Rags to Riches* is: STANZA #1 – REFRAIN – STANZA #2 – instrumental bridge – repeat REFRAIN – repeat STANZA #2. Of course, as the decade ended, rock 'n' roll introduced even more radical departures to the structure of popular music.

Classic 50s EASY-POP Hits

American EASY-POP recordings in the fifties were characterized by a sunny and bracing lyricism. More than one hundred quintessential 50s EASY-POP standards are identified in chapter 3, along with the singers that recorded them.

References from Chapter 2:

Gammond, Peter and Clayton, Peter. *Dictionary of Popular Music*. New York: Philosophical Library, Inc, 1961.

Gillett, Charlie. *The Sound of the City — The Rise of Rock 'n' Roll*. New York: Dell Publishing, 1970.

Harris, James. *Philosophy at 33 $^1/_3$ rpm — Themes of Classic Rock Music*. Chicago: Open Court Publishing, 1993.

Whitcomb, Ian. *After the Ball*. London: Allen Lane the Penguin Press, 1972.

Songs have been a part of our lives. We have sung them, hummed them, whistled and played them. We have heard them on the radio and on records, in music stores, or on the stage and on the screen. Songs have made us laugh and made us cry, pervaded our sleep and perhaps most importantly, have given us memories.

Robert Lissauer in *Encyclopedia of American Popular Song* (1991)

Chapter 3

Classic EASY-POP Songs of the Fifties

The versatile popular singers, the unique arrangements that backed them, the infectious lyrics, and the finger-snapping beat, characterize the recordings that are remembered as quintessential 50s EASY-POP songs. Chapter 2 defined 50s EASY-POP music—this chapter describes one hundred of the classic hit songs that recall the decade. These records ranked at, or near, the top of the popularity polls and stayed there for three months or more.

Popular music in America reflects the textures and nuances of the time. Especially for youngsters growing up during the fifties, there is an association of events with popular music. Each of these songs will evoke a memory for adults who came-of-age in the fifties. Chart 3.1 lists classic 50s EASY-POP hit songs and the singers who recorded them. Following the chart, there is a year-by-year detailing of the most memorable 50s EASY-POP recordings—a discography of the favorite songs each year—providing an annual snapshot of musical tastes and popular singers.

Classic EASY-POP Hit Songs of the fifties

(Recordings ranked at or near the top of the charts for three months or more, listed alphabetically by artist)

•*Rag Mop* 1950
Sentimental Me 1950
•*Undecided* 1951
•*You You, You* 1953
Ames Brothers

•*I Can Dream, Can't I*
1950
I Wanna Be Loved 1950
Andrews Sisters

Diana 1957
Lonely Boy 1959
Put Your Head on My Shoulder 1959
Paul Anka

Venus 1959
Bobby Sox to Stockings
1959
Frankie Avalon

Banana Boat Song 1957
Harry Belafonte

•*Because of You* 1951
•*Cold, Cold Heart* 1951
•*Rags to Riches* 1953
•*Stranger in Paradise*
1953
Tony Bennett

April Love 1957
Love Letters in the Sand
1957
Don't Forbid Me 1957
Pat Boone

•*Music! Music! Music!*
1950
•*Till I Waltz Again with You* 1952
•*Ricochet* 1953
Teresa Brewer

The Three Bells 1959
The Browns

Ivory Tower* 1956
Cathy Carr

•*Hold Me, Thrill Me, Kiss Me* 1952
Karen Chandler

Band of Gold 1955
Don Cherry

•*Mr. Sandman* 1954
Lollipop 1958
Chordettes

•*Come On-A My House*
1951
•*Half-As-Much* 1952
•*Tenderly* 1952
This Ole House 1954
•*Hey There* 1954
Rosemary Clooney

•*Mona Lisa* 1950
Orange Colored Sky 1950
•*Too Young* 1951
Nat King Cole

Hoop-Dee-Doo 1950
A Bushel and a Peck 1950
•*If* 1951
•*Don't Let the Stars Get in Your Eyes* 1952
No Other Love 1953
•*Wanted* 1954
Hot Diggity 1956
Round and Round 1957
•*Catch a Falling Star*
1958
Perry Como

•*Hold My Hand* 1954
Don Cornell

•*Sh-Boom** 1954
Earth Angel* 1955
Crew-Cuts

Dream Lover 1959
Mack the Knife 1959
Bobby Darin

My Heart Cries for You
1950
Vic Damone

•*A Guy is a Guy* 1952
When I Fall in Love 1952
If I Give My Heart to You 1954

•*Secret Love* 1954
Whatever Will Be, Will Be (Que Sera, Sera) 1956
Everybody Loves a Lover 1958
Doris Day

Teach Me Tonight 1954
DeCastro Sisters

It's All in the Game 1958
Tommy Edwards

Bye, Bye, Love 1957
Wake Up Little Susie
1957
All I Have To Do is Dream 1958
Everly Brothers

•*Any Time* 1951
•*Wish You Were Here*
1952
•*I'm Walking Behind You* 1953
•*Oh! My Pa-Pa* 1953
•*I Need You Now* 1954
Heart 1955
Dungaree Doll 1955
Eddie Fisher

The Big Hurt 1959
Miss Toni Fisher

Hearts of Stone* 1954
Fontane Sisters

Heart and Soul 1952
•*Three Coins in the Fountain* 1954
Love is a Many-Splendored Thing 1955
Four Aces

•*I Get So Lonely* 1954
Four Knights

Moments to Remember
1955
No, Not Much 1956
Standing on the Corner
1956
Four Lads

Chart 3.1. Classic 50s EASY-POP Hit Songs   (Chart continues on the next page)

Classic EASY-POP Hit Songs of the fifties (continued)

26 Miles *(Santa Catalina)* 1958
Big Man 1958
Four Preps

Lipstick on Your Collar
1959
Connie Francis

•**Kiss of Fire** 1952
Georgia Gibbs

Wayward Wind 1956
Gogi Grant

Unchained Melody 1955
Al Hibbler

Everyday 1957
Buddy Holly

•**Battle of New Orleans**
1959
Johnny Horton

Young Love * 1957
Tab Hunter

Sorry *(I Ran All the Way Home)* 1959
Impalas

•**Why Don't You
Believe Me** 1952
How Important Can It Be
1955
Joni James

•**Little Things Mean a
Lot** 1954
Kitty Kallen

•**Cry of the Wild Goose**
1950
•**Jezebel** 1951
Moonlight Gambler 1956
Frankie Laine

•**That's Amore** 1953
**Memories are Made of
This** 1955
Dean Martin

•**I Get Ideas** 1951
Tony Martin

Chances Are 1957
It's Not for Me to Say 1957
Johnny Mathis

Sincerely * 1955
Sugartime 1957
McGuire Sisters

•**My Heart Cries for You**
1950
The Roving Kind 1950
•**My Truly, Truly Fair**
1951
Singing the Blues 1956
**Heartaches by the
Number** 1959
Guy Mitchell

**Nel Blu Dipinto Di Blu
(Volare)** 1958
Domenico Modugno

**That's All I Want from
You** 1954
Jaye P. Morgan

Poor Little Fool 1958
Never Be Anyone Else
1959
Ricky Nelson

•**The Tennessee Waltz**
1950
•**All My Love** 1950
•**I Went to Your
Wedding** 1952
•**Doggie in the Window**
1953
Patti Page

•**How High the Moon**
1951
•**Mockin' Bird Hill** 1951
•**Vaya Con Dios** 1953
Les Paul & Mary Ford

My Prayer 1956
The Great Pretender
1956
Platters

Love Me Tender 1956
Teddy Bear 1957
•**Don't** 1958
•**A Fool Such As I** 1959
Elvis Presley

•**Cry** 1951
**Just Walkin' in the
Rain** 1956
Johnnie Ray

Don't You Know 1959
Della Reese

Tammy 1957
Debbie Reynolds

Honeycomb 1957
**Oh! Oh! I'm Falling in
Love Again** 1958
Jimmie Rodgers

•**Song from
'Moulin Rouge'** 1953
Felicia Sanders

My Heart Cries for You
1950
Sweet Violets 1951
Dinah Shore

•**Young at Heart** 1954
Learnin' the Blues 1955
Frank Sinatra

•**Shrimp Boats** 1951
• **You Belong to Me** 1952
•**Jambalaya** 1952
Jo Stafford

Bonaparte's Retreat 1950
•**Wheel of Fortune** 1952
Rock and Roll Waltz 1955
Kay Starr

**To Know Him is to Love
Him** 1958
Teddy Bears

The Breeze and I 1955
Caterina Valente

Crying in the Chapel *
1953
June Valli

Goodnight, Irene 1950
The Weavers

Let Me Go Lover 1954
Joan Weber

• Record sold more than a million copies   * record was a cover of an original R&B artist

Chart 3.1.   Classic 50s EASY-POP Hit Songs

1950 News Headlines:

North Korea Invades South Korea, United States Enters Korean Conflict
Postmaster Cuts Residential Mail Delivery from Twice-a-Day to Once-a-Day
Blacklisting of Performers with Alleged Communist Affiliations Spreads
President Harry Truman Seizes Railroads to Avert Strike
Bomb Shelter Plans become Widely Available

Popular Culture in 1950:

Favorite singers:
Perry Como
Patti Page
Ames Brothers

Most popular film stars:
John Wayne
Betty Hutton
Photoplay Magazine Gold Medal Awards

Most Popular films:

#1 *Cinderella* (a Walt Disney animated film featuring popular song *Bibbidy Bobbidy Boo*)
#2 *King Solomon's Mines* (starring Deborah Kerr and Stewart Granger)
#3 *Annie Get Your Gun* (a musical starring Betty Hutton and Howard Keel)
#4 *Cheaper By The Dozen* (starring Clifton Webb, Jeanne Crain, and Myrna Loy)
#5 *Father of the Bride* (starring Spencer Tracy and Elizabeth Taylor)
from Susan Sackett's Billboard Box Office Hits, p.86-91

Most Popular TV programs:

#1 *Texaco Star Theater* (comedy series starring 'Mr. Television,' Milton Berle)
#2 *Fireside Theater* (weekly thirty-minute dramatic series hosted by Gene Raymond)
#3 *Your Show of Shows* (ninety-minute variety series starring Sid Caesar and Imogene Coca)
#4 *Philco Television Playhouse* (weekly 'Golden Age' dramatic anthology series)
#5 *Colgate Comedy Hour* (series with rotating hosts including Dean Martin & Jerry Lewis)
from Alex McNeil's Total Television, p.897

Mass Media Facts:

First appearance for AC Nielsen's television rating services
Party lines make up 75% of US telephone lines
ABC televises 'Opening Night at the Metropolitan Opera'
'Miss TV USA' beauty pageant won by Edie Adams
In 1950, there were 150,000 TV sets in the United States
Movie attendance fell by 25% between 1946 and 1950

First Appeared in 1950:

Smokey the Bear, Minute Rice, Corning Ware, Hula Hoops,
the Diner's Club, the FBI's Ten-Most-Wanted Program, and Sugar Pops
from Gordon's Columbia Chronicles p.390

Two Unforgettable EASY-POP Recordings of 1950:

The Tennessee Waltz recorded by **Patti Page** introduced November 18
Written by Pee Wee King & Redd Stewart   Orchestra conducted by Jack Rael

While they were waltzing, Patti Page's best friend stole her sweetheart in this huge hit that remained at the top of the charts for 13 weeks. One of the biggest hits of all time, second only to Bing Crosby's *White Christmas*, the record sold more than ten million copies. Legendary jazzman, Buck Clayton provided the record's memorable trumpet refrain. The song was originally intended to be the 'B' side of the forgettable holiday novelty song *Boogie Woogie Santa Claus*.

Mona Lisa recorded by **Nat King Cole** introduced June 10
Written by Ray Evans & Jay Livingston   Orchestra conducted by Les Baxter

Selling more than three million records—this faux-Italian ballad, originally titled *Prima Donna*, was a number one hit all summer. Fragments of the Oscar-winning song were heard in the film 'Captain Carey, U.S.A.' sung by a blind Italian street performer questioning whether the enigmatic woman in the Leonardo de Vinci painting is real or just a lovely work of art. Nat King Cole introduced the novelty tune *Orange Colored Sky* on his TV show and it became a second hit for him at the end of the year.

More Classic Fifties EASY-POP Hit Singles from 1950:
(eight additional hit recordings listed in alphabetical order)

All My Love recorded by **Patti Page** introduced August 26
Music by Maurice Ravel, Adapted by Paul Durand, Lyric by Mitchell Parish
Orchestra conducted by Harry Geller

The towering and challenging *All My Love* was the second big hit recording for Patti Page in 1950 after her *Tennessee Waltz*. Harry Geller provided an exotic arrangement that added "eye-yi-yi's" & "oh-oh-oh's" to an infectious melody based on Ravel's *Bolero*.

The Cry of the Wild Goose recorded by **Frankie Laine** introduced Feb. 11
Written by Terry Gilkyson   Orchestra conducted by Harry Geller

Frankie Laine's rough style is evident in this swirling, melodramatic wondering-fool or heart-at-rest recording. This #1 hit followed his #1 hit a year earlier with the western-themed 'clippity-cloppity' mega-hit *Mule Train*. Tennessee Ernie Ford also had a hit with *The Cry of the Wild Goose*.

Goodnight, Irene recorded by the **Weavers** introduced July 8
Written by Huddie Ledbetter & John Lomax   Orchestra conducted by Gordon Jenkins

This historic group, that made folk music a popular phenomenon, had their biggest hit with *Goodnight, Irene*, selling more than two million copies.

Hoop-Dee-Doo by **Perry Como** & the **Fontane Sisters** introduced June 3
Written by Frank Loesser & Milton DeLugg   Orchestra conducted by Mitchell Ayres

Perry Come and the Fontane Sisters had the #1 version of this exhilarating polka; Kay Starr and Doris Day also had hits with this bouncy, fast paced tune. A second Perry Como duet, *A Bushel and A Peck* with Betty Hutton, charted in 1950 too.

I Can Dream Can't I recorded by the **Andrews Sisters** introduced Sept. 4, 1949
Written by Sammy Fain & Irving Kahal   Orchestra conducted by Gordon Jenkins

Patty Andrews was backed by her sisters, Maxine and LaVerne, on this million-selling recording and again on their final #1 hit, *I Wanna Be Loved* in 1950.

Music! Music! Music! recorded by **Teresa Brewer** introduced February 4
Written by Stephen Weiss & Bernie Baum   Accompanied by the Dixieland All Stars

Recorded when 5-foot-2 Teresa Brewer was barely 19 years old, this contagious, Dixieland, nickel-in-the-nickelodeon song fit her like a glove. It became a runaway hit and had the entire country singing all year.

My Heart Cries for You recorded by **Guy Mitchell** introduced December 9
Written by Carl Sigman & Percy Faith   Orchestra conducted by Mitch Miller
also *My Heart Cries for You* recorded by **Dinah Shore** introduced December 9
and *My Heart Cries for You* recorded by **Vic Damone** introduced December 30

Three singers had top-ten versions of this song adapted from a French folk tune *Chanson de Marie Antoinette*. Guy Mitchell had a second top-ten hit in 1950 with *The Roving Kind*, adapted from the 1800s English folk song *The Pirate Ship*.

Sentimental Me recorded by **Ames Brothers** introduced January 28
Written by Jim Morehead & Jimmy Cassin   Orchestra conducted by Roy Ross

The Ames Brothers, Ed, Gene, Joe, and Vic, had two #1 hits in 1950. On the flip side of the ballad *Sentimental Me*, they released their novelty hit *Rag Mop*.

Novelty and Instrumental hit records during 1950:

Bonaparte's Retreat
recording by **Kay Starr** introduced May 27

Chattanooga Shoe Shine Boy
ragtime recording by **Red Foley** introduced April 29

If I Knew You Were Comin' I'd've Baked a Cake
novelty song by **Eileen Barton** introduced March 25

La Vie En Rose
English language version by French chanteuse **Edith Piaf** introduced October 21

Sam's Song and Simple Melody
duet recordings by **Bing and Gary Crosby** introduced July 29

The Thing
novelty recording by **Phil Harris** introduced December 2

The Third Man Theme
instrumental by **Anton Karas** introduced April 29
and instrumental by **Guy Lombardo** introduced May 6

Tzena, Tzena, Tzena
Israeli folk recording by the **Weavers** introduced July 1

Popular long-playing record albums released in 1950:
(compilations of songs were available on either one 33^1/$_3$ rpm 10" disc or as a set of 45rpm records)

'Ella Sings Gershwin Songs' recorded by **Ella Fitzgerald**
Decca album with eight songs including *Someone to Watch over Me, Nice Work if You Can Get It, Lady Be Good*, and *But Not for Me*

'The Toast of New Orleans' recorded by **Mario Lanza**
Four songs on two 45s from the film including *Be My Love* and *Bayou Lullaby*

'Young Man with a Horn' recorded by **Doris Day**
and **Harry James**
Columbia movie soundtrack with eight songs: *Too Marvelous for Words, With a Song in My Heart, The Very Thought of You*, and *I May be Wrong*

'Oh, You Beautiful Doll' recorded by **Tony Martin**
RCA album includes six songs *Peg O' My Heart, The Very Thought of You, Come Josephine in My Flying Machine*, and
I Want You to Want Me (to Want You)

'Merry Christmas' recorded by **Bing Crosby**
8 songs on this Decca holiday re-issue include *White Christmas* and *Silent Night*

1951 News Headlines:

President Truman Relieves General Douglas MacArthur who laments:
"Old soldiers never die, they just fade away"

22nd Amendment Takes Effect Limiting the President to Two Terms

US Tests Atomic Bomb Near Las Vegas

West Germany is Granted Sovereignty

Ethel and Julius Rosenberg are Found Guilty of Treason and Sentenced to Death

Popular Culture in 1951:

Favorite singers: Most popular film stars:
Guy Mitchell   **Mario Lanza**
Jo Stafford   **Doris Day**
Mills Brothers   Photoplay Magazine Gold Medal Awards

Most Popular films:

#1 *Quo Vadis* (biblical epic starring Robert Taylor, Deborah Kerr, and Peter Ustinov)
#2 *Alice in Wonderland* (Walt Disney's animated film version of the Lewis Carroll classic)
#3 *Showboat* (stars Kathryn Grayson, Howard Keel, Ava Gardner, Marge & Gower Champion)
#4 *David and Bathsheba* (epic starring Gregory Peck and Susan Hayward)
#5 *The Great Caruso* (biopic starring Mario Lanza and Ann Blyth)
from Susan Sackett's Billboard Box Office Hits, p.92-97

Most Popular TV programs:

#1 *Arthur Godfrey's Talent Scouts* (celebrity guests introduce aspiring talent)
#2 *Texaco Star Theater* (sixty-minute comedy/variety series starring Milton Berle)
#3 *I Love Lucy* (premier season of situation comedy starring Lucille Ball and Desi Arnaz)
#4 *The Red Skelton Show* (popular comedian hosts his own comedy/variety series)
#5 *Colgate Comedy Hour* (weekly series with rotating hosts including Abbott and Costello)
from Alex McNeil's Total Television, p.897

Mass Media Facts:

First coast-to-coast telecast: President Truman's address from San Francisco Peace Conference
First telecast of an NFL championship football game on the Dumont network
In Cleveland, radio disc jockey Alan Freed introduces the term rock 'n' roll
Univac I is the first mass-produced computer
5¢ phone calls increase to 10¢ in most large American cities

First Appeared in 1951:

Dennis the Menace, Sugarless chewing gum, Power steering on new Chryslers,
Trading Stamps, and Pushbutton-controlled garage doors.
from Gordon's Columbia Chronicles p.399

Two Unforgettable EASY-POP Recordings of 1951:

How High The Moon recorded by **Les Paul & Mary Ford** introduced March 31
Music by Morgan Lewis, Lyrics by Nancy Hamilton

Accompanied by Les Paul on guitar

This Grammy 'Hall of Fame' award winner was originally introduced by Alfred Drake in the 1940 Broadway musical 'Two for the Show.' In this multi-track hit recording, Les Paul superimposed several guitar parts behind breezy-voiced Mary Ford's close microphone harmony. Her light-hearted delivery, his guitar and their overdubbing technique produced another hit in 1951, *Mockin' Bird Hill*, that was also recorded by Slim Whitman and Patti Page.

Any Time recorded by **Eddie Fisher** introduced December 8
Written by Herbert 'Happy' Lawson   Orchestra conducted by Hugo Winterhalter

Young Eddie Fisher's first million-selling hit *Any Time* was a 1921 vaudeville tune, successfully revived in 1948 by his RCA labelmate, country star Eddy Arnold. Eddie Fisher's big voice version of *Any Time* was one of several songs recorded during his two-year tour of duty in the US Army Special Services. The song zoomed to #2 on the charts and it might have been even more successful if the flamboyant, bravura baritone had been able to promote it.

More Classic Fifties EASY-POP Hit Singles from 1951:
(eight additional hit recordings listed in alphabetical order)

Because of You recorded by **Tony Bennett** introduced June 23
Music by Arthur Hammerstein, Lyrics by Dudley Wilkinson

Orchestra conducted by Percy Faith

Legendary ballad vocalist Tony Bennett's first #1 hit recording was *Because of You*, originally published in 1940 and featured in the 1951 film 'I Was an American Spy.' A month later he had a second #1 hit with *Cold, Cold Heart*.

Come On-A My House recorded by **Rosemary Clooney** introduced July 7
Written by Ross Bagdasarian, William Saroyan   Orchestra conducted by Mitch Miller

Rosemary Clooney's first #1 hit *Come On-A My House* was from the off-Broadway musical 'The Son.' The raucous Mitch Miller arrangement, similar to her 1952 record *Botch-A-Me*, features Stan Freeman on the harpsichord.

Cry recorded by **Johnnie Ray** (with the Four Lads) introduced November 24
Written by Churchill Kohlman   Produced by Mitch Miller

This first #1 hit recording for the passionate, soulful, vocal style that Johnnie Ray introduced in 1951 sold more than two million copies.

If recorded by **Perry Como** introduced January 13
Written by Robert Hargreaves, Stanley Damerell, & Touchard Evans
Orchestra conducted by Mitchell Ayres

One of Perry Como's more dramatic recordings, the song, originally published in 1934, was also recorded in 1951 by Jo Stafford, Billy Eckstine, Dean Martin, the Ink Spots, and Vic Damone.

Jezebel recorded by **Frankie Laine** introduced May 5
Written by Wayne Shanklin   Orchestra conducted by Mitch Miller

Frankie Laine's husky, masculine, baritone voice is exploited in this heavy, 'man-done-wrong' recording produced by Columbia record's A&R man, Mitch Miller.

My Truly, Truly Fair recorded by **Guy Mitchell** introduced June 2
Written by Bob Merrill   Orchestra conducted by Mitch Miller

Easy, likable Guy Mitchell sings songs and brings trinkets to his 'Truly Fair' in this million-selling, quintessential fifties hit with a mariner spirit, a contagious melody, a cheerful Mitch Miller arrangement, and an infectious upbeat chorus.

Sweet Violets recorded by **Dinah Shore** introduced July 7
Original folk song written in 1882 by Joseph Emmet
Arranged by Charles Grean & Cy Coben   Orchestra conducted by Henri Rene

Following her 1948 smash *Buttons & Bows*, Dinah Shore hit #3 with a lilting version of the folk song *Sweet Violets* in 1951. The humorously surprising lyrics were cleaned-up a bit for Dinah Shore's recording. She had an earlier hit in 1951 with her starry-eyed Tony Martin duet, *A Penny a Kiss*.

Too Young recorded by **Nat King Cole** introduced April 14
Written by Sid Lippman & Sylvia Dee   Orchestra conducted by Les Baxter

This they-tell-us-we're-to-young-to-be-in-love song was another huge hit for Nat King Cole with Les Baxter again conducting a lush Nelson Riddle arrangement—the same collaboration that produced *Mona Lisa*.

Three other EASY-POP hit singles released during 1951:

I Get Ideas
recording by **Tony Martin** introduced April 16

Shrimp Boats
recording by **Jo Stafford** introduced November 10

Undecided
recording by the **Ames Brothers** introduced September 29

Novelty, Country, and Folk hit records during 1951:

Be My Love
#1 hit recorded by popular operatic tenor **Mario Lanza** introduced March 10

Mockin' Bird Hill
version of this hit song by **Patti Page** introduced February 24

On Top of Old Smokey
a southern folk recording by the **Weavers** introduced March 30

Sin (It's No Sin)
country recording by **Eddie Howard** introduced April 29
also recorded by the **Four Aces** introduced September 15

Sound Off
novelty military recording by the **Vaughn Monroe** introduced April 21

Popular long-playing record albums released in 1951:
(compilations of songs were available on either one 33⅓ rpm 10" disc or as a set of 45rpm records)

'Les Paul's New Sound (vol.2)' recorded by Les Paul and Mary Ford
Six songs on this Capitol album include *In the Good Old Summertime, Three Little Words, The Lonesome Road,* and *I'm Forever Blowing Bubbles*

'Mr. Music' recorded by Bing Crosby
Decca album with the Andrews Sisters and Dorothy Kirsten. Songs include *High On the List, Accidents Will Happen, Milady,* and *Life Is So Peculiar*

'Swing and Dance with Frank Sinatra' recorded by Frank Sinatra
Columbia album with 8 songs including *Should I* and *When You're Smiling*

'Mario Lanza sings Christmas Songs' recorded by Mario Lanza
RCA album: *The First Noel, O Come All Ye Faithful, Away in a Manger, Oh Little Town of Bethlehem,* and *Silent Night*

1952 News Headlines:

Dwight Eisenhower defeats Adlai Stevenson to become 34th US President

Poliomyelitis epidemic strikes more than 50,000

King George IV of England Dies, Elizabeth II is Crowned Queen

Atomic Energy Commission Tests H-Bomb at Eniwetok Atoll

In Denmark, George Jorgensen is surgically transformed into Christine Jorgensen

Popular Culture in 1952:

Favorite singers:
Eddie Fisher
Teresa Brewer
Four Aces

Most popular film stars:
Gary Cooper
Susan Hayward
Photoplay Magazine Gold Medal Awards

Most Popular films:

#1 *This is Cinerama* (innovative three screen process features spectacular roller-coaster ride)

#2 *The Greatest Show on Earth* (starring Betty Hutton, Cornel Wilde, and Charlton Heston)

#3 *The Snows of Kilimanjaro* (starring Gregory Peck, Susan Hayward, and Ava Gardner)

#4 *Ivanhoe* (lavish crusade epic starring Robert Taylor and Elizabeth Taylor)

#5 *Hans Christian Andersen* (starring Danny Kaye as the beloved Danish storyteller)
from Susan Sackett's Billboard Box Office Hits, p.98-103

Most Popular TV programs:

#1 *I Love Lucy* (second season of filmed situation comedy starring Lucille Ball and Desi Arnaz)

#2 *Arthur Godfrey's Talent Scouts* (celebrity guests 'discover' new performers)

#3 *Arthur Godfrey and His Friends* (variety hour with a continuing cast of performers)

#4 *Dragnet* (thirty-minute weekly police drama starring Jack Webb as Sergeant Joe Friday)

#5 *Texaco Star Theater* (vaudeville-style comedy/variety series starring Milton Berle)
from Alex McNeil's Total Television, p.898

Mass Media Facts:

NBC premieres the morning 'Today Show' with wry, low-key Dave Garroway

FCC lifts 4-year freeze on TV Broadcast Licenses and new TV stations sign-on

Sony introduces the pocket-sized Transistor Radio

Lucille Ball's pregnancy was incorporated into her TV Show 'I Love Lucy'

Argentina's Eva Peron Dies

The 'Penny Postcard' increases to 2¢

First Appeared in 1952:

Holiday Inn, 'Mad' comics, Fiberglass, Kent filter-tip cigarettes,
Telephone Area Codes, BMW, and Kellogg's Sugar Frosted Flakes
from Gordon's Columbia Chronicles p.408

Two Unforgettable EASY-POP Recordings of 1952:

Wheel of Fortune recorded by **Kay Starr** introduced February 16
Written by Bennie Benjamin & George Weiss
Orchestra conducted by Harold Mooney

Opening with its instantly recognizable clicking spinning wheel, Kay Starr's first platinum record stayed at #1 for ten weeks in the spring of 1952. While the *Wheel of Fortune* is turning, turning, turning, brassy Kay Starr is yearning for love in this era-defining slice of adult pop. She also had hits in 1952 with *Comes A-Long A-Love* and her own gospel-flavored *Kay's Lament*.

You Belong To Me recorded by **Jo Stafford** introduced August 9
Written by Chilton Price with Pee Wee King and Redd Stewart
Orchestra conducted by Paul Weston

Whether he's flying over the ocean in a silver plane or seeing the pyramids along the Nile, Jo Stafford let him know *You Belong To Me*. Patti Page and Dean Martin also recorded *You Belong To Me* but it was Jo Stafford who sold two million copies of her all-time biggest recording in the fall of 1952 and followed it with another hit *Jambalaya* in the same year.

More Classic Fifties EASY-POP Hit Singles from 1952:
(eight additional hit recordings listed in alphabetical order)

Don't Let the Stars Get in Your Eyes by **Perry Como** Dec 6
Written by Slim Willet (aka Winston L. Moore), Cactus Pryor, Barbara Trammel
Orchestra conducted by Mitchell Ayres

This country cross-over song was recorded by dozens of artists but the #1 version was by Perry Como. The decade's most popular singer recorded dozens of these animated, fast-paced hits like *Catch a Falling Star* and *Hot Diggity*.

A Guy is a Guy recorded by **Doris Day** introduced March 15
Written by Oscar Brand   Orchestra conducted by Paul Weston

In this song, a disarming Doris Day admits that she is not surprised that he follows her down the street because she knew that he would. Based on the 1719 British song *A Knave is a Knave* this novelty was Doris Day's #1 hit of 1952 but she also charted with her dreamy, memorable version of *When I Fall in Love* from the film 'One Minute to Zero.'

Half As Much recorded by **Rosemary Clooney** introduced May 3
Written by Curley Williams   Orchestra conducted by Percy Faith

This plaintive, if-you-loved-me-half-as-much-as-I-love-you, recording was a million-selling number one hit for Rosemary Clooney in 1952. She also had a hit with her unforgettable version of *Tenderly*.

Hold Me, Thrill Me, Kiss Me by **Karen Chandler** introduced Oct. 25
Written by Harry Noble   Orchestra conducted by Jack Pleis

This teen lover's lament, Karen Chandler's debut recording, rose to the top five. The song hit the top ten again when Mel Carter recorded it in 1965.

I Went To Your Wedding recorded by **Patti Page** introduced August 30
Written by Jessie Mae Robinson   Orchestra conducted by Jack Rael

Written by one of the few black female songwriters and inspired by her niece's wedding, this ultimate, melodramatic, lost-love song was #1 for ten weeks. The groom's mother was crying as Patti Page cries too. She sings the verses over a simple guitar arrangement, then full-voice as the orchestra swells behind her.

Kiss of Fire recorded by **Georgia Gibbs** introduced April 19
Written by Lester Allen & Robert Hill   Orchestra conducted by Glenn Osser

Adapted from *Choclo,* an Argentine tango, this steamy I-must-have-your-kiss-although-it-dooms-me song was #1 for seven weeks. It was also a hit for Tony Martin and for Toni Arden in the spring of 1952.

Till I Waltz Again With You by **Teresa Brewer** introduced Dec 13
Written by Sidney Prosen   Orchestra conducted by Jack Pleis

Teresa Brewer's million-selling plaintive and dreamy young-lovers-have-to-part song was her favorite hit recording. This popular song was also recorded by the Harmonicats, Dick Todd, and Russ Morgan in 1953.

Why Don't You Believe Me recorded by **Joni James** introduced Oct 17
Written by Lew Douglas, Luther King Laney, Leroy Rodde
Orchestra conducted by Lew Douglas

This was the first of many #1 EASY-POP hits that young newcomer Joni James would chart. There were also hit versions by Patti Page and Margaret Whiting.

Two other EASY-POP hit singles released during 1952:

Heart and Soul
a hit recording by the **Four Aces** introduced October 25

Wish You Were Here
another hit recording by **Eddie Fisher** introduced September 6

Novelty and Instrumental hit records during 1952:

Auf Wiederseh'n Sweetheart
recorded by **Vera Lynn** introduced July 12

Blue Tango
instrumental recording by **Leroy Anderson** introduced July 5

Delicado
instrumental recording by **Percy Faith** introduced July 5

Glow-Worm
novelty recording by the **Mills Brothers** introduced December 6

High Noon (Do Not Forsake Me)
western film title recording by **Frankie Laine** introduced July 12

It's In the Book
spoken word recording by **Johnny Standley** introduced November 22

Slow Poke
novelty recording by **Pee Wee King** introduced January 5

Popular long-playing record albums released in 1952:
(compilations of songs were available on either one 33$\frac{1}{3}$ rpm 10" disc or as a set of 45rpm records)

'I'm in the Mood for Love' recorded by **Eddie Fisher**
RCA album with 8 songs including *You'll Never Know, That Old Feeling, Hold Me, Everything I Have is Yours,* and *I've Got You under My Skin*

'Johnnie Ray' recorded by **Johnnie Ray**
Columbia album with 8 songs including *Walkin' My Baby Back Home, All of Me, Don't Take Your Love from Me, Give Me Time,* and *Don't Blame Me*

'Unforgettable' recorded by **Nat King Cole**
12 songs on three Extended Play 45s include *Mona Lisa, Hajji Baba,* and *Too Young*

'TV Favorites' recorded by **Perry Como**
8 songs on four RCA Victor 45s including *Black Moonlight* and *While We're Young*

1953 News Headlines:

Communist Premier of the Soviet Union, Joseph Stalin, Dies at 72

Edmund Hillary and Tenzing Norkay Reach Peak of Mount Everest

Earl Warren is Nominated Chief Justice of the Supreme Court

Easter Egg Rolling is Revived at the White House

Studies Indicate a Correlation between Heart Disease and Diets High in Animal Fat

Popular Culture in 1953:

Favorite singers:

Tony Bennett

Kay Starr

Chordettes

Most popular film stars:

Alan Ladd

Marilyn Monroe

Photoplay Magazine Gold Medal Awards

Most Popular films:

#1 *Peter Pan* (a Disney animated film featuring the memorable pixie character, Tinker Bell)

#2 *The Robe* (starring Richard Burton, Jean Simmons, and Victor Mature)

#3 *From Here to Eternity* (starring Burt Lancaster, Deborah Kerr, and Frank Sinatra)

#4 *Shane* (classic western starring Alan Ladd, Jean Arthur, Van Heflin, and Brandon deWilde)

#5 *How to Marry a Millionaire* (starring Marilyn Monroe, Betty Grable, & Lauren Bacall)

from Susan Sackett's Billboard Box Office Hits, p.104-109

Most Popular TV programs:

#1 *I Love Lucy* (smash hit situation comedy featuring a pregnant Lucille Ball and Desi Arnaz)

#2 *Dragnet* (second season of realistic police drama starring Jack Webb as Sergeant Joe Friday)

#3 *Arthur Godfrey's Talent Scouts* (celebrities bring new acts, audience selects winner)

#4 *You Bet Your Life* (comedian Groucho Marx hosted this half-hour filmed quiz show)

#5 *The Bob Hope Show* (America's premier comedian in this once-a-month variety series)

from Alex McNeil's Total Television, p.898

Mass Media Facts:

First appearance of 3-D movies: 'Bwana Devil' and 'House of Wax'

First coast-to-coast 'Oscar' telecast of the Academy Awards with host Bob Hope

55% of American families own a television set

RCA demonstrates videotape recording

FCC adopts NTSC as the color standard for TV in the US, developed by RCA

IBM starts building commercial computers

First Appeared in 1953:

TV Guide magazine, Chevrolet Corvette, DC-7 propeller airplane,
Conelrad emergency broadcast system, and Playboy magazine

from Gordon's Columbia Chronicles p.390

Two Unforgettable EASY-POP Recordings of 1953:

The Doggie in the Window recorded by **Patti Page** introduced Jan. 31
Written by Bob Merrill   Orchestra conducted by Jack Rael

Patti Page sold more than four million copies of this simple and unpretentious musing of a lady pricing a puppy with a waggily tail. Earlier Bob Merrill's song had been turned down by Mindy Carson. This famous and successful novelty recording was produced by Mercury A&R man Joe Reisman who also provided the memorable 'arf-arf' yaps, while the violinist provided the more guttural barks.

You, You, You by the **Ames Brothers** introduced June 27
Music by Lotar Olias, English Lyrics by Robert Mellin,
original German lyrics by Walter Rothenberg Orchestra conducted by Hugo Winterhalter

Stand-out harmony and an uncomplicated singing style on a simple bouncy ballad *You, You, You* provided the biggest hit for the Ames Brothers (actually brothers Ed, Vic, Gene, and Joe Urick). This vocal quartet, with few equals, saw *You, You, You* dominate the charts for two months during the summer of 1953

More Classic Fifties EASY-POP Hit Singles from 1953:
(eight additional hit recordings listed in alphabetical order)

Crying in the Chapel recorded by **June Valli** introduced August 1
Written by Artie Glenn   Orchestra conducted by Joe Riesman

Crying in the Chapel was written in 1953 by Artie Glenn for his high-school son, Darrell Glenn, to record and it became a local hit in Knoxville, Tennessee. The top-ten version by June Valli, who released records all during the fifties, was her most memorable recording. Elvis Presley had a top-ten hit with *Crying in the Chapel* in 1965.

I'm Walking Behind You recorded by **Eddie Fisher** introduced May 9
Written by Billy Reid   Orchestra conducted by Hugo Winterhalter

Eddie Fisher brought his trademark zest to this recording of the British song *I'm Walking Behind You (on your wedding day)* with soprano Sally Sweetland. Frank Sinatra also recorded a hit version of this wedding-of-a-girlfriend song. An even more emotional Eddie Fisher had a second #1 hit in 1953 with *Oh! My Pa-Pa*, an unusual tribute since he and his father were not close.

No Other Love recorded by **Perry Como** introduced June 20
Written by Richard Rodgers & Oscar Hammerstein II

Orchestra conducted by Henri Rene

The music for this song from 1953's Broadway musical 'Me & Juliet' was originally composed as the *Southern Cross* theme for the 1952 TV documentary series 'Victory at Sea.'

Rags to Riches recorded by **Tony Bennett** introduced September 19
Written by Richard Adler & Jerry Ross   Orchestra conducted by Percy Faith

Tony Bennett's unique phrasing and intonation were evident in both of his memorable up-tempo 1953 hit recordings *Rags to Riches* and **Stranger in Paradise**.

Ricochet recorded by **Teresa Brewer** introduced October 3
Written by Larry Coleman, Joe Darion, & Norman Gimbel

Orchestra conducted by Jack Pleis

While this upbeat, spirited, fast-paced, recording with offbeat you-began-to-ricochet-like-a-rifle-bullet lyric was not her favorite, producer Bob Thiele felt it would be a big hit and suit her unique talent. He was right.

Song from 'Moulin Rouge' recorded by **Felicia Sanders** introduced Apr 4
Written by Bill Engvick & Georges Auric   Orchestra conducted by Percy Faith

Often considered an instrumental recording, this lush Percy Faith arrangement does not introduce vocalist Felicia Sanders until the last half of the record.

That's Amore recorded by **Dean Martin** introduced November 14
Written by Harry Warren & Jack Brooks   Orchestra conducted by Dick Stabile

Probably the most famous 50s Italian love song, Dean Martin introduced his signature moon-hits-your-eye-like-a-big-pizza-pie tune in the film 'The Caddy' co-starring his comic partner Jerry Lewis.

Vaya Con Dios recorded by **Les Paul** and **Mary Ford** introduced June 20
Written by Inez James, Buddy Pepper, & Larry Russell   Accompanied by Les Paul

The last number one hit for this duo, *Vaya Con Dios (May God Be With You)*, stayed at the top of the charts all summer in 1953.

Novelty and Instrumental hit records during 1953:

April in Portugal
instrumental recording by **Les Baxter** introduced March 4

C'est Si Bon
novelty recording by **Eartha Kitt** introduced July 18

I Believe
inspirational recording by **Frankie Laine** introduced February 21

St. George and the Dragonet
comedy recording by **Stan Freberg** introduced October 10

Your Cheating Heart
country/pop recording by **Joni James** introduced February 21

Popular long-playing record albums released in 1953:
(compilations of 8 songs were available on either one 33$\frac{1}{3}$ rpm 10" disc or as a set of 45 rpm records)

'I Believe' inspirational songs recorded by **Perry Como**
RCA album songs include *I Believe, Nearer My God to Thee,* and *Abide with Me*

'By the Light of the Silvery Moon' recorded by **Doris Day**
Columbia album songs include *Light of the Silvery Moon, If You Were the Only Girl, Be My Little Baby Bumble Bee, Ain't We Got Fun,* and *Just One Girl*

'Black Coffee' recorded by **Peggy Lee**
Decca album songs include *Black Coffee, It Ain't Necessarily So, Love Me or Leave Me, You're My Thrill, I Didn't Know What Time It Was,* and *There's a Small Hotel*

'RCA Victor Presents Eartha Kitt' recorded by **Eartha Kitt**
Eight songs including *C'est Si Bon, Uska Dara,* and *I Want to be Evil*

'Let There Be Love' recorded by **Joni James**
MGM album songs include *My Romance, The Nearness of You, You're Nearer, Love is Here to Stay, You're My Everything,* and *I'll Be Seeing You*

'Dinah Shore Sings the Blues' recorded by **Dinah Shore**
Songs include *Basin Street Blues, Bye Bye Blues,* and *Nashville Blues*

'The Kay Starr Style' recorded by **Kay Starr**
RCA album songs include *Side by Side, It's The Talk of the Town,* and *Too Busy*

1954 News Headlines:

Supreme Court Rules: Racial Segregation in Public Education is Unconstitutional

British Agree to Return Suez Canal to Egypt within Two Years

Vietnam Is Divided into North and South at the 17th Parallel

Largest Thermonuclear Blast Occurs at Bikini Atoll

Surgeon Sam Sheppard Is Accused of Wife's Murder

Popular Culture in 1954:

Favorite singers:
Nat King Cole
Rosemary Clooney
Crew-Cuts

Most popular film stars:
William Holden
June Allyson
Photoplay Magazine Gold Medal Awards

Most Popular films:

#1 *White Christmas* (starring Bing Crosby, Donald O'Conner, and Rosemary Clooney)

#2 *20,000 Leagues Under the Sea* (starring Kirk Douglas and James Mason)

#3 *Rear Window* (Alfred Hitchcock thriller starring James Stewart and Grace Kelly)

#4 *The Caine Mutiny* (starring Humphrey Bogart, Jose Ferrer, and Van Johnson)

#5 *The Glenn Miller Story* (biopic starring James Stewart and June Allyson)

from Susan Sackett's Billboard Box Office Hits, p110-115

Most Popular TV programs:

#1 *I Love Lucy* (fourth season of situation comedy series starring Lucille Ball and Desi Arnaz)

#2 *The Jackie Gleason Show* (weekly comedy variety series starring 'the Great One')

#3 *Dragnet* (terse, "just-the-facts" police drama starring Jack Webb as Sergeant Joe Friday)

#4 *You Bet Your Life* (contestants are foils for comedian Groucho Marx on this quiz show)

#5 *Toast of the Town* (News columnist, Ed Sullivan, hosts long-running variety series)

from Alex McNeil's Total Television, p.899

Mass Media Facts:

Color TV broadcasts begin and color TV sets are marketed for $1,000

Pianist Liberace becomes a TV sensation with his candelabras and wide smiles

Marilyn Monroe and Joe DiMaggio marry on Jan. 14 and file for divorce Oct. 5

The first 'Miss America' pageant is televised: Lee Ann Meriweather wins

Transistor radios and stereo music tapes go on sale

US shaken by Edward R. Murrow TV documentary on Senator Joseph McCarthy

First Appeared in 1954:

Frozen TV dinners, the Cha-Cha, US Air Force Academy, 'Duck Tail' haircuts,

Veterans' Day (replacing Armistice Day), and the breath-inhaler alcohol detector

from Gordon's Columbia Chronicles p.390

Two Unforgettable EASY-POP Recordings of 1954:

Young At Heart recorded by **Frank Sinatra** introduced February 13
Music by Johnny Richards, Lyrics by Carolyn Leigh
Orchestra conducted by Nelson Riddle

Frank Sinatra was the first performer to record this breezy, upbeat ballad, which became another million-selling hit for him. Carolyn Leigh added lyrics to Johnny Richards's instrumental composition called *Moonbeam*. The song, delivered in a straightforward way by the greatest crooner of the decade, was such a hit that a movie he was filming at the time with Doris Day was renamed to coincide with the name of the song, and the song was included in the opening and closing credits of the movie, which was released as 'Young at Heart.'

Mr. Sandman recorded by the **Chordettes** introduced October 30
Written by Pat Ballard   Arranged by Archie Bleyer

Beginning with thirteen 'bum-bum-bum-bums' then the deep voice asking 'yes?' plus the reference to 'wavy hair like Liberace,' it just had to be the Chordettes' biggest hit. Archie Bleyer's simple background doesn't clutter the vocals and the Chordettes single *Mr. Sandman* rocketed them to major chart success. Originally written by Pat Ballard for a male singer, the sensational Chordettes' vocal arrangement plus the saucy flavor imparted by translating it from a man's plea to a girl's plea, kept *Mr. Sandman* at the top the charts for seven weeks.

More Classic Fifties EASY-POP Hit Singles from 1954:
(eight additional hit recordings listed in alphabetical order)

Hearts of Stone recorded by the **Fontane Sisters** introduced December 11
Written by Eddy Ray & Rudy Jackson   Orchestra conducted by Billy Vaughn

Otis Williams & the Charms released an earlier recording of *Hearts of Stone* but the Fontane Sisters' cover with a chorus of 'do, do, wat, do, do, wa, da' scored #1.

Hold My Hand recorded by **Don Cornell** introduced September 11
Written by Jack Lawrence & Richard Myers   Orchestra conducted by Jerry Carr

Prominently featured in the Dick Powell/Debbie Reynolds comedy film 'Susan Slept Here,' Don Cornell charted the biggest hit of his career with *Hold My Hand*.

I Need You Now recorded by **Eddie Fisher** introduced September 4
Written by Jimmie Crane & Al Jacobs
Orchestra conducted by Hugo Winterhalter

Bobby-sox idol, Eddie Fisher, in his full-voiced lyric baritone sweetness, belted-out this ballad to number one on the charts.

Let Me Go Lover recorded by **Joan Weber** introduced December 4
Written by Al Hill & Jenny Lou Carson
Orchestra conducted by Jimmy Carroll

Teresa Brewer, Patti Page, and Peggy Lee all recorded *Let Me Go Lover* but no one hit the low note on 'lover' like Joan Weber did on her #1 version. It was her only top-one-hundred recording.

Little Things Mean a Lot recorded by **Kitty Kallen** introduced April 17
Written by Edith Lindeman & Carl Stutz   Orchestra conducted by Jack Pleis

Blowing a kiss from across the room, Kitty Kallen's only number one hit song *Little Things Mean a Lot* was also recorded five years later by Joni James.

Secret Love recorded by **Doris Day** introduced January 9
Written by Sammy Fain & Paul Francis Webster
Orchestra conducted by Ray Heindorf

Doris Day introduced her number one hit record *Secret Love* in the musical film 'Calamity Jane' and it was the Oscar winning song that year.

That's All I Want From You by **Jaye P. Morgan** introduced Nov 27
Written by M. Rotha (real name: Fritz Rotta)
Orchestra conducted by Hugo Winterhalter

Jaye P. Morgan recorded *(A Little Love That Slowly Grows) That's All I Want from You* during her first session at RCA. It was a million-selling record and heralded the arrival of a new star in EASY-POP music.

This Ole House recorded by **Rosemary Clooney** introduced August 7
Written by Stuart Hamblen   Orchestra conducted by Buddy Cole

Her two #1 hits in 1954 included the raucous novelty recording of *This Old House* balanced with her touching version of **Hey There** from 'Pajama Game.'

Five other EASY-POP hit singles released during 1954:

(Oh Baby Mine) I Get So Lonely (When I Dream About You)
hit recording by the **Four Knights** introduced January 23

If I Give My Heart to You
sentimental hit recording by **Doris Day** introduced September 11

Teach Me Tonight
hit recording by the **DeCastro Sisters** introduced October 9

Three Coins in the Fountain
movie title theme recorded by the **Four Aces** introduced May 22

Wanted
another hit ballad by **Perry Como** introduced April 10

Novelty and Rock 'n' Roll hit records during 1954:

The *Happy Wanderer (Val-de-ri, Val-de-ra)*
recording by **Frank Weir** and his orchestra introduced May 1

Sh-Boom
rock and roll cover recording by the **Crew-Cuts** introduced April 29

Popular long-playing record albums released in 1954:
(compilations of 8 songs were available on either one 33⅓ rpm disc or as a set of 45rpm records)

'May I Sing to You' recorded by **Eddie Fisher**
Eight songs include *Begin the Beguine, Nature Boy, Night and Day, Where the Blue of the Night Meets the Gold of the Day,* and *April Showers*

'Songs in a Mellow Mood' recorded by **Ella Fitzgerald**
Includes *Stardust, Nice Work If You Can Get It, My Heart Belongs to Daddy, People Will Say We're in Love, Imagination,* and *I'm Glad There is You*

'Songs for Young Lovers' recorded by **Frank Sinatra**
Sinatra's first 'concept' album and first collaboration with Nelson Riddle. Songs include *My Funny Valentine, A Foggy Day,* and *I Get A Kick Out of You*

'Swing Easy' recorded by **Frank Sinatra**
Sinatra's second Capitol album with Nelson Riddle arrangements. Songs include *Just One of Those Things, Wrap Your Troubles in Dreams,* and *All of Me*

1955 News Headlines:

Supreme Court Orders School Segregation to End

Richard Daley Becomes Mayor of Chicago

The Minimum Wage Rises from 75¢ to $1.00

Labor Unions AFL and CIO Merge, George Meany Becomes President

Film Star James Dean Dies in Car Crash at 24

Popular Culture in 1955:

Favorite singers:

Frank Sinatra

Judy Garland

Fontane Sisters

Most popular film stars:

William Holden

Jennifer Jones

Photoplay Magazine Gold Medal Awards

Most Popular films:

#1 *Lady and the Tramp* (a Walt Disney animated film featuring the voice of Peggy Lee)

#2 *Cinerama Holiday* (a travelogue in the 'Cinerama' three-screen format)

#3 *Mister Roberts* (starring Henry Fonda, James Cagney, William Powell, and Jack Lemon)

#4 *Battle Cry* (a war film starring Van Heflin, Aldo Ray, Mona Freeman, and James Whitmore)

#5 *Oklahoma* (Rodgers & Hammerstein musical starring Gordon MacRae and Shirley Jones)

from Susan Sackett's Billboard Box Office Hits, p.116-121

Most Popular TV programs:

#1 *The $64,000 Question* (Hal March hosted quiz show that became an overnight sensation)

#2 *I Love Lucy* (fifth season of situation comedy starring Lucille Ball and Desi Arnaz)

#3 *The Ed Sullivan Show* (New name for long-running variety series 'Toast of the Town')

#4 *Disneyland* (hour-long anthology series: cartoons; nature stories; and 'Davy Crockett')

#5 *The Jack Benny Program* (half-hour comedy series with a group of supporting players)

from Alex McNeil's Total Television, p.899

Mass Media Facts:

President Eisenhower holds the first televised presidential press conference

Disneyland opens in Anaheim, California

Eppie Lederer begins 'Ask Ann Landers' advice column in the Chicago Sun-Times

United States Post Office inaugurates Certified Mail

Children's program 'Kukla, Fran, and Ollie' begins telecasting from Chicago

Eddie Fisher and Debbie Reynolds marry

First Appeared in 1955:

Ford Thunderbird, McDonald's, Crest toothpaste, Gorton's Fish Sticks,

roll-on deodorant, and Colonel Sanders' Kentucky Fried Chicken

from Gordon's Columbia Chronicles p.435

Two Unforgettable EASY-POP Recordings of 1955:

Sincerely by the **McGuire Sisters** introduced January 8
Written by Harvey Fuqua & Alan Freed   Orchestra conducted by David Jacobs

Sincerely was the first and the biggest hit for the McGuire Sisters—showing off their trademark close harmony. It was a cover of the original 1955 release by the rhythm and blues group, the Moonglows. Ironically, the Moonglow's recording of *Sincerely* was very similar to the 1951 Dominoes' tune *That's What You're Doing To Me*. Harvey Fuqua, who started the Moonglows (with lead singer Bobby Lester) wrote *Sincerely* with his mentor, the legendary Alan Freed, who is best-known as the radio disc-jockey who coined the term 'rock 'n roll.'

Memories Are Made of This by **Dean Martin** introduced Dec 3
Written by Terry Gilkyson, Richard Dehr, Frank Miller
                    Backed by the Easy Riders (Terry Gilkyson, Richard Dehr, Frank Miller)

Dean Martin was backed by the Easy Riders singing 'sweet sweet' on this light and peppy recording that offered a recipe for fifties philosophy for life—a girl, a boy, some grief, some joy. The song is from the film 'The Seven Hills Of Rome' where it was sung by Mario Lanza. The song's writer, Terry Gilkyson, had performed with the legendary folk group The Weavers in the early 1950s.

More Classic Fifties EASY-POP Hit Singles from 1955:
(eight additional hit recordings listed in alphabetical order)

Band of Gold recorded by **Don Cherry** introduced December 3
Written by Bob Musel & Jack Taylor   Orchestra conducted by Ray Conniff

With its unusual choral backing and a Ray Conniff arrangement, *Band of Gold*, was the most successful hit single for easy-going, singer/golfer Don Cherry.

The Breeze and I recorded by **Caterina Valente** introduced April 9
Music by Ernesto Lecuona, Lyrics by Al Stillman
                    Orchestra conducted by Werner Muller

This wistful song, in which the singer laments that only the *Breeze and I* are aware of her love, begins with castinets and "la-la-la". The song was originally written as *Andalucia* and it was a 1940 hit for Jimmy Dorsey with Bob Eberly singing Al Stillman's lyrics.

Heart recorded by **Eddie Fisher** introduced May 14
Written by Richard Adler & Jerry Ross

Orchestra conducted by Hugo Winterhalter

Eddie Fisher's energetic recording of this rousing number from the Broadway musical 'Damn Yankees' made the top-ten, so did his end-of-the-year recording of the teen-oriented *Dungaree Doll*.

How Important Can It Be? recorded by **Joni James** introduced Feb. 19
Written by Bennie Benjamin, George Weiss

Orchestra conducted by Tony Aquaviva

Youthful Joni James reflects the feelings of fifties teenage girls in this song that questions the importance of past romantic relationships to a new-found love.

Learnin' the Blues recorded by **Frank Sinatra** introduced May 7
Written by Dolores Vicki Silvers   Orchestra conducted by Nelson Riddle

With the tables empty and the dance floor deserted, Frank Sinatra's signature release, with classic Nelson Riddle arrangement, was a #1 hit record.

Love is a Many-Splendored Thing by the **Four Aces** Aug. 27
Written by Sammy Fain & Paul Francis Webster

Orchestra conducted by Jack Pleis

Two lovers kiss on a high and windy hill to a soaring melody in this title song from the William Holden/Jennifer Jones romantic film 'Love is a Many-Splendored Thing.' It was a number one hit for the Four Aces in the fall of 1955.

Moments to Remember by the **Four Lads** introduced September 3
Written by Al Stillman & Robert Allen   Orchestra conducted by Ray Ellis

An unidentified woman opens with "January to December" and then "never quite watched the show" at the drive-in movie in this sentimental Four Lads' hit.

Rock and Roll Waltz recorded by **Kay Starr** introduced December 31
Written by Roy Alfred & Shorty Allen

Orchestra conducted by Hugo Winterhalter

Kay Starr tried her hand at a rock/pop song with her successful mom-and-dad-waltzing-to-a-rock-song recording that reached the top of the charts.

Novelty, Rock, and Instrumental hit records during 1955:

Ain't That A Shame
cover recording by **Pat Boone** introduced September 17

Autumn Leaves
instrumental recording by **Roger Williams** introduced October 29

Ballad of Davy Crockett
record by **Fess Parker** introduced March 12; by **Bill Hayes** introduced March 26

Cherry Pink and Apple Blossom White
mambo instrumental recording by **Perez Prado** introduced March 5

Dance With Me Henry
cover recording by **Georgia Gibbs** introduced May 14

Earth Angel
cover recording by **Crew-Cuts** introduced February 5

Rock Around the Clock
rock 'n' roll recording by **Bill Haley & his Comets** introduced July 9

Sixteen Tons
work song recorded by **Tennessee Ernie Ford** introduced November 26

Unchained Melody
top-ten instrumental recording by **Les Baxter** introduced April 9
top-ten vocal version by **Al Hibbler** introduced April 9
top-ten vocal version by **Roy Hamilton** introduced April 23

The *Yellow Rose of Texas*
choral ensemble recording by **Mitch Miller & his Gang** introduced September 3

Popular long-playing record albums released in 1955:
(compilations of songs were available on either one 33⅓ rpm 12" disc or as a set of 45rpm records)

'Miss Show Business' recorded by **Judy Garland**
Twelve songs including *Rock-a-Bye Your Baby with a Dixie Melody, Danny Boy, Happiness is Just a Thing Called Joe,* and *Over the Rainbow*

'In the Wee Small Hours' recorded by **Frank Sinatra**
Another classic collaboration with Nelson Riddle.
Twelve melancholy ballads include *In the Wee Small Hours, I'll Be Around, I Get Along Without You Very Well, Mood Indigo, What is This Thing Called Love,* and *When Your Lover Has Gone*

1956 News Headlines:

Ike (Dwight Eisenhower) re-elected President, Defeats Adlai Stevenson

Dr. Jonas Salk's Polio Vaccine goes on the Market

Congress Inaugurates the Interstate Highway System

Former Milwaukee Schoolteacher Golda Meir Becomes Prime Minister of Israel

Grace Kelly Marries Prince Rainier of Monaco

Popular Culture in 1956:

Favorite singers:
Pat Boone
Joni James
Four Lads

Most popular film stars:
Rock Hudson
Kim Novak
Photoplay Magazine Gold Medal Awards

Most Popular films:

#1 *The Ten Commandments* (a biblical epic starring Charlton Heston as Moses)

#2 *Around the World in 80 Days* (Jules Verne classic starring David Niven & Cantinflas)

#3 *Giant* (Edna Ferber saga starring Rock Hudson, Elizabeth Taylor, and James Dean)

#4 *Seven Wonders of the World* (a travelogue in the 'Cinerama' three-screen format)

#5 *The King and I* (Rodgers & Hammerstein musical starring Deborah Kerr and Yul Brynner)
from Susan Sackett's Billboard Box Office Hits, p.122-127

Most Popular TV programs:

#1 *I Love Lucy* (final season of situation comedy series starring Lucille Ball and Desi Arnaz)

#2 *The Ed Sullivan Show* (Elvis Presley appeared on this long-running variety series)

#3 *General Electric Theater* (filmed anthology series of contemporary adventures)

#4 *The $64,000 Question* (Hal March hosted the 2nd season of this big-money quiz show)

#5 *December Bride* (Spring Byington stars as an attractive widow in this situation comedy)
from Alex McNeil's Total Television, p.900

Mass Media Facts:

First transatlantic telephone cable system begins service to Europe

Elvis Presley's appearance on the Ed Sullivan TV show attracts record audience

NBC's Chet Huntley and David Brinkley bring star system to network news

Drive-in movie theaters peak at 7,000

CBS moves production of shows from NYC to Television City in California

Marilyn Monroe and Arthur Miller marry

First Appeared in 1956:

Liquid Paper, disposable Pampers, Imperial margarine, Salem menthol cigarettes, Comet cleansing powder, and Ovaltine's Captain Midnight decoders
from Gordon's Columbia Chronicles p.444

Two Unforgettable EASY-POP Recordings of 1956:

Whatever Will Be, Will Be (Que Sera, Sera) by **Doris Day** June 23
Written by Jay Livingston & Ray Evans   Orchestra conducted by Frank DeVol

Alfred Hitchcock assigned the gifted team of Jay Livingston and Ray Evans to write a simple lullaby for his suspense film 'The Man Who Knew Too Much' and it proved to be the biggest hit of Doris Day's recording career. The phrase came from the Italian family motto, 'Che, Sera, Sera' in the film 'The Barefoot Contessa.' The motto in the movie was Italian, but the writers switched the Italian 'Che' to the Spanish 'Que' because more people spoke Spanish in the US. *Que Sera, Sera* received the 1956 Academy Award for best original song.

Love Me Tender recorded by **Elvis Presley** introduced October 20
Written by Elvis Presley & Vera Matson (actually Ken Darby)
Accompanied by the Ken Darby Trio

This pensive, haunting ballad was the title song from Elvis Presley's first film. It was co-written by Ken Darby and Elvis Presley. Vera Matson, credited as a co-writer, was the wife of Ken Darby. The melody is an adaptation of the Civil War era song called *Aura Lee.* Elvis Presley put subdued emotion into the song and the result was spectacular. It was one of five #1 hits he released in 1956 including rock 'n' roll hits *Heartbreak Hotel, Don't Be Cruel, Hound Dog*, and *I Want You, I Need You, I Love You.*

More Classic Fifties EASY-POP Hit Singles from 1956:
(eight additional hit recordings listed in alphabetical order)

Hot Diggity recorded by **Perry Como** introduced March 10
Written by Al Hoffman & Dick Manning   Orchestra conducted by Mitchell Ayers

Perry Como was joined by the Ray Charles Singers (no relation to rock icon, Ray Charles) in this popular number one hit *Hot Diggity, Dog Ziggity, Boom What You Do To Me* novelty song.

Ivory Tower recorded by **Cathy Carr** introduced March 17
Written by Jack Fulton & Lois Steele   Orchestra conducted by Dan Belloc

This only hit song for Cathy Carr was a cover of an original recording by the R&B group the Charms. Gale Storm also covered it. All were top-ten hits.

Just Walking in the Rain recorded by **Johnnie Ray** introduced Sept. 1
Written by Johnny Bragg & Robert Riley   Orchestra conducted by Ray Conniff

Again tortured by love lost, but slightly more subdued than his 1951 trademark smash hit *Cry*, this Johnnie Ray recording reached number two on the charts.

Moonlight Gambler recorded by **Frankie Laine** introduced December 1
Written by Bob Hilliard & Phil Springer   Orchestra conducted by Ray Conniff

Frankie Laine's brash vibrancy and dynamic style, gambling on love or not gambling at all, was evident again in *Moonlight Gambler*, the final hit of his twenty-year recording career.

My Prayer recorded by the **Platters** introduced July 7
Written by Georges Boulanger & Jimmy Kennedy

Written in 1939, *My Prayer* was based on Georges Boulanger's *Avant de Mourir*. The R&B group the Platters had two recordings that rode the top of the charts in 1956—***The Great Pretender*** and then *My Prayer*.

No, Not Much recorded by the **Four Lads** introduced January 21
Written by Al Stillman & Robert Allen   Orchestra conducted by Ray Ellis

There is a disarming sarcasm in this I-Don't-Want-My-Arms-Around-You-*NO-NOT-MUCH* classic fifties hit. The bright, easy-to-sing-along-with song was typical Four Lads. The melodic group had another 1956 hit with ***Standing on the Corner*** from the Broadway musical 'Most Happy Fella.'

Singing the Blues recorded by **Guy Mitchell** introduced October 27
Written by Melvin Endsley   Produced by Mitch Miller

Mitch Miller arranged a whistling opening and ever popular and likable Guy Mitchell would "cry-eye-eye-eye over you" in this POP/country standard that was also a hit for Marty Robbins.

The *Wayward Wind* recorded by **Gogi Grant** introduced April 28
Written by Herb Newman & Stan Lebowsky   Orchestra conducted by Buddy Bregman

Buddy Bregman created an ethereal arrangement for jazz/pop singer Gogi Grant, Billboard magazine's Most Popular Female vocalist in 1956. This next-of-kin to the *Wayward Wind* favorite song stayed on the charts for more than half of 1956.

Novelty, Rock, and Instrumental hit records during 1956:

The Green Door
rock 'n' roll recording by **Jim Lowe** introduced November 3

It's Almost Tomorrow
recording by the **Dream Weavers** introduced November 12, 1955

Lisbon Antigua
instrumental recording by **Nelson Riddle** introduced February 25

Moonglow (Theme from 'Picnic')
instrumental by **Morris Stoloff** introduced June 2

The Poor People of Paris
instrumental recording by **Les Baxter** introduced March 17

Tonight You Belong to Me
novelty recording by **Patience & Prudence** introduced August 4

Popular long-playing record albums released in 1956:
(compilations of songs were available on either one 33⅓ rpm 12" disc or as a set of 45rpm records)

'Calypso' recorded by **Harry Belafonte**
The first million-selling album by a single artist, twelve West Indian songs
include: *Day-O, Jamaica Farewell, I Do Adore Her, Come Back Liza,* and
Man Smart (Woman Smarter)

'Judy' recorded by **Judy Garland**
Twelve songs including *Come Rain or Come Shine, I Feel a Song Comin' On,
Lucky Day, April Showers, I Will Come Back,* and *Dirty Hands, Dirty Face*

'Ella Fitzgerald Sings the Cole Porter Songbook'
34 songs include *In the Still of the Night, Night and Day, You're the Top,
Too Darn Hot, Begin the Beguine, So In Love, Anything Goes, I Love Paris,
I Get a Kick Out of You, Easy to Love,* and *It's De-Lovely*

'The **Complete Manhattan Tower**'
recorded by **Gordon Jenkins Orchestra**
A complete work for orchestra and vocalists. Twelve songs include *Married I
Can Always Get, I'm Learnin' My Latin,* and *New York's My Home*

'Songs for Swinging Lovers' recorded by **Frank Sinatra**
Supreme Frank Sinatra collaboration with Nelson Riddle, 12 up-tempo standards
include: *You Make Me Feel So Young, Too Marvelous for Words,
Pennies from Heaven,* and *I've Got You Under My Skin*

1957 News Headlines:

Soviet Union Launches the First Man-made Space Satellite, Sputnik 1

Jimmy Hoffa becomes President of the Teamsters Union

Arkansas National Guard Blocks Black High School Students in Little Rock

Supreme Court's Roth Decision Sets Community Standards for Obscenity

Popular Culture in 1957:

Favorite singers:
Johnny Mathis
Dinah Shore
McGuire Sisters

Most popular film stars:
Rock Hudson
Deborah Kerr
Photoplay Magazine Gold Medal Awards

Most Popular films:

#1 *The Bridge on the River Kwai* (British film starring William Holden and Alec Guinness)

#2 *Peyton Place* (film of Grace Metalious' steamy novel starring Lana Turner and Hope Lange)

#3 *Sayonara* (film of James Michener's novel starring Marlon Brando and Miyoshi Umeki)

#4 *Old Yeller* (starring Dorothy McGuire, Fess Parker, Tommy Kirk, and Kevin Corcoran)

#5 *Raintree County* (saga starring Montgomery Clift, Elizabeth Taylor, and Eva Marie Saint)
from Susan Sackett's Billboard Box Office Hits, p.128-133

Most Popular TV programs:

#1 *Gunsmoke* (James Arness stars as Marshall Matt Dillon in this 'adult' western's 3rd season)

#2 *The Danny Thomas Show/Make Room for Daddy* (thirty-minute situation comedy)

#3 *Tales of Wells Fargo* (Dale Robertson stars as agent Jim Hardie in this western)

#4 *Have Gun, Will Travel* (Richard Boone stars as Paladin, a college-educated gunslinger)

#5 *I've Got a Secret* (Garry Moore hosts four celebrity panelists in this quiz show)
from Alex McNeil's Total Television, p.900

Mass Media Facts:

Alan Freed's nightly rock and roll music radio show reaches a national audience

University professor Charles Van Doren wins on TV quiz show 'Twenty-One'

Industry support sends first 'merit scholars' to college

Film superstar Humphrey Bogart dies

FORTRAN becomes the first high-level computer programming language

Quiz show fraud rocks U.S. television

First Appeared in 1957:

Hula Hoops, the Slinky, Silly Putty, and
the Ford Motor Company introduces the Edsel
from Gordon's Columbia Chronicles p.453

Two Unforgettable EASY-POP Recordings of 1957:

April Love recorded by **Pat Boone** introduced October 28
Music by Sammy Fain, Lyrics by Paul Francis Webster
From the film 'April Love' directed by Henry Levin

The title song from his popular film 'April Love' co-starring Shirley Jones was nominated for an Academy Award—energetic and talented Lionel Newman was the music director on the film. The lilting, April-love-is-for-the-very-young song was Pat Boone's fifth top-rated song in the mid fifties. With his white buck shoes and clean-cut image, smooth baritone Pat Boone scored two more number one hits in 1957: *Love Letters in the Sand* and *Don't Forbid Me.*

Round and Round recorded by **Perry Como** introduced February 23
Written by Lou Stallman & Joe Shapiro Orchestra conducted by Mitchell Ayres

Relaxed and amiable Perry Como was a singer who didn't have to prove anything with his voice—no fuss, no affect, no attitude. His #1 hit, the quint-essential *Round and Round* was on the charts for more than half of 1957. Dozens of these exhilarating, up-tempo, bouncy, hits like *Papa Loves Mambo* and *Tina Marie*, were recorded in the mid-fifties by the decade's most successful singer.

More Classic Fifties EASY-POP Hit Singles from 1957:
(eight additional hit recordings listed in alphabetical order)

Chances Are recorded by **Johnny Mathis** introduced September 16
Written by Al Stillman & Robert Allen   Orchestra conducted by Ray Conniff

Chances Are was one of two #1 hits for Johnny Mathis in 1957, also *It's Not for Me to Say*, both exemplify the smooth, sensitive, subtle side of the fifties sound.

Diana recorded by **Paul Anka** introduced July 15
Written by Paul Anka   Orchestra conducted by Don Costa

Diana, Paul Anka's first recording shot to #1 and spent half-a-year on the charts. The music was based on a popular Latin rhythm called cha-lypso, a modified cha-cha done to a calypso beat. 15-year-old Paul Anka wrote *Diana*, a song describing his unrequited love for his little sister's 20-year-old babysitter.

Everyday recorded by **Buddy Holly** introduced November 11

Niki Sullivan (rhythm guitar), Joel Mauldin (bass), Jerry Alison (drums)

Written by Charles Harden (Buddy Holly) & Norman Petty

Goin' faster than a roller coaster, Buddy Holly and the Crickets' *Everyday*, with Norman Petty playing a celeste, was the 'B' side of the popular rock hit *Peggy Sue*. Buddy Holly and the Crickets also had a rock hits in 1957 with *That'll Be the Day* and *Oh, Boy!* all recorded in Clovis, New Mexico.

Honeycomb recorded by **Jimmie Rodgers** introduced August 12

Written by Bob Merrill   Orchestra conducted by Hugo Peretti

This folk-flavored song's catchy melody and lyrics coupled with Jimmie Rodgers distinctive, lilting voice caught on fast—rocketing this, his first recording, to #1. According to this light and breezy song, the honey from a million trips made my baby's lips.

Sugartime recorded by the **McGuire Sisters** introduced December 30

Written by Charlie Phillips & Odis Echols   Orchestra conducted by Neal Hefti

Popular favorite *Sugartime* was a huge hit recording during 1957 and 1958 but, unfortunately, it was the last top-ten hit for the McGuire Sisters.

Tammy recorded by **Debbie Reynolds** introduced July 22

Written by Jay Livingston & Ray Evans

Orchestra conducted by Joseph Gershenson

She heard the cottonwoods whispering above in the title song from the film 'Tammy and the Bachelor.' It was the only number one hit for America's sweetheart and popular film star Debbie Reynolds.

(Let Me Be Your) *Teddy Bear* recorded by **Elvis Presley** introduced June 24

Written by Kal Mann & Bernie Lowe   With the Jordanaires

Tigers play rough and you don't love lions enough so Elvis Presley wants to be a *Teddy Bear* in this song from his second film 'Loving You.' He also had #1 rock hits with *Too Much, All Shook Up,* and the title song from his third film *Jailhouse Rock*.

Young Love recorded by **Tab Hunter** introduced January 12

Written by Carole Joyner & Ric Cartey   Orchestra conducted by Billy Vaughn

Film star and heartthrob, Tab Hunter, recorded this cover of country singer Sonny James' original recording—both versions topped the charts in 1957.

Calypso, Rock, and Instrumental hit records during 1957:

Around the World
instrumental by **Victor Young** introduced May 20 and **Mantovani** introduced June 10

Banana Boat Song (Day-O)   and   *Island in the Sun*
calypso recordings by **Harry Belafonte** introduced January 12 and June 3

Bye Bye Love
first hit for the rock era duo, the **Everly Brothers** introduced May 20

Little Darlin'
cover recording by the **Diamonds** introduced March 16

Love Is Strange
popular recording by **Mickey & Sylvia** introduced January 5

Marianne
calypso recording by **Terry Gilkyson &** the **Easy Riders** introduced February 6

My Special Angel
Country/EASY-POP recording by **Bobby Helms** introduced October 14

So Rare
instrumental recording by **Jimmy Dorsey** introduced February 23

Wake Up Little Susie
second hit in 1957 for the **Everly Brothers** introduced September 30

White Sport Coat (and a Pink Carnation)
recording by country crossover singer **Marty Robbins** introduced April 13

Popular long-playing record albums released in 1957:
(compilations of songs were available on 33¹/₃ rpm 12" discs)

'Day by Day' recorded by **Doris Day**
Songs include *But Not for Me, Gypsy in My Soul,* and *But Beautiful*

'Ella Fitzgerald Sings the Rodgers and Hart Songbook'
34 songs including *Blue Room, Isn't It Romantic,* and *Mountain Greenery*

'Wonderful, Wonderful' recorded by **Johnny Mathis**
Twelve songs include *Day In, Day Out* and *That Old Black Magic*

'The Beat of My Heart' recorded by **Tony Bennett**
Twelve songs include *Let's Face the Music and Dance, I Get a Kick Out of You, Let There Be Love, Lullaby of Broadway,* and *Just One of Those Things*

'Swing Around Rosie' recorded by **Rosemary Clooney**
Includes *Blue Moon, 'Deed I Do, Too Close for Comfort,* and *Goody Goody*

'A Swinging Affair' recorded by **Frank Sinatra**
Forceful, brassy collaboration with Nelson Riddle, 12 jazzy standards include:
Night and Day, From this Moment On, If I Had You, and *Oh! Look at Me Now*

1958 News Headlines:

Castro-Led Rebels Seize Provincial Capital in Cuba

Alaskans Vote to Become the 49th State

Explorer I, First U.S. Satellite is Launched from Cape Canaveral

Pope Pius XII Dies, Pope John XXIII is Elected

Charles DeGaulle Becomes French Premier

Popular Culture in 1958:

Favorite singers:

Bobby Darin

Doris Day

Everly Brothers

Most popular film stars:

Tony Curtis

Debbie Reynolds

Photoplay Magazine Gold Medal Awards

Most Popular films:

#1 *South Pacific* (Rodgers & Hammerstein musical starring Rossano Brazzi and Mitzi Gaynor)

#2 *Auntie Mame* (Patrick Dennis' story of his eccentric aunt starring Rosalind Russell)

#3 *Cat on a Hot Tin Roof* (Elizabeth Taylor/Paul Newman in Tennessee Williams' scorcher)

#4 *No Time for Sergeants* (military comedy starring Andy Griffith)

#5 *Gigi* (original musical starring Leslie Caron, Louis Jourdan, and Maurice Chevalier)

from Susan Sackett's Billboard Box Office Hits, p.134-139

Most Popular TV programs:

#1 *Gunsmoke* (James Arness stars as Marshall Matt Dillon in this half-hour 'adult' western)

#2 *Wagon Train* (hour-long western following a California-bound wagon train each season)

#3 *Have Gun, Will Travel* (2nd season of western with Richard Boone as gunslinger, Paladin)

#4 *The Rifleman* (western saga of a struggling homesteader and his motherless son)

#5 *The Danny Thomas Show/Make Room for Daddy* (thirty-minute family comedy)

from Alex McNeil's Total Television, p.901

Mass Media Facts:

U.S. Defense Department creates ARPA, forerunner of the Internet

The Kingston Trio's *Tom Dooley* begins a folk music vogue

Lana Turner's boyfriend Johnny Stompanato fatally stabbed by her 14-year-old daughter

Elizabeth Taylor, Eddie Fisher, and Debbie Reynolds love triangle is publicized

Elvis Presley is inducted into the Army

Brigitte Bardot becomes the new sex symbol

First Appeared in 1958:

Stereo LP records, Chevrolet Impala, Sweet 'n' Low, Pizza Hut,

Green Giant canned beans, and Cocoa Krispies

from Gordon's Columbia Chronicles p.390

Two Unforgettable EASY-POP Recordings of 1958:

Catch a Falling Star by **Perry Como** introduced January 13
Written by Paul Vance & Lee Pockriss   Orchestra conducted by Mitchell Ayres

The Ray Charles singers back Perry Como again on this Joe Reisman arrangement that was based on a classical theme from Brahms' *Academic Festival Overture*. In March of 1958, the RIAA (Recording Industry Association of America) certified their first-ever 'gold record' to *Catch a Falling Star*. It was the last number one hit for the decade's favorite singer. In 1959, Perry Como won the very first Grammy Award for Best Male Vocal Performance.

---

26 Miles (Santa Catalina) by the **Four Preps** introduced January 20
Written by Bruce Belland & Glen Larson

Although the song says Santa Catalina, the island of romance, is "26 miles across the sea," it is actually just 22 miles from Los Angeles. Geography aside, the teenage quartet was able to capture a youthful spirit in their two biggest hit recordings that were both released in 1958. *26 Miles*, written by two members of the group, Bruce Belland and Glen Larson, hit the top of the charts early in the year and later the same year a second Four Preps song written by the duo *Big Man* topped the charges again.

More Classic Fifties EASY-POP Hit Singles from 1958:
(eight additional hit recordings listed in alphabetical order)

Don't recorded by **Elvis Presley** introduced January 27
Written by Jerry Leiber & Mike Stoller   with the Jordanaires

One pop song-writing team that Elvis Presley worked with was the prolific Jerry Leiber and Mike Stoller, who wrote *(Don't say) Don't (when I hold you this way)*. Elvis Presley recorded two more top hits in 1957—the rock 'n' roll *Hard Headed Woman* and the more playful *Wear My Ring Around Your Neck*.

Everybody Loves a Lover recorded by **Doris Day** introduced July 21
Written by Richard Adler & Robert Allen Orchestra conducted by Frank DeVol

This lively, peppy, girlish recording utilizes the multi-track voice overdub that lets Doris Day sing a duet with herself. The technique was frequently employed in 50s recordings. Everybody did love Doris Day but it was her last top-forty hit.

It's All in the Game recorded by **Tommy Edwards** introduced August 18
Written by Charles Dawes & Carl Sigman   Orchestra conducted by Leroy Holmes

The music for this #1 hit song was written by US Vice President Charles Dawes in 1912 as *Melody in A Major*. The lyrics were written by Carl Sigman in 1951, the year Tommy Edwards first recorded it. He re-recorded the song in 1958.

Lollipop recorded by the **Chordettes** introduced March 10
Written by Beverly Ross & Julius Dixon Orchestra conducted by Archie Bleyer

Lollipop is the penultimate girl-group hit from the late 50s. The Chordettes' infectious full round-like arrangement with its 'lollypop, lollypop, oh, lolly, lolly, lolly, lollypop' also included a finger-in-the-mouth pop.

Nel Blu Dipinto Di Blu (Volare) by **Domenico Modugno** introduced Aug 18
Written by Domenico Modugno, English lyrics by Mitchell Parish

Volare – Oh! Oh! was the only hit recording for Italian singer/actor Domenico Modugno. His Italian version was #1 and stayed on the charts for sixteen weeks. In English it was a hit for the McGuire Sisters and for Dean Martin.

Oh! Oh! I'm Falling in Love Again by **Jimmie Rodgers** Feb. 17
Written by Al Hoffman & Dick Manning   Orchestra conducted by Hugo Peretti

The muted, rock-influenced arrangement on this brisk recording compliments Jimmie Rodgers high, sweet voice and acoustic guitar. He also had strong sellers in 1958 with his pop-oriented folk songs *Secretly* and *Are You Really Mine*.

Poor Little Fool recorded by **Ricky Nelson** introduced July 7
Written by Shari Sheeley   Combo supervised by Jimmy Haskell & Ozzie Nelson

Ricky Nelson originally dismissed recording what would become his first #1 single because he felt it sounded "too much like Elvis" whom he idolized.

To Know Him is To Love Him by the **Teddy Bears** introduced Sept. 22
Music and Lyrics by Phil Spector

This song launched Phil Spector's career. He was a senior in high school when he created the only number one hit recording for the Teddy Bear trio of Phil Spector, Carol Conners (real name Annette Kleinbard), and Marshall Leib.

Novelty, Rock, and Instrumental hit records during 1958:

All I Have to Do is Dream
recorded by the **Everly Brothers** introduced May 12

At the Hop
rock 'n' roll recording by **Danny and the Juniors** introduced January 6

Chanson d'Amour *(Song of Love)*
recording by **Art and Dotty Todd** introduced April 14

Donna / La Bamba *(B-side)*
hits by Latin rock 'n' roll singer **Ritchie Valens** introduced November 24

Don't Let Go
pop/rock recording by **Roy Hamilton** introduced January 13

He's Got the Whole World
gospel recording by **Laurie London** introduced March 24

Patricia
mambo instrumental recording by **Perez Prado** introduced June 16

Purple People Eater
novelty recording by **Sheb Wooley** introduced June 9

Tequila
instrumental recording by the **Champs** introduced March 17

That Old Black Magic
duet by **Louis Prima & Keely Smith** introduced November 3

Witch Doctor
novelty recording by **David Seville** introduced April 28

Popular long-playing record albums released in 1958:
(compilations of songs were available on 33⅓ rpm 12" discs)

'Johnny's Greatest Hits' recorded by **Johnny Mathis**
First example of a 'Greatest Hits' album. Twelve songs include: *Chances Are, Twelfth of Never, It's Not for Me to Say, No Love,* and *Wonderful! Wonderful!*

'The Very Thought of You' recorded by **Nat King Cole**
12 songs include *For All We Know* and *The More I See You*

'Ella Fitzgerald Sings the Irving Berlin Songbook'
32 songs including *Cheek to Cheek, Always, Puttin' on the Ritz,* and *Blue Skies*

'Come Fly With Me' recorded by **Frank Sinatra**
Light-hearted collaboration with Billy May includes: *Around the World, Let's Get Away from It All, Autumn in New York,* and *Isle of Capri*

1959 News Headlines:

Hawaii Becomes the 50th State to be Added to the Union

Eisenhower and Khrushchev Meet at Camp David - Khrushchev Tours U. S.

Fidel Castro Takes Havana, Batista Flees

Castro Visits the U.S. and is Warmly Received

Oklahoma Repeals Prohibition that came with Statehood in 1907

Popular Culture in 1959:

Favorite singers:

Andy Williams

Connie Francis

Four Preps

Most popular film stars:

Rock Hudson

Doris Day

Photoplay Magazine Gold Medal Awards

Most Popular films:

#1   *Ben-Hur* (blockbuster chariot-race epoch starring Charlton Heston and Stephen Boyd)

#2   *Sleeping Beauty* (an elaborate Walt Disney animated film)

#3   *The Shaggy Dog* (slapstick comedy starring Fred McMurray and Kevin Corcoran)

#4   *Operation Petticoat* (comedy starring Cary Grant and Tony Curtis)

#5   *Darby O'Gill and the Little People* (starring Albert Sharpe and Sean Connery)

from Susan Sackett's Billboard Box Office Hits, p.140-146

Most Popular TV programs:

#1   *Gunsmoke* (the 5th season of this 20-year-running western series starring James Arness)

#2   *Wagon Train* (Ward Bond starred as wagon-master in this hour-long, big-western series)

#3   *Have Gun, Will Travel* (Richard Boone stars as gun-for-hire, Paladin, in this western)

#4   *The Danny Thomas Show/Make Room for Daddy* (half-hour situation comedy)

#5   *The Red Skelton Show* (visual comedian performed comedy sketches with guest stars)

from Alex McNeil's Total Television, p.901

Mass Media Facts:

Charles Van Doren admits his TV quiz role was fixed

Rock stars, Buddy Holly, Ritchie Valens, and Big Bopper killed in plane crash

New computer COBOL programming language uses plain English

Scented SMELL-O-VISION movies: 'Scent of Mystery' and 'Behind the Great Wall' released

86% of Americans own a TV set

First Appeared in 1959:

Barbie dolls, Microchips, the Grammy Awards, Xerox plain paper copier,
Ektachrome high-speed film, and Princess telephones in five colors

from Gordon's Columbia Chronicles p.390

Two Unforgettable EASY-POP Recordings of 1959:

Mack the Knife recorded by **Bobby Darin** introduced August 24
Written by Kurt Weill, Bert Brecht, & Marc Blitzstein from 'The Threepenny Opera'

Mack the Knife, written in 1928 as *Moritat* or *Theme from the Threepenny Opera*, became Bobby Darin's signature song. 'Mack' is the character Macheath, the murderer, in *The Threepenny Opera*. The light melody makes this feel like an upbeat song but it contrasts sharply with the lyrics about a criminal. Bobby Darin also recorded the bouncy 50s pop hit *Dream Lover,* which he wrote himself.

Venus recorded by **Frankie Avalon** introduced February 9
Written by Ed Marshall   Orchestra conducted by Peter DeAngelis

From the angelic choir's opening notes, *Venus* was the first #1 hit for Frankie Avalon. The song about a man who prays to the goddess, Venus, to send him a woman who is basically her human equivalent was originally offered to Al Martino who turned down the song. Frankie Avalon's *Bobby Sox to Stockings* was also a top-ten hit in 1959.

More Classic Fifties EASY-POP Hit Singles from 1959:
(eight additional hit recordings listed in alphabetical order)

The *Battle of New Orleans* by **Johnny Horton** introduced April 27
Written by Jimmy Driftwood

Country singer Johnny Horton died in an automobile accident the year after he hit the top of the POP charts in 1959 with *The Battle of New Orleans.* It was written by Jimmy Driftwood, an Arkansas high school history teacher, who often wrote songs to help students learn about historical events.

The *Big Hurt* recorded by **Miss Toni Fisher** introduced November 16
Written by Wayne Shanklin

In this heartbreaking #3 hit, Miss Toni Fisher describes her valiant attempt to go on until her 'big hurt' ends. Signet Records founder Wayne Shanklin used a flange phasing shift to create the swirling, whooshing sound that gives the recording of *The Big Hurt* a unique and identifiable sound. It was Miss Toni Fisher's only record to break into the top-twenty.

Don't You Know recorded by Della Reese introduced September 21
Written by Bobby Worth   Orchestra conducted by Glenn Osser

Don't You Know was the only top-ten EASY-POP hit for singer/actress Della Reese. It displays her unique delivery and her distinctive diction.

Heartaches By The Number by Guy Mitchell introduced Oct. 5
Written by Harlan Howard   Produced by Mitch Miller

Guy Mitchell's jaunty pop/country recordings began in 1950 with *My Heart Cries For You* and ended in 1959 with another one, *Heartaches by the Number*. Guy Mitchell opines that while he loves her more every day, she loves him less.

Lipstick on Your Collar recorded by Connie Francis introduced May 18
Written by George Goehring & Edna Lewis

One of the most popular female vocalists of the sixties began recording in the late fifties with frothy, girlish teenybopper songs like *Lipstick on Your Collar (told a tale on you)* in 1959.

Lonely Boy recorded by Paul Anka introduced June 1
Written by Paul Anka   Orchestra conducted by Don Costa

In addition to *Lonely Boy,* from the campy Mamie Van Doren film 'Girl's Town,' nineteen-year-old Paul Anka had another chart topper with **Put Your Head on My Shoulder** in 1959.

Sorry *(I Ran All the Way Home)* by the Impalas introduced March 16
Written by Artie Zwirn & Harry Giosasi   Orchestra conducted by Ray Ellis

This bright, brash POP/doo-wop apology was an overnight success and the only hit recording for the Impalas with sweet-voiced lead singer Joe 'Speedo' Frazier.

The Three Bells recorded by the Browns introduced July 27
Written by Dick Manning & Jean Villard   Produced by Chet Atkins

The bells rang first for Jimmy Browns' birth, then again for his marriage, and finally his death in this pop/folk song from Maxine, Bonnie, and Jim Ed Brown. It was based on a song called *While The Angelus Was Ringing*, a hit in France for both Les Compagnons De La Chanson and Edith Piaf.

Novelty, Rock, and Instrumental hit records during 1959:

(Now and Then There's) A Fool Such As I
another hit recording by **Elvis Presley** introduced March 23

Come Softly To Me
recording by the **Fleetwoods** introduced April 13

El Paso
pop/country recording by **Marty Robbins** introduced November 9

('Til) I Kissed You
another hit recording by the **Everly Brothers** introduced August 17

My Heart Is An Open Book
recording by **Carl Dobkins, Jr.** introduced April 13

Never Be Anyone Else for Me
another hit recording by teen idol **Ricky Nelson** introduced February 23

Personality
hit recording by R&B artist **Lloyd Price** introduced April 27

Shout
R&B / gospel recording by the **Isley Brothers** introduced September 21
Joey Dee and the Starliters released an even bigger hit in 1962

Smoke Gets in Your Eyes
rock 'n' roll recording by the **Platters** introduced January 19

Popular long-playing record albums released in 1959:
(compilations of songs available on 33$\frac{1}{3}$ rpm 12" discs)

'Ella Swings Lightly' recorded by **Ella Fitzgerald**
Sixteen songs including *Just You, Just Me, My Kinda Love*, and
Gotta Be This or That

'The Exciting Connie Francis' recorded by **Connie Francis**
Twelve songs include *There Will Never Be Another You* and
Come Rain or Come Shine

'Eydie Sings Show Stoppers' recorded by **Eydie Gorme**
Songs include *Guys and Dolls, You're Just in Love, Johnny One Note,*
Thou Swell, I Don't Care, and *Always True to You in My Fashion*

'Heavenly' recorded by **Johnny Mathis**
Twelve songs including *Moonlight Becomes You, A Lovely Way to Spend an*
Evening, Hello Young Lovers, A Ride on a Rainbow, That's All, and *Misty*

'Come Dance With Me' recorded by **Frank Sinatra**
Swinging collaboration with Billy May: *Saturday Night (Is the Loneliest Night),*
Day In – Day Out, Just in Time, Cheek to Cheek, and *Something's Gotta Give*

A Closer Look at the Singers

Teresa Brewer, Rosemary Clooney, Doris Day, Joni James, Jaye P. Morgan, Patti Page, and Kay Starr alternated at the top of the polls with hit songs during the 1950s. Female singing legends Judy Garland, Peggy Lee, Eartha Kitt, Dinah Shore, and Sarah Vaughan performed great popular standards in movies, on television, and on records. Chapter 4 provides brief biographies of thirty-seven of the decade's most popular female vocalists and the successful 50s EASY-POP standards they recorded.

Perry Como, Eddie Fisher, Johnny Mathis, and Guy Mitchell regularly topped the fifties popular music charts, while singing legends Tony Bennett, Nat King Cole, and Frank Sinatra were establishing their legacy as superstars of adult POP standards. Paul Anka, Harry Belafonte, Pat Boone, and Bobby Darin introduced their own unique sounds while Elvis Presley, Buddy Holly, Sam Cooke, and Ricky Nelson introduced rock 'n' roll sounds. Chapter 5 describes thirty-seven of the decade's most popular male vocalists and their fifties-style EASY-POP hits.

The rich harmony of the Ames Brothers, the Chordettes, the Crew-Cuts, the Fontane Sisters, the Four Lads, the McGuire Sisters, and the Platters added bright melodies to the popular music hit parade throughout the decade. Chapter 6 details thirty-seven of the decade's most popular duets, trios, and quartets along with their most famous recordings.

References from Chapter 3:

Gordon, Lois and Gordon, Alan. *The Columbia Chronicles of American Life 1910-1992*. New York: Columbia University Press, 1995.

McNeil, Alex. *Total Television*. New York: Viking Penguin Inc., 1984.

Sackett, Susan. *Billboard Box Office Hits*. New York: Billboard Books, 1990.

Whitburn, Joel. *Billboard Book of Top 40 Hits*. Seventh Edition. New York: Billboard Books, 2000.

Whitburn, Joel. *Pop Hits, Singles & Albums 1940-1954*. New York: Billboard Books, 2002.

Whitburn, Joel. *Top Pop Albums 1955-1996*. New York: Billboard Books, 1996.

Whitburn, Joel. *Top Pop Singles 1955-1986*. New York: Billboard Books, 1987.

Cheerfulness, sir, is the principle ingredient in the composition of health.

Irish Actor, Arthur Murphy (1727-1805)

Chapter 4

Quintessential Girl Singers of the 50s

Chapter 3 presented a hundred of the most popular songs of the 50s. This chapter describes thirty-seven of the decade's most popular female vocalists who recorded those fifties-style EASY-POP hits.

In the 1950s, female vocalists were called 'girl' singers. Using the word 'girl' to refer to adult women did not have the pejorative connotation that it might have today. In many cases though, female vocalists did portray a girlish attitude and demeanor—and the lyrics often suggested a young singer. It was a decade for women. Doris Day was the most popular box-office movie star, Dinah Shore won annual Emmy's for the best TV variety series, and Teresa Brewer, Joni James, Jaye P. Morgan, Patti Page, and Kay Starr all had dozens of hit songs during the decade.

A list of the 'Quintessential Girl Singers of the Fifties' along with their most memorable recording of the decade is provided in chart 4.1. Following the chart, there are brief biographies of each of these beguiling women that include a roster of some of their successful 50s EASY-POP hits.

Quintessential Girl Singers of the Fifties

Artist	Famous EASY-POP Hit Song in the fifties	year released
Toni Arden	*Kiss of Fire*	1952
Pearl Bailey	*Takes Two To Tango*	1952
Teresa Brewer	*Till I Waltz Again with You*	1952
Cathy Carr	*Ivory Tower**	1956
Mindy Carson	*Wake the Town and Tell the People*	1955
Karen Chandler	*Hold Me, Thrill Me, Kiss Me*	1952
Rosemary Clooney	*Half As Much*	1952
Dorothy Collins	*My Boy, Flat Top*	1955
Doris Day	*Whatever Will Be, Will Be (Que Sera, Sera)*	1956
Miss Toni Fisher	*The Big Hurt*	1959
Connie Francis	*Lipstick on Your Collar*	1959
Judy Garland	*The Man That Got Away*	1954
Georgia Gibbs	*Kiss of Fire*	1952
Eydie Gorme	*Too Close for Comfort*	1956
Gogi Grant	*The Wayward Wind*	1956
Joni James	*Why Don't You Believe Me*	1952
Kitty Kallen	*Little Things Mean a Lot*	1954
Eartha Kitt	*C'est Si Bon*	1953

Chart 4.1. Quintessential Girl Singers of the Fifties
(Chart continues on the next page)

Quintessential Girl Singers of the Fifties (continued)

Artist	Famous EASY-POP Hit Song in the fifties	year released
Peggy Lee	Fever	1958
Julie London	Cry Me a River	1955
Vera Lynn	Auf Wiederseh'n Sweetheart	1952
Gisele MacKenzie	Hard to Get	1955
Jane Morgan	Fascination	1957
Jaye P. Morgan	That's All I Want from You	1954
Patti Page	The Tennessee Waltz	1950
Della Reese	Don't You Know	1959
Debbie Reynolds	Tammy	1957
Dinah Shore	Sweet Violets	1951
Jo Stafford	You Belong to Me	1952
Kay Starr	Wheel of Fortune	1952
Gale Storm	I Hear You Knocking*	1955
Caterina Valente	The Breeze and I	1955
June Valli	Crying in the Chapel*	1953
Sarah Vaughan	Make Yourself Comfortable	1954
Dinah Washington	What A Diff'rence A Day Makes	1959
Joan Weber	Let Me Go Lover	1954
Margaret Whiting	Moonlight in Vermont	1954

* These recordings were covers of recordings from the original artists

Chart 4.1. Quintessential Girl Singers of the Fifties

Toni Arden

Famous EASY-POP hit single during the 50s: *Kiss of Fire*   1952
Toni Arden also had hits with *I Can Dream Can't I* in 1949,
Too Young in 1951, *I'm Yours* in 1952, and *Padre* in 1958.
Recording career with hits on the charts: 1949-1958   Record Labels: Columbia, Decca

Antoinette Aroizzone, often described as a 'little girl with a big voice,' grew up in Jackson Heights, Queens, New York. Her father sang with New York's Metropolitan Opera. Instead of following in his footsteps, she chose to sing with the big bands, joining Al Trace in 1945 and performing with piano-playing band leader Joe Reichman in 1946. She made her first big impression performing on the bill at New York's Copacabana nightclub with Dean Martin and Jerry Lewis. She performed with Bing Crosby on his radio show and with Jimmy Durante on his TV show. In 1949, an appearance on Ed Sullivan's 'Toast of the Town' got her a recording contract with Columbia Records. The intensity of her 1952 version of *Kiss of Fire*, a tune based on an Argentine tango and backed by Percy Faith's orchestra, rivaled Georgia Gibbs #1 version and Tony Martin's #6 version, but placed just below the top-ten. She moved to Decca Records where she recorded her million-selling record *Padre* in 1958. Later in the decade Toni Arden recorded albums of Italian melodies.

Pearl 'Pearlie Mae' Bailey (born March 29, 1918)

Famous EASY-POP hit single during the 50s: *Takes Two to Tango*   1952
This was the only top-ten hit recording for Pearl Bailey.
Recording career with hits on the charts: 1952   Record Label: Coral

Vocalist, movie and stage actress, Pearl Bailey, the daughter of a minister, was born in Newport News, Virginia. An irrepressible show business personality, she won a singing contest at Harlem's Apollo Theater in 1938 and was featured with big bands led by Cab Callo-way and Cootie Williams. In 1946, she gave an award-winning performance in the Broadway musical 'St. Louis Woman.' Her move from Columbia Records, where she recorded duets with Frank Sinatra, to Coral Records resulted in her brassy hit *Takes Two to Tango* where Pearlie Mae's irreverent personality, sultry style, and irascible spirit come across. In 1952, she married jazz drummer Louis Bellson. Beginning with her role as a fortune-teller in 'Carmen Jones' in 1954, she appeared in films and stage shows, including 'Hello Dolly' in 1967. She hosted her own television variety show in 1970. Pearl Bailey died in 1990.

Teresa Brewer (born May 7, 1931)

Famous EASY-POP hit during the 50s: ***Till I Waltz Again with You*** 1952
Teresa Brewer also had hits with *Music! Music! Music!* in 1950,
Ricochet in 1953, *Jilted* and *Let Me Go Lover* in 1954, *A Tear Fell* and
A Sweet Old-Fashioned Girl in 1956, and *You Send Me* in 1957.
Recording career with hits on the charts: 1950-1961   Record Label: Coral

Born Theresa Breuer in Toledo, Ohio, this child prodigy debuted on
the Major Bowes Amateur Hour at age 5 and toured with the show
until she was 12. She scored her first big hit as an exuberant and
startlingly brassy teenager in 1950 with the diabolically catchy
Music! Music! Music! She was backed on the recording by the
Dixieland All-Stars and the record was on every jukebox in the
country. Cute and bouncy, 5-foot-2, 100 pound, Teresa Brewer was
ideally suited to the tastes of the American public in the fifties. Bing
Crosby called her "the Sophie Tucker of the Girl Scouts." In 1953,
she appeared with Rhonda Fleming and Guy Mitchell in the film
'Those Redheads from Seattle' and starred in a summer TV series
with Mel Torme. In the 1960s, she broadened her act to include a
wide sampling of Americana, from country music and pop, to swing
and be-bop. In 1972, she married record producer Bob Thiele and
emerged as a blues and jazz singer, recording with Count Basie and
Duke Ellington.

Cathy Carr (born June 28, 1936)

Famous EASY-POP hit single during the 50s: ***Ivory Tower*** 1956
This was the only top-ten hit recording for Cathy Carr.
Recording career with hits on the charts: 1956-1959   Record Label: Fraternity

Cathy Carr was a songstress from the Bronx, New York. As a child
she appeared on 'The Children's Hour,' a local television show in
New York City. A singer and dancer with the USO, she performed
with big-band leader Sammy Kaye. In 1953, she signed with Fraternity Records, a small company based in Cincinnati, Ohio, and scored
a big hit with her cover version of the song *Ivory Tower*. Gale Storm
also had a cover version of this song on Dot Records, but it was originally recorded by the R&B group, Otis Williams & the Charms on
Deluxe Records. Cathy Carr's follow-up recording, *Heart Hideaway*
did not break into the top-twenty and her move to Roulette Records
did not produce any more hit recordings. In 1958, Cathy Carr tried to
repeat her success with a cover of Phil Spector's *To Know Him is to
Love Him*. Her version was overlooked in favor of the original by the
Teddy Bears on Dore Records.

Mindy Carson (born July 16, 1927)

Famous POP hit during the 50s: ***Wake the Town and Tell the People*** 1955
Mindy Carson also had hits with *Candy and Cake* and *My Foolish Heart*
in 1950 and *Since I Met You Baby* in 1956.
Recording career with hits on the charts: 1946-1956   Labels: RCA & Columbia

Mindy Carson, born in New York City, got her first break in 1946 on
the 'Stairway To The Stars' radio program which starred Paul
Whiteman and Martha Tilton. In 1949, she had her own CBS radio
series with announcer Don Pardo. That fall she starred in her NBC
television variety show that featured violinist Florian Zabach and
Earl Sheldon's orchestra. At RCA Victor, accompanied by the Henri
Rene orchestra, she recorded a happy novelty tune *Candy And Cake*
with a ballad, *My Foolish Heart*, on the 'B' side, but it was the ballad
that became the bigger hit. At Columbia Records in 1952, A&R chief
Mitch Miller paired her with Guy Mitchell on *Cause I Love You
That's-A-Why* and *Tell Us Where The Good Times Are*. In 1955,
Mindy Carson recorded her biggest hit *Wake The Town And Tell The
People* and charted again in 1957 with a pop cover of Ivory Joe
Hunter's *Since I Met You Baby*. She appeared on Broadway in the
short-lived 1958 boxing musical 'The Body Beautiful' by Sheldon
Harnick & Jerry Bock.

Karen Chandler [aka Eve Young] (born September 1, 1923)

Famous EASY-POP hit during the 50s: ***Hold Me, Thrill Me, Kiss Me*** 1952
This was the only 50s top-ten hit recording for Karen Chandler.
Recording career with hits on the charts: 1948-1956   Record Label: Coral

Karen Chandler was born Eva Alice Nadauld in Rexburg, Ohio.
Under the stage name Eve Young, she toured with the Benny
Goodman Orchestra in the late forties. Eve Young's first recorded
success came with *Cuanto La Gusta* introduced by Carmen Miranda
in the Elizabeth Taylor / Jane Powell film 'A Date with Judy' in
1948. She followed this with *My Darling, My Darling* with the
Benny Goodman orchestra and the Drugstore Cowboy's Jack
Lathrop. Changing her name to Karen Chandler in 1952, she married
Coral records conductor/arranger, Jack Pleis, whose orchestra accom-
panied her on her million-selling hit recording of *Hold Me, Thrill Me,
Kiss Me*. It had been a number one hit for Gene Austin in 1927. It
was also recorded in 1953 by Frankie Laine and again by Mel Carter
in 1965. Karen Chandler paired with popular western singer Jimmy
Wakely to record *Tonight You Belong To Me* in 1956 but sisters
Patience & Prudence had the hit version.

Rosemary Clooney (born May 23, 1928)

Famous EASY-POP hit single during the 50s: *Half as Much* 1952
Rosemary Clooney also had hits with *Come On-A My House* in 1951,
Tenderly and *Botch-A-Me* in 1952, *Hey There, Mambo Italiano,
Count Your Blessings Instead of Sheep,* and *This Ole House* in 1954,
and *Mangos* in 1957.
Recording career with hits on the charts: 1951-1960   Record Label: Columbia

Rosemary Clooney was born in Maysville, Kentucky. She and her sister, Betty, won a spot on radio station WLW in Cincinnati and by 1947 they were on the road with Tony Pastor's orchestra. One of the most popular singers of the fifties, her background in jazz made her an excellent lyric interpreter with intelligent phrasing and skillful timing. Her early hits came with novelty tunes but her dramatic qualities became more evident as the years went on. Her direct and attractive style was often described as 'diction with intimacy.' In 1954, she starred with Bing Crosby, Danny Kaye, and Vera-Ellen in the blockbuster film 'White Christmas' and then with Guy Mitchell in the western satire film 'Red Garters.' After a semi-retirement in the 70s, Rosemary Clooney returned with renewed power and confidence. Her resiliency and energy validates her position among the fine jazz-based vocalists in American music. Rosemary Clooney died on June 29, 2002.

Dorothy Collins (born November 18, 1926)

Famous EASY-POP hit single during the 50s: *My Boy, Flat Top* 1955
Dorothy Collins also had a top-twenty hit with *Seven Days* in 1956.
Recording career with hits on the charts: 1955-1960   Record Label: Coral

This cute, wholesome Canadian singer with the slight lisp, was born Marjorie Chandler in Windsor, Ontario. In the late forties she sang with the Raymond Scott orchestra and married the orchestra leader. The fast-paced simple trifle *My Boy – Flat Top* was her most successful recording. Dorothy Collins is one of the most underrated singers in pop music. Every Saturday evening in the fifties, America's sweetheart starred on the legendary NBC-TV series 'Your Hit Parade.' The delightful singer opened each week's program, appearing inside the Lucky Strike cigarette pack logo, chirping "Be Happy-Go-Lucky, Be Happy, Go Lucky Strike." In 1971, she was nominated for a Tony award for her starring role in the original cast of the legendary Broadway musical, Stephen Sondheim's 'Follies.' Dorothy Collins died in 1994.

Doris Day (born April 3, 1924)

Famous EASY-POP hit: ***Whatever Will Be, Will Be*** *(Que Sera, Sera)* 1956
Doris Day also hit with *A Guy is a Guy* in 1952, *Secret Love* in 1954, and
Everybody Loves a Lover, *Tunnel of Love*, and *Teacher's Pet* in 1958.
Recording career with hits on the charts: 1947-1962   Record Label: Columbia

Doris Kappelhoff was born in Cincinnati where her dreams of being a dancer ended in an automobile accident when she was 14. She began taking vocal lessons and before she was 20 she was a singer with Les Brown's band. In 1956 and 1957, she was voted 'most popular singer' in the national disc jockey poll. Her recording success was over-shadowed by movies, as Doris Day became the #1 box office star of the late 50s and early 60s. Playing the quintessential all-American girl, the perpetually pure ingénue was cast opposite masculine icons Rock Hudson and Clark Gable. Her forty films were as varied as 'Calamity Jane,' 'Pillow Talk,' 'Love Me or Leave Me,' and 'The Man Who Knew Too Much' directed by Alfred Hitchcock. Doris Day displayed a relentlessly bright, sunny persona. Ironically, her personal life was troubled. She entered into abusive marital relationships and in 1968 pursued legal action against corrupt managers who lost all of her career earnings. Ultimately, she recovered 22 million dollars in the largest civil suit ever awarded in California. Her fresh-faced looks, sensual innocence, and strikingly pure vocal style summed up a glamorous era. She retired to Carmel, California.

Miss Toni Fisher (born February 12, 1931)

Famous EASY-POP hit single during the 50s: ***The Big Hurt*** 1959
This was the only top-ten hit recording for Miss Toni Fisher.
Recording career with hits on the charts: 1959 - 1962   Record Label: Signet

Miss Toni Fisher (as she was always billed) was born in Los Angeles and had three recordings that made the Billboard top 100 charts. Her only major hit song was *The Big Hurt* in 1959. Producer Wayne Shanklin, her collaborative partner, gave the arrangement a unique and identifiable, phase shift effect, creating a swirling, whooshing sound. It was on the top seller charts for almost four months. She also recorded *How Deep Is The Ocean* in 1960. While there were three top-ten versions of this Irving Berlin classic in 1932, Toni Fisher's record did not fare as well with it's best showing as #93 on the charts. The final recording charted by Toni Fisher and released on Big Top records in 1962 was *West of the Wall*, the sad story of lovers separated by the infamous Berlin Wall. It barely placed in the top 40.

Connie Francis (born December 12, 1938)

Famous EASY-POP hit single during the 50s: *Lipstick on Your Collar* 1959
Connie Francis also had hits with *Who's Sorry Now* and *My Happiness* in
1958 and *Everybody's Somebody's Fool* in 1960.
Recording career with hits on the charts: 1957-1969   Record Label: MGM Records

When she was just three years old, this Italian American girl, born
Concetta Rosa Maria Franconero in Newark, New Jersey, started
playing the accordion and at age ten she was accepted on the TV
series 'StarTime.' After three weeks, she was advised to concentrate
on singing. Just as she was about to accept a pre-med scholarship to
New York University, her 1957 recording of *Who's Sorry Now* began
a string of top-forty hits. She had ten consecutive million-selling
records and by 1967 became the biggest-selling recording artist. With
an affinity for languages, Connie Francis became one of the first pop
singers to release her songs in other languages. She recorded the title
song from her 1961 movie 'Where the Boys Are' in six languages.
Her Italian and Jewish albums transformed Francis from a teenage
idol to a mature performer. In the seventies, during a stage performance, she was raped at her hotel and sidelined for several years, but
returned to performing in 1989.

Judy Garland (born June 10, 1922)

Famous POP hit single during the 50s: *The Man That Got Away* 1954
also: *Without a Memory* in 1953 and *Comes Once in a Lifetime* in 1962
Recording career with hits on the charts: 1939 - 1954   Labels: Columbia & Capitol

Frances Gumm, born in Grand Rapids, Michigan, began performing
as the youngest of the Gumm Sisters, co-starred with Mickey Rooney
in a successful series of teenage 'backlot musicals' at MGM, and shot
to stardom in 1939 singing *Over the Rainbow* in 'The Wizard of Oz.'
In 1950, she filmed her outstanding song & dance number *Get Happy*
in the MGM film 'Summer Stock.' Scheduled to star in 'Annie Get
Your Gun' she was fired a few weeks into filming by MGM for fail-
ing to appear for work. Her legacy included classic movie and live
performances but also personal setbacks and career difficulties. In
1952, she played the Palace Theater in New York for a hugely successful 19-week run and recorded her second most famous song *The
Man That Got Away* from her comeback hit musical 'A Star Is Born'
in 1954. Her electrifying Carnegie Hall concert in 1961 was another
triumph and the album of the concert won five Grammy awards. Judy
Garland died of an accidental overdose of pills on June 22, 1969. Her
daughter Liza Minnelli carries on the classic Garland tradition.

Georgia Gibbs (born August 17, 1920)

Famous EASY-POP hit single during the 50s: *Kiss of Fire* 1952
She also had hits with *Tweedle Dee* and *Dance with Me Henry* in 1955.
Recording career with hits on the charts: 1950-1958   Record Labels: Coral & Mercury

Born Fredda Gibbons in Worcester, Massachusetts, she sang on the Lucky Strike radio show in the late 30s and then with Artie Shaw's band in 1942. On the Garry Moore-Jimmy Durante radio show in the late 40s, Garry Moore dubbed her "Her Nibs, Miss Gibbs." Her first chart hit was *If I Knew You Were Comin I'd've Baked a Cake* in 1950. Like many white pop singers she recorded cover versions of R&B hits for a pop audience. Her cover of *Tweedle Dee* outsold LaVern Baker's original and her version of *The Wallflower*, renamed *Dance With Me Henry* outsold Etta James' original. She was very adaptable during the 50s recording ballads, covers, novelties, cha-cha-cha as well as her #1 hit, the tango-tinged *Kiss of Fire* adapted from the Argentine *El Choclo*. Toni Arden and Tony Martin also had top-twenty versions of *Kiss of Fire* in 1952.

Eydie Gorme (born August 16, 1931)

Famous EASY-POP hit single during the 50s: *Too Close for Comfort* 1956
Eydie Gorme also had hits with *Fini* in 1954 and
You Need Hands in 1958.
Recording career with hits on the charts: 1954-1972   Labels: Coral & ABC-Paramount

Born Edith Gormezano in the Bronx, she was raised by her Turkish and Spanish immigrant Jewish parents, graduated high school in 1946, and worked as a translator, using her fluency in Spanish. She also sang with big bands before going on her own in 1952. Eydie Gorme caught her big break and her life's partner when she and Steve Lawrence were booked on the original 'Tonight Show' then hosted by Steve Allen. When they sang together the industry buzzed. Steve & Eydie, as they are always known, were married in Las Vegas in 1957. As a solo performer, every time she would sing her 1957 record *Guess Who I Saw Today? (...I Saw You!)*, from the Broadway Review 'New Faces of 1952,' it was a showstopper. Lively and talented Eydie Gorme enjoyed several hit singles, none bigger than 1963's *Blame It On The Bossa Nova* and none more impressive than her 1967 Grammy Award winning version of *If He Walked Into My Life Today* from the stage musical 'Mame.' Steve and Eydie are the parents of two sons, David—who serves today as his parents' musical director—and Michael, who died at age 23 in 1986.

Gogi Grant (born September 20, 1924)

Famous EASY-POP hit single during the 50s: *The Wayward Wind* 1956
Gogi Grant also had a top-ten hit with *Suddenly There's A Valley* in 1955.
Recording career with hits on the charts: 1955 - 1958   Record Label: Era

Jazz-pop singer, Gogi Grant, was born Myrtle Audrey Arinsberg in Philadelphia, but moved to Los Angeles at age 12. She began her singing career using her married name, Audrey Brown. In 1952, she was renamed Gogi Grant by RCA-Victor executive Dave Kapp. She moved to Era records where her first release was the top-ten hit *Suddenly There's a Valley*. During the last fifteen minutes of her next recording session at Era, she recorded her legendary 1956 hit, *The Wayward Wind* and then was voted Most Popular Female Vocalist by Billboard magazine. But despite the awards she was unable to follow up her smash hit record, never again breaking into the top fifty. She did release five albums in the late fifties and she dubbed all of the vocals for Ann Blyth's portrayal of 1920s torch singer Helen Morgan in the 1957 Warner Brothers' film co-starring Paul Newman. The best-selling soundtrack album from 'The Helen Morgan Story' featured twenty songs she recorded for the film. Gogi Grant retired in 1967.

Joni James (born September 22, 1930)

Famous POP hit single during the 50s: *Why Don't You Believe Me* 1952
Joni James also had hits with *Have You Heard, Your Cheatin' Heart,*
Almost Always, and *My Love, My Love* in 1953 and
How Important Can It Be? and *You Are My Love* in 1955.
Recording career with hits on the charts: 1952-1960   Record Label: MGM Records

Born Joan Carmello Babbo in a poor neighborhood on the Southeast side of Chicago, she studied ballet and drama from age twelve and modeled during high school. In the late 1940's, she toured Canada as a dancer. In 1952, while appearing in a TV commercial she was spotted by executives at MGM records, signed a contract, recorded *Why Don't You Believe Me*, and became an overnight sensation. She released an incredible number of hits over the next three years and married her orchestral arranger/conductor Anthony 'Tony' Aquaviva. Joni James belongs to that elite group of recording artists who have sold over 100 million records worldwide. Like many Americans of Italian descent, Joni James was extremely proud of her ancestry and her Italian album *Ti Voglio Bene* with some songs in English and some in Italian was unique at the time. She retired in 1964.

Kitty Kallen (born May 25, 1922)

Famous POP hit single during the 50s: *Little Things Mean a Lot* 1954
Kitty Kallen also had hits with *In the Chapel in the Moonlight* in 1954,
Go On With the Wedding (with Georgie Shaw) in 1956,
If I Give My Heart to You in 1959, and *My Coloring Book* in 1963.
Recording career on the charts: 1949-1962 Record Labels: Mercury, Decca, Columbia

Band singer Kitty Kallen was born in Philadelphia, began her career as a child performer on 'The Children's Hour' radio program, and later roomed with Dinah Shore as they both sought their big break. In 1943, she was the vocalist on Jimmy Dorsey's recording of *They're Either Too Young or Too Old* and in 1945, the vocalist on Harry James' *I'm Beginning to See the Light*. Her solo career began in the early fifties at Mercury records where she recorded several hits but she released her biggest hits in the mid fifties with her move to Decca records and new accompaniment by Jack Plies' Orchestra. *Little Things Mean a Lot* was one of the biggest hits of the post war era. Her recording sold more than two million copies and Joni James would have another top-40 hit with it in 1959. Four months later Kitty Kallen was on top of the charts again with *In the Chapel in the Moonlight*. In 1955, she made her film debut in Universal's 'The Second Greatest Sex.' A quarter century of recordings from big band to pop, Kitty Kallen was a continuing fixture in American pop music.

Eartha Kitt (born January 17, 1927)

Famous EASY-POP hit single during the 50s: *C'est Si Bon* 1953
Eartha Kitt also had a hit with *Santa Baby* in 1953.
Recording career with hits on the charts: 1953-1954 Record Label: RCA Victor

Sixteen years after her birth on a cotton plantation in Carolina in 1928, Eartha Mae Kitt won a scholarship to Katherine Dunham's dance school. On a tour to Paris in the 40s she stayed to dance and sing in the cabaret circuit. Legendary film director Orson Welles discovered here there and praised her as "the most exciting woman alive." In 1950, she returned to the United States and the New York nightclub scene with bookings at the Blue Angel and the Village Vanguard. Eartha Kitt epitomized the stereotypical sophisticated, seductive, exotic, sex-kitten chanteuse. Rising to fame with her striking, slinky presence and throaty purr voice, she became a sensation in Broadway's 'New Faces of 1952.' Always a performer at heart, her act translated best in a live setting. Eartha Kitt's alluring vamp persona was so vivid and highly mannered that she is still easily identifiable today, more than fifty years after her initial splash.

Peggy Lee (born May 26, 1920)

Famous EASY-POP hit single during the 50s: **Fever** 1957
Peggy Lee also had hits with *Lover* in 1952 and *Mr. Wonderful* in 1956.
Recording career on the charts: 1945-1969   Record Labels: Decca & Capitol

A leading POP and jazz singer, Peggy Lee was born Norma Deloris Egstrom in Jamestown, North Dakota. The seventh of eight children, her mother died when she was four years old. She became famous singing with Benny Goodman's orchestra in the early forties and went solo in the late forties. At the Doll House in Palm Springs, California, unable to shout above the clamor, she snared the audience attention by lowering her voice with a soft and 'cool' style that has become her trademark. Her captivating style is a distinctive combination of delicate and driving, husky and seductive. She and her then-husband Dave Barbour co-wrote many of her early hits including *It's a Good Day* and *Manana*. Even after their divorce they continued their song-writing collaboration. Few vocalists had her staying power singing everything from jazz to blues, and singing it with a beat. She appeared in several major motion pictures including 'The Jazz Singer' in 1953 and as a despondent singer in 'Pete Kelly's Blues' in 1955, earning her an Academy Award nomination as best supporting actress. She wrote the lyrics and supplied several voices for the Walt Disney animated feature 'Lady and the Tramp' in 1955.

Julie London (born September 26, 1926)

Famous EASY-POP hit single during the 50s: **Cry Me a River** 1955
This was the only top-ten hit recording for Julie London.
Recording career with hits on the charts: 1955 - 1956   Record Label: Liberty

Born Julie Peck in Santa Rosa, California, she sang as a teenager in a West Coast band, attended Hollywood Professional High School, and after graduation was discovered by talent agent Sue Carol (the wife of actor Alan Ladd) while working as an elevator operator. She appeared in her first film 'Nabonga' in 1944. Her first recording was a breathy *Cry Me a River* written by former high school classmate Arthur Hamilton and performed in the Jayne Mansfield film 'The Girl Can't Help It.' Hollywood DJ Jack Wagner, another former classmate, impressed with her talent, sultry looks, and smoky-voice, promoted her records. In 1955, Julie London married Jack Webb, the star of the 'Dragnet' TV series, who produced the film 'Pete Kelly's Blues,' in which Julie appeared. She later married Bobby Troup who moved her to the Liberty label where she recorded more than 30 albums. She played Dixie McCall in the 70s TV series 'Emergency!' produced by ex-husband Jack Webb.

Vera Lynn (born March 20, 1919)

Famous hit single during the 50s: *Auf Wiederseh'n Sweetheart* 1952
Vera Lynn also had hits with *Yours* in 1952 and *We'll Meet Again* in 1954.

Recording career with hits on the charts: 1948-1957   Record Label: London

British singer, Dame Vera Lynn, whose career flourished during World War II, was born Vera Margaret Welch in London. Nicknamed 'The Forces Sweetheart' by British troops stationed abroad she sent them messages during her incredibly popular BBC radio series 'Sincerely Yours.' In 1939, she first recorded *We'll Meet Again*—the hopeful lyrics and her unaffected style appealed to people separated during the war. That song, as well as her record *The White Cliffs of Dover* are typical of the wartime morale effort. After the war, she heard a song in a German pub, found the music, had lyrics written, and recorded *Auf Wiederseh'n Sweetheart*, the first song by a British artist to top the charts in the United States. Several of her recordings made the US charts in the fifties including *My Son, My Son,* a #1 hit in England in 1954 and *Don't Cry My Love* in 1957. In 1976, she was appointed a DBE (Dame Commander of the Order of the British Empire).

Gisele MacKenzie (born January 10, 1927)

Famous EASY-POP hit single during the 50s: *Hard to Get* 1955
Gisele MacKenzie also hit with *The Star You Wished Upon Last Night* in 1956.

Recording career on the charts: 1952-1956   Record Labels: Capitol, X, and Vik

Born Gisèle Marie-Louise Marguerite LaFlèche in Winnipeg, Manitoba, Canada, of French-Scottish descent, she studied violin, piano, and voice at the Royal Conservatory in Toronto and hosted her own Canadian Broadcasting Corporation radio program 'Meet Gisele.' She adopted her father's second given name, MacKenzie, as her professional name when she moved to Los Angeles in 1950. There she sang with Percy Faith's orchestra on CBS radio, joined Bob Crosby on CBS TV's 'Club 15' in 1951, and began a long association with comedian Jack Benny in 1953. She often played violin duets with Jack Benny; the contrast of their playing abilities serving as the basis of a wry comedy routine. With her crystalline, resonant singing voice, perfect pitch, and her even, flowing style, she was a regular performer on NBC TV's 'Your Hit Parade' from 1953 to 1957 (sharing the spotlight with fellow Canadian, the Ontario-born singer Dorothy Collins) and in 1957, starred in her own NBC TV series. Her single recordings included *Hard to Get*, accompanied by Richard Maltby, and *Pepper-Hot Baby* for the 'X' label, a subsidiary of RCA Victor and *The Star You Wished Upon Last Night* for Vik Records.

Jane Morgan (born December 25, 1920)

Famous EASY-POP hit single during the 50s: ***Fascination*** 1957
Jane Morgan also had hits with *The Day the Rains Came* in 1958
and *With Open Arms* in 1959.
Recording career with hits on the charts: 1956 - 1959   Record Label: Kapp

Born in Boston as Florence Catherine Currier but raised in Florida, Jane Morgan attended the famous Juilliard School of Music in New York City, studying opera during the day and singing in nightclubs at night. After four successful years as a singer at the 'Club des Champs Elysees' in Paris, she made the transition back to America as a night-club singer at the St. Regis Hotel in New York City. Signed to Kapp records in the mid 50s, she was teamed with pianist Roger Williams to record *Two Different Worlds*. One year later she hit number seven with her theme *Fascination*, based on the old French composition *Valse Tzigane*, and featured in the Billy Wilder film 'Love in the Afternoon' starring Gary Cooper and Audrey Hepburn. *The Day the Rains Came* and *With Open Arms* followed. Her last hit was the title song from the 1959 movie 'Happy Anniversary' starring David Niven.

Jaye P. Morgan (born December 3, 1931)

Famous EASY-POP hit during the 50s: ***That's All I Want From You*** 1954
Jaye P. Morgan also had hits with *Life is Just a Bowl of Cherries* in 1953
and *The Longest Walk, Danger! Heartbreak Ahead,*
and *Pepper-Hot Baby* in 1955.
Recording career with hits on the charts: 1953-1960   Record Labels: Derby and RCA

Born in Mancos, Colorado, Mary Margaret Morgan began her career performing for family and friends. Moving to California she attended Verdugo Hills High School, serving as class treasurer and getting the nickname Jaye P, after the banker J. P. Morgan. She sang at school assemblies and following graduation, landed a spot as vocalist with the Frank DeVol orchestra. Her first hit was *Life is Just a Bowl of Cherries* in 1953. Beginning in 1954, sassy, dusky-voiced Jaye P. Morgan spent five years recording top 40 hits for RCA Victor. From 1954 to 1955, she was a vocalist on the television quiz program 'Stop the Music' and in 1956, she starred in her own television show accompanied by her singing siblings: Duke, Bob, Charlie, and Dick, (The Morgan Brothers) as a summer replacement for Eddie Fisher's 'Coke Time.' Today she is most often associated with her boisterous comic antics as a panelist and judge on Chuck Barris' low-brow 1970s cult hit TV game series 'The Gong Show.'

Patti Page (born November 8, 1927)

Famous EASY-POP hit single during the 50s: *The Tennessee Waltz* 1950
Also *All My Love* in 1950, *Mockin' Bird Hill, Would I Love You,* and
Detour in 1951, *I Went to Your Wedding* in 1952, *Doggie in the
Window* and *Changing Partners* in 1953, *Cross Over the Bridge* in
1954, *Allegheny Moon* in 1956, *Old Cape Cod* in 1957, and *Left Right
Out of Your Heart* in 1958.

Recording career with hits on the charts: 1948-1968   Record Label: Mercury

With her sincere phrasing and smooth style, Patti Page was the best
selling female vocalist during the 1950s. One of eleven children,
Clara Ann Fowler was born in Claremore, Oklahoma, and raised in
Tulsa. When another singer, billed as 'Patti Page' for the 'Page Milk
Company Show' on radio, left, 18-year-old Clara Fowler took her
place and name. Orchestra leader and saxophonist, Jack Rael heard
the program and became her personal manager. Using a multiple-
voice technique on her recording of *Confess*, she was the first pop
artist to overdub harmony onto her own lead vocals. Her record *The
Tennessee Waltz*, the first hit crossover from country to pop, was #1
for an astounding 13 weeks, stayed on the charts for six months, and
sold more than ten million copies. Many of her songs—*Mister and
Mississippi, Detour* and *Cross Over the Bridge*—have a strong pre-
rock 'n' roll beat. In 1998, she won a Grammy as 'Best Traditional
Pop Singer.'

Della Reese (born July 6, 1931)

Famous EASY-POP hit single during the 50s: ***Don't You Know*** 1959
Della Reese also had a top-twenty hits with *And That Reminds Me (of you)*
in 1957 and *Not One Minute More* in 1959.

Recording career with hits on the charts: 1957-1966   Record Labels: Jubilee and RCA

Before shortening her name, Delloreese Patricia Early was born in
Detroit and began singing in church when she was six years old. She
was hired by Mahalia Jackson to sing with her troupe in the 1940s.
Later the full-voiced, rich alto singer joined the female gospel group,
'The Meditation Singers' and performed with Erskine Hawkins' R&B
orchestra early in the 1950s. An appearance at Detroit's famed
'Flame Show Bar' helped develop her individual, tough and brassy
style. She was voted 'The Most Promising Singer' in 1957 by
Billboard, Cashbox, Variety, the Disc Jockeys of America, and the
Jukebox Operators Association. She appeared in the film 'Lets Rock'
in 1958. The actress and singer appeared on many TV series
including her own, 'Della' in 1970, in 'Chico and the Man' in the late
seventies, and 'Touched By An Angel' with Roma Downey in 1994.

Debbie Reynolds (born April 1, 1932)

Famous EASY-POP hit single during the 50s: *Tammy*   1957
Debbie Reynolds also had a hit with *Aba Daba Honeymoon* in 1951.
Recording career with hits on the charts: 1951-1960   Record Label: Coral

America's sweetheart, Mary Francis Reynolds, was born in El Paso, Texas. Her film career began in 1948 after the sixteen-year-old won the Miss Burbank beauty contest. The perky, wholesome, girl-next-door appeared in Hollywood musicals including the genre's defining film 'Singing in the Rain' with Gene Kelly and Donald O'Conner. With her adorable face and saucy sparkle, she personified cheerful bounce and youthful innocence and was one of the ten most popular stars of 1954. She was the loveable, scrappy little juvenile delinquent in 'Susan Slept Here,' and an independent young woman in 'Give a Girl a Break,' 'Athena,' 'Hit the Deck,' 'The Catered Affair,' and 'Bundle of Joy.' In 1957, she introduced her million-selling #1 hit *Tammy* in the comedy film 'Tammy and the Bachelor.' She married Eddie Fisher in 1955, they divorced in 1959, writer/actress Carrie Fisher is their daughter. In 1973, Debbie Reynolds starred on Broadway in the acclaimed musical revival of 'Irene.'

Dinah Shore (born March 1, 1917)

Famous EASY-POP hit single during the 50s: *Sweet Violets*   1952
Dinah Shore also had hits with *My Heart Cries for You* in 1950,
A Penny a Kiss in 1951, *Whatever Lola Wants (Lola Gets)* in 1955,
and *Chantez, Chantez* in 1957.
Recording career with hits on the charts: 1940-1957   Record Labels: Columbia & RCA

Dinah Shore, born Frances Rose Shore in Winchester, Tennessee, was one of the most popular entertainers of the forties and fifties. Stricken with polio at 18 months of age, she recovered using the Sister Kenny mental and muscle-exercising therapy. She graduated from Vanderbilt University in 1938, majoring in Sociology. With her low-pitched, velvet-covered voice, she became a solo star almost immediately after her brief stay with Xavier Cugat's band. Her sparkling popularity in the late forties included radio shows and records—*Shoofly Pie and Apple Pan Dowdy, The Gypsy,* and *Buttons and Bows.* She appeared in a dozen films including the underrated 'Aaron Slick from Punkin Crick' in 1952. Her cheery optimism and southern down-home charm brought the greatest fame with her top rated Emmy-award-winning television series in the fifties and sixties that she always ended singing "See the USA in your Chevrolet" followed by her exuberant hand-blown signature kiss to her audience.

Jo Stafford (born November 12, 1917)

Famous EASY-POP hit single during the 50s: ***You Belong To Me*** 1952
Jo Stafford also had hits with *No Other Love* in 1950, *Shrimp Boats* in
1951, *Jambalaya* in 1952, and *Make Love to Me* in 1954.

Recording career with hits on the charts: 1944-1957 Record Label: Columbia

Classically trained and technically gifted, Jo Stafford was born in
Coalinga, California. She was a member of Tommy Dorsey's vocal
group, the Pied Pipers whose recordings included *Candy, Yes Indeed*,
and *Manhattan Serenade* in the early forties. At Capitol records she
recorded *Say Something Sweet to Your Sweetheart* in 1948 and *Whispering Hope* in 1949, both with Gordon MacRae, then a string of solo
hits in the fifties. Admired for the range, warmth, and purity of her
voice, Jo Stafford is considered one of the most versatile singers of
the era. At Columbia Records she was the first artist to sell twenty-
five million records. She was accompanied on her recordings by her
husband and top-flight arranger Paul Weston and his Orchestra. As a
lark, the couple released a bad-lounge-act comedy album—he was the
inept Jonathan Edwards playing on an untuned piano and she was
Darlene Edwards, an off-key singer. The 1961 cult favorite won the
Grammy for Best Comedy Album. Jo Stafford died in 2008.

Kay Starr (born July 21, 1922)

Famous EASY-POP hit single during the 50s: ***Wheel of Fortune*** 1952
also *Hoop-Dee-Doo* and *Bonaparte's Retreat* in 1950, *Comes A-Long
A-Love* in 1952, *Side by Side* and *Half a Photograph* in 1953, *If You
Love Me* and *The Man Upstairs* in 1954, *Rock 'n' Roll Waltz* in 1955.

Recording career with charted hits: 1948-1962 Record Labels: Capitol and RCA

Cherokee/Irish Kay Starr was born Katherine LaVerne Starks on an
Indian reservation in Dougherty, Oklahoma. She started singing with
Joe Venuti's orchestra at age 15 and got a break with Glenn Miller's
orchestra, filling-in for an ailing Marion Hutton, before launching a
solo career. She was comfortable in big bands, jazz, country, blues or
pop and was especially fond of numbers with hand-clappin' rhythm.
She signed with Capitol records and in 1950 struck back-to-back gold
with *Bonaparte's Retreat* and the lively polka *Hoop-Dee-Doo*. Her
biggest signature hit, *Wheel of Fortune* with its 'click, click, click'
opening and brassy sound was prime 50s adult pop. Her controlled
power and the strong emotional undertow in her voice made her an
appealing live performer. She moved to RCA Victor records in 1955
and went straight to the top of the charts with *Rock and Roll Waltz*. In
the 90s she performed with Helen O'Connell and Margaret Whiting
in the oldies '3 Girls 3' tour.

Gale Storm (born April 5, 1922)

Famous EASY-POP hit single during the 50s: *I Hear You Knocking*　1955
Gale Storm also had hits with *Memories Are Made of This* and *Teenage Prayer* in 1955, *Why Do Fools Fall In Love* and *Ivory Tower* in 1956, and *Dark Moon* in 1957.
Recording career with hits on the charts: 1955 - 1957　　Record Label: Dot

Tenacious Gale Storm, real name Josephine Owaissa Cottle, was born in Bloomington, Texas, the youngest of five children. She entered a 'Gateway to Hollywood' talent contest and walked away with a movie contract. She is best remembered for her early fifties television work as the star of her own hit series 'My Little Margie' playing a scheming, meddlesome daughter trying to circumvent her father's parental control. She appeared as the headliner at the Thunderbird Hotel in Las Vegas and by 1955 the dynamic singer was recording for Randy Wood's Dot label where she won a gold record with her cover version of Smiley Lewis' *I Hear You Knocking.* She also starred in the less well-remembered 'Gale Storm Show/Oh Susanna' in the late 50s. During the 1970s she struggled with alcoholism and the stigma attached to the disease, but is now alcohol free.

Caterina Valente (born January 14, 1931)

Famous EASY-POP hit single during the 50s: *The Breeze and I*　1955
This was the only top-ten hit recording for Caterina Valente.
Recording career on the US charts: 1955　　Record Label: Decca

The Valentes were Italian citizens making their home in Paris when Caterina, the youngest of four children was born. Her Spanish father played classical accordion and her Italian mother was a dancer and musician. In the early 50s she began a solo career singing in German, French, Italian, and Spanish. She introduced herself to European audiences with her recordings of *Istanbul* and *I Love Paris.* Her recording, *Malaguena,* in German, led to her first English recording of *Andalucia* retitled *The Breeze and I.* In 1955, Gordon MacRae presented her on the 'Colgate Comedy Hour' television series as the 'Malaguena' girl and *The Breeze and I* became a worldwide hit. Her effervescent talent made her Europe's most successful female recording artist. Charismatic Caterina Valente is a true world citizen having sung in twelve different languages. She also plays guitar and has acted in fifteen films, including 'Mannequins for Rio' sometimes appearing with her brother Silvio Francesco. Another brother Pietro Valente is an actor and musician.

June Valli (born June 30, 1930)

Famous EASY-POP hit single during the 50s: *Crying In the Chapel* 1953
June Valli also had a hit with *I Understand* in 1954.
Recording career on the charts: 1952-1960   Record Labels: RCA Victor & Mercury

June Valli was born in the Bronx, New York. She got her start with a win on Arthur Godfrey's 'Talent Scouts' TV program. She was a featured vocalist along with Dorothy Collins, Snooky Lanson, and Russell Arms on the pop music television show 'Your Hit Parade.' After a two year stint Giselle McKenzie replaced her. She also appeared on 'The Big Show' hosted by Tullulah Bankhead. Signing a contract with RCA Victor in the early fifties, she recorded her two biggest hits *Crying in the Chapel* and *I Understand*. The country-twinged *Crying in the Chapel* was written by Artie Glenn and originally recorded by his son, country singer Darrell Glenn, covered by the R&B group the Orioles, and recorded in 1965 by Elvis Presley. June Valli's dramatic 1953 version was her only top-ten hit. She married Chicago disc jockey Howard Miller and in the late fifties moved to Mercury records where she recorded her last chart hit *Apple Green* in 1960. June Valli died in 1993 at the age of 64.

Sarah Vaughan (born March 27, 1924)

Famous EASY-POP hit during the 50s: *Make Yourself Comfortable* 1954
Sarah Vaughan also had hits with *Whatever Lola Wants* in 1955,
Mister Wonderful in 1956, and *Broken-Hearted Melody* in 1959.
Recording career on the charts: 1947-1966   Record Labels: Columbia & Mercury

Sarah Lois Vaughan was born in Newark, New Jersey, studied piano, and before she was twenty, won an amateur contest at the Apollo Theater with a sizzling rendition of *Body and Soul*. Ella Fitzgerald called her the world's 'greatest singing talent.' During a career that spanned nearly fifty years, she was a singer's singer, influencing everyone from Mel Torme to Anita Baker. The suppleness of her voice was shaded by a luscious timbre—she was the incomparable 'Sassy' Sarah Vaughan. As is typical of a jazz-derived popular artist, much of her work has been in a jazz context, but she was also extremely commercial in a pop setting. In the early fifties she enlarged her audience, recording show tunes *Whatever Lola Wants* from 'Damn Yankees' and the title song from 'Mr. Wonderful.' Her three-octave range, with its swooping highs and sensual lows could be moody, misty, or swinging. Her songs work on many levels and she ends up taller than her material. Sarah Vaughan died in 1990 at age sixty-six.

Dinah Washington (born August 29, 1924)

Famous POP hit during the 50s: ***What a Diff'rence a Day Makes*** 1959
Dinah Washington also had hit duets with Brook Benton on
Baby (You've Got What It Takes) and
A Rockin' Good Way (To Mess Around and Fall in Love) in 1960.
Recording career with hits on the charts: 1959-1963   Record Label: Mercury

Controversial rhythm & blues vocalist and pianist Dinah Washington was born Ruth Lee Jones in Tuscaloosa, Alabama, and raised in Chicago. In the early forties she was singing and playing piano in Salle Martin's gospel choir as Ruth Jones, while performing in the evenings as Dinah Washington in clubs with Lionel Hampton. Her gritty, penetrating voice, excellent timing, crystal-clear enunciation, and bluesy phrasing created her own distinctive style. *What a Diff'rence a Day Makes* won a Grammy Award for Best R&B Performance and it was her biggest hit. Her album, with its reliance on strings, was criticized by critics as being too commercial but it was a huge success and she continued to favor pop songs rather than blues and jazz. In 1960, she had top-ten hit duets with Brook Benton: *Baby* and *A Rockin' Good Way*. The seven-time-married Dinah Washington died of an accidental overdose of diet pills and alcohol in 1963 before she was forty.

Joan Weber (born December 12, 1936)

Famous EASY-POP hit single during the 50s: ***Let Me Go Lover***   1954
This was the only top-ten hit recording for Joan Weber.
Recording career with hits on the charts: 1954-1955   Record Label: Columbia

Fifties songstress Joan Weber was born in Paulsboro, New Jersey. She was eighteen years old when her manger brought the strong-voiced teen to the attention of Mitch Miller the A&R head at Columbia Records. He had the song *Let Me Go, Devil*, a warning against alcohol, rewritten as *Let Me Go, Lover*. The song, first heard on an episode of the CBS-TV dramatic anthology series 'Studio One,' was recorded by several female singers—Teresa Brewer had a version that went to #6, Patti Page had a #8 version, and Sunny Gale's recording went to #71—but it was unknown eighteen-year-old Joan Weber whose version was a number one hit for four weeks and remained on the charts for sixteen weeks. Often cited as a one-hit-wonder, she did record *Who'll Be My Judge*, an overlooked, should-have-been hit in 1957. Joan Weber died on May 13, 1981, in a mental institution in Ancora, New Jersey, at age 45.

Margaret Whiting (born July 22, 1924)

Famous EASY-POP hit single during the 50s: ***Moonlight in Vermont*** 1954
Margaret Whiting also had hits with *A Tree in the Meadow* and
Far Away Places in 1948, *Slippin' Around* in 1949,
A Bushel and a Peck and *Blind Date* in 1950,
Good Morning Mr. Echo in 1951, and *The Money Tree* in 1956.
Recording career with hits on the charts: 1946-1967   Record Label: Capitol

Born in Detroit and raised in Hollywood, 'Maggie' Whiting was the sister of actress/singer Barbara Whiting. Their father, successful songwriter Richard A. Whiting, author of *On the Good Ship Lollipop, Till We Meet Again*, and *Ain't We Got Fun*, worked for popular songwriter Johnny Mercer. In 1942, when Johnny Mercer and two partners launched Capitol Records, teen-aged Margaret Whiting was the first artist to be engaged. Capitol's arranger/conductor Paul Weston was particularly successful working with female singers and between 1946 and 1954 she recorded more than 40 hit singles. Following her #1 pairing with country & western film star Jimmy Wakely in 1949 on *Slippin Around,* she recorded two more hit duets with him in 1950: *A Bushel and a Peck* and *Broken Down Merry-Go-Round.* Later that year, she teamed with Bob Hope on the novelty hit *Blind Date*. On her 1954 recording of *Moonlight in Vermont* she was accompanied by her husband Joe 'Fingers' Carr. It was a remake of her 1945 classic.

Brief biographies of less well-known girl singers Betty Johnson, Peggy King, and Margie Rayburn are included in Chapter 9 'Fifty Fabulous, all-but-forgotten, EASY-POP Songs.'

References from Chapter 4:

Bogdanov, Vladimir, Woodstra, Chris and Erlewine, Stephen Thomas, editors. *All Music Guide: The Definitive Guide to Popular Music.* 4th Edition. San Francisco: Backbeat Books, 2001.

Larkin, Colin. *The Virgin Encyclopedia of Fifties Music.* Third Edition. London: Virgin Books Limited, 2002.

If a man does not keep pace with his companions, perhaps it is because he hears a different drummer. Let him step to the music he hears, however measured or far away.

Henry David Thoreau (1817-1862)

Chapter 5

Quintessential Guy Singers of the 50s

Chapter 3 presented popular songs of the 50s and chapter 4 described the girl singers. This chapter describes thirty-seven of the decade's most popular male vocalists and their fifties-style EASY-POP hits.

The 1950s were the golden decade for male vocalists. Universally recognized, outstanding singers of the twentieth century were creating their memorable recordings during the post-war era. Tony Bennett, Nat King Cole and Frank Sinatra secured their place as icons of adult POP standards in the fifties. Perry Como and Eddie Fisher regularly topped the fifties popular music charts and late in the decade they were joined by Paul Anka, Pat Boone, and Johnny Mathis. Harry Belafonte started the calypso craze and Elvis Presley, Buddy Holly, Sam Cooke, and Ricky Nelson introduced rock 'n' roll elements into their traditional 50s recordings.

A list of 'Quintessential Guy Singers of the Fifties' along with their most memorable recording of the decade is shown in chart 5.1. Following the chart, there are brief biographies of each of these unforgettable men and a listing of some of their successful 50s EASY-POP songs.

Quintessential Guy Singers of the Fifties

Artist	Famous EASY-POP Hit Song in the fifties	year released
Paul Anka	*Diana*	1957
Frankie Avalon	*Venus*	1959
Harry Belafonte	*The Banana Boat Song (Day-O)*	1957
Tony Bennett	*Stranger in Paradise*	1953
Brook Benton	*It's Just a Matter of Time*	1959
Pat Boone	*April Love*	1957
Don Cherry	*Band of Gold*	1956
Nat King Cole	*Mona Lisa*	1950
Perry Como	*Don't Let the Stars Get in Your Eyes*	1952
Sam Cooke	*You Send Me*	1957
Don Cornell	*Hold My Hand*	1954
Bing Crosby	*True Love* (with Grace Kelly)	1953
Vic Damone	*On The Street Where You Live*	1956
Bobby Darin	*Dream Lover*	1959
Johnny Desmond	*The Yellow Rose of Texas*	1955
Tommy Edwards	*It's All in the Game*	1958
Eddie Fisher	*Any Time*	1951
Al Hibbler	*Unchained Melody*	1955
Buddy Holly	*Everyday*	1957

Chart 5.1. Quintessential Guy Singers of the Fifties

(Chart continues on the next page)

Quintessential Guy Singers of the Fifties (continued)

Artist	Famous EASY-POP Hit Song in the fifties	year released
Johnny Horton	The Battle of New Orleans	1959
Tab Hunter	Young Love*	1957
Frankie Laine	Jezebel	1951
Mario Lanza	Be My Love	1950
Julius LaRosa	Eh Cumpari	1953
Steve Lawrence	Pretty Blue Eyes	1959
Dean Martin	That's Amore	1953
Tony Martin	I Get Ideas	1951
Al Martino	Here in My Heart	1952
Johnny Mathis	Chances Are	1957
Guy Mitchell	Heartaches by the Number	1959
Ricky Nelson	Poor Little Fool	1958
Elvis Presley	Love Me Tender	1956
Lloyd Price	Personality	1959
Johnnie Ray	Cry	1951
Jimmie Rodgers	Honeycomb	1957
Frank Sinatra	Young at Heart	1954
Andy Williams	Canadian Sunset	1956

* These recordings were covers of recordings from the original artists

Chart 5.1. Quintessential Guy Singers of the Fifties

Paul Anka (born July 30, 1941)

Famous EASY-POP hit single during the 50s: *Diana* 1957
Paul Anka also had hits with *Lonely Boy* and *Put Your Head on My Shoulder* in 1959 and *Puppy Love* in 1960.
Recording career with hits on the charts: 1957-1983   Record Label: ABC Paramount

Born in Ottawa, Canada, to parents of Lebanese Christian descent, child prodigy Paul Anka knew at age 13 that he wanted to be a singer/songwriter. On a trip to New York he auditioned for ABC producer Don Costa and sang his own composition, *Diana,* a love song to a former baby sitter. His father had to fly to New York to sign his son's contract. The teenager's evocative song jumped to #1 and launched his career. Hit *Puppy Love* was written for his old flame Walt Disney's Mouseketeer, Annette Funicello. Among his dozen top-ten hits were two more #1 songs: *Lonely Boy* and *You're Having My Baby.* A millionaire while still a minor, he wrote Frank Sinatra's signature song *My Way,* Buddy Holly's *It Doesn't Matter Any More*, and Tom Jones' hit *She's a Lady.* When Johnny Carson debuted as host of NBCs 'Tonight Show' in 1962, Paul Anka wrote one of the most recognized theme songs in TV history for his nightly entrance.

Frankie Avalon (born September 18, 1939)

Famous EASY-POP hit single during the 50s: *Venus* 1959
Avalon also had hits with *Bobby Sox to Stockings* and *Why* in 1959.
Recording career with hits on the charts: 1958-1962   Record Label: Chancellor

Born Francis Avallone in South Philadelphia, the teen played in bands in Atlantic City, New Jersey, and was back-up trumpet for Rocco and the Saints. He cut his first solo in 1958 but had been making recordings for several years prior to that as a trumpeter, not a singer. Photogenic Frankie Avalon first came to the attention of American Bandstand's Dick Clark while still in high school. He was managed by music impresario Bob Marcucci who wanted a singer with the right good looks. *Venus* on Marcucci's Chancellor label was Frankie Avalon's first #1 hit and between 1958 and 1962, he charted 13 singles in the Billboard Top 40. In 1959, Frankie Avalon appeared in the Warner Brothers western film 'Guns of the Timberland' with Alan Ladd and Gilbert Roland. He is often remembered for his frequent teaming with Annette Funicello in a series of six surfer-beach-party films, beginning with 'Beach Party' in 1963. Frankie Avalon and his wife Kay have eight children and he operates his own health care products business.

Harry Belafonte (born March 1, 1927)

Famous POP hit during the 50s: ***The Banana Boat Song (Day-O)*** 1957
Harry Belafonte also had hits with *Scarlet Ribbons* in 1952
and *Jamaica Farewell* in 1955.
Recording career with hits on the charts: 1952-1957   Record Label: RCA Victor

Harold Belafonte, Jr., born in Harlem, but partly raised in Jamaica, dropped out of school in the ninth grade and joined the US Navy. With little life direction, he was attracted to the arts. In the late 1940s he was part of the legendary Negro Ensemble Theater and he studied at the famed Dramatic Workshop in New York City alongside Marlon Brando. He signed a recording contract in 1952 and reached the peak of his recording success from 1956 to 1962. Starting as a 'straight pop' singer in New York City nightclubs, he began to specialize in happy-go-lucky folk music and West Indian calypso. His clear, silky voice, his good looks, and his assimilation of folk and world rhythms made him a national sensation—unparalleled for an African-American pop star before the civil rights movement. He also appeared in eight films including 'Calypso,' 'Carmen Jones,' and the controversial 'Island in the Sun' in 1957. In 1959, his live LP re-cording 'Belafonte at Carnegie Hall' spent three years on the charts.

Tony Bennett (born August 3, 1926)

Famous EASY-POP hit single during the 50s: ***Stranger in Paradise*** 1953
Tony Bennett also had hits with *Because of You* and *Cold, Cold Heart* in 1951, *Rags to Riches* in 1953, *There'll Be No Teardrops Tonight* in 1954, and *In the Middle of an Island* in 1957.
Recording career with hits on the charts: 1951-2007   Record Label: Columbia

The son of an Italian-born immigrant grocer, Anthony Benedetto was born in the Astoria section of Queens and attended the High School of Industrial Arts in Manhattan, where he nurtured two passions— singing and painting. His boyhood idols included Bing Crosby and Nat King Cole, both big influences on his easy, natural singing style. After singing in the US Army band, a break came in 1949 when Bob Hope noticed him working with Pearl Bailey in Greenwich Village and added him to his show at the Paramount Theater. Then Columbia A&R man, Mitch Miller, heard about the athletic kid with the golden voice and signed him to a contract. Early success came with a string of chart-topping singles. Rock 'n' roll caused his career to sag, but he came back with his smash signature hit in 1962: *I Left My Heart in San Francisco*. Still popular in the 21st century, the jazzy performer now sports the rumpled face of a singer who has weathered life.

Brook Benton (born September 19, 1931)

Famous POP hit single during the 50s: ***It's Just a Matter of Time*** 1959
Brook Benton also had hits with *Baby (You've Got What It Takes)* and
A Rockin' Good Way (To Mess Around and Fall in Love) in 1960, both
were duets with Dinah Washington.
Recording career with hits on the charts: 1958-1970   Record Label: Mercury

Silky smooth soul singer and songwriter, Brook Benton was born
Benjamin Franklin Peay in Camden, South Carolina. He began his
career with the Camden Jubilee Singers and moved to New York in
1948 to join gospel groups—Bill Langford's Spiritual Singers, the
Langfordaires, the Golden Gate Quartet, and the Jerusalem Stars. He
recorded under the name Benjamin Peay in 1953 and then teamed
with writer/producer Clyde Otis to create a violin-studded variation
on the R&B sound. His own composition, *It's Just A Matter Of Time*
was this rich baritone's first big hit but he is widely known for his
sixties recordings of *Rainy Night in Georgia* and *Fools Rush In*. His
pairing with Dinah Washington produced two big hits in 1960, *Baby*
and *A Rockin' Good Way*. Brook Benton died in New York City in
1988 of complications from spinal meningitis.

Pat Boone (born June 1, 1934)

Famous EASY-POP hit single during the 50s: ***April Love***   1957
Pat Boone also had hits with *Friendly Persuasion (Thee I Love)* and
Don't Forbid Me in 1956 and *Love Letters in the Sand* in 1957.
Recording career with hits on the charts: 1955-1966   Record Label: Dot

Pat Boone is associated with his EASY-POP recordings *Love Letters in
the Sand, Friendly Persuasion,* and *April Love*—but his big hits also
included rock 'n' roll covers of *Ain't That A Shame, Long Tall Sally,*
and *I Almost Lost My Mind.* On his cover recordings he added his
own twists to rock & roll, polished rough edges, and made them more
palatable to audiences raised on soothing traditional pop. This great-
great grandson of America's frontier hero, Daniel Boone, was born in
Jacksonville, Florida. After high school in Nashville, Tennessee,
where he was student body president, he married Shirley Foley,
daughter of country star Red Foley. He appeared on TVs 'Ted Mack's
Amateur Hour,' the 'Arthur Godfrey Show,' and eventually his own
weekly TV show on ABC. With his trademark white buck shoes, perfectly combed hair, and radiant smile, Pat Boone was the very essence
of American values at a time when rock & roll seemed threatening.
At the box office, he had a string of successful films including 'State
Fair,' 'Journey to the Center of the Earth,' and 'April Love.'

Don Cherry (born January 11, 1924)

Famous EASY-POP hit single during the 50s: ***Band of Gold*** 1956
Don Cherry also had a hit with *Thinking of You* in 1950.
Recording career with hits on the charts: 1950-1956 Record Labels: Decca & Columbia

Singer/golfer Don Cherry was born in Wichita Falls, Texas, the youngest of three children. After high school graduation, he entered and won the city's Junior Golf Championship. A month after the U.S. entered World War II, he was drafted into the Army-Air Corps. When his four-year service was complete, he competed in golf tournaments during the day and performed at night. His mellow baritone voice touched people and he sang briefly with the Tommy Dorsey and Victor Young orchestras. He had a record deal with Decca in the early fifties where he recorded *Thinking of You* and *Vanity*, then moved to Columbia where he recorded his million-selling *Band of Gold*. On TV he appeared on the 'Mike Douglas Show,' 'Merv Griffin Show,' and the 'Johnny Carson Tonight Show.' He left the musical field in the late fifties to become a professional golfer.

Nat King Cole (born March 17, 1917)

Famous EASY-POP hit single during the 50s: ***Mona Lisa*** 1950
Nat King Cole also had hits with *Too Young* in 1951, *Pretend* in 1953,
Answer Me, My Love in 1954, *Darling Je Vous Aime Beaucoup* in
1955, *A Blossom Fell* in 1956, and *Ballerina* in 1957.
Recording career with hits on the charts: 1943-1966   Record Label: Capitol

One of the most popular singers of his generation, Nathaniel Adams Coles, son of a Baptist church pastor, was born in Montgomery, Alabama, in 1919, raised in Chicago, and christened Nat 'King' Cole by a Los Angeles club owner in 1937. Beginning his career as a jazz pianist, he formed an innovative, drummerless trio, the hugely popular King Cole Trio in 1939 with guitarist Oscar Moore and bassist Wesley Prince. Nat King Cole conquered the pop charts in the fifties as a mild-mannered, warm-voiced singer of orchestrated 1950s ballads like *Mona Lisa* and *Unforgettable* and breezy, countrified 1960s sing-alongs like *Ramblin' Rose* and *Those Lazy-Hazy-Crazy Days of Summer*. His rich, husky, careful enunciation was backed by various orchestras including Nelson Riddle's and Billy May's. The 1957 hit *Send For Me* with its guitars, sax, and gritty vocal was as close as he got to rock and roll. He appeared in films 'Saint Louis Blues' and 'Cat Ballou' as well as hosting his own TV series. Daughter Natalie Cole is also a recording star. Nat King Cole died of lung cancer in 1965.

Perry Como (born May 18, 1912)

Famous hit during the 50s: ***Don't Let the Stars Get in Your Eyes*** 1952
Perry Como also had hits with *If* in 1952, *No Other Love* in 1953, *Wanted* in 1954, *Tina Marie* in 1955, *Hot Diggity* in 1956, *Round and Round* in 1957, and *Catch a Falling Star* and *Magic Moments* in 1958.

Recording career with hits on the charts: 1943-1974   Record Label: RCA Victor

He was born Pierino Como in Canonsburg, Pennsylvania, to immigrants from Palena, Italy. Perry Como left the barbershop he opened while attending high school to sing with Freddie Carlone's band in 1933 and by 1937 he was a featured vocalist with Ted Weems orchestra. In 1943, he was signed by RCA Victor and became one of the most successful performers of the twentieth century. He left a legacy of lighthearted songs and romantic ballads. Often accompanied by the Mitchell Ayres Orchestra and the Ray Charles Singers, Perry Como sold more than one hundred million records and had fourteen tunes that were number one hits. He also recorded two classic fifties Christmas Songs: *It's Beginning to Look a Lot like Christmas* with the Fontane Sisters and *Home for the Holidays.* Television was made for his laid-back style and personality. He hosted top rated NBC TV shows from 1948-1963. Wearing a cardigan sweater, he appeared extremely relaxed and his intimate and personal baritone voice complemented his affability and sincerity. Perry Como died in 2001.

Sam Cooke (born January 22, 1931)

Famous EASY-POP hit single during the 50s: ***You Send Me*** 1957
Sam Cooke had another pop hit with *Chain Gang* in 1960.

Recording career with hits on the charts: 1957-1966   Record Labels: Keen & RCA

Sam Cooke, a Baptist minister's son, was born in Mississippi and grew up in Chicago. An 'A' student, he sang in choirs and at 19 was the lead singer of the 'Soul Stirrers.' After six years in gospel music, Sam Cooke burst onto the pop scene with *You Send Me*. The song's innovative blend of gospel, pop, and R&B stayed on the charts for six months, rising to #1 in both the R&B and pop markets. He recorded secular songs in 1956 as 'Dale Cook' on Specialty records, then a string of hits on Keen records led to a contract with RCA. His records sold to white teenagers yet he never lost his credibility with his core black audience. During his short 8-year pop career he wrote many of the songs that he recorded including *You Send Me, Chain Gang, Only Sixteen*, and *Cupid*. Sam Cooke was among the original inductees into the Rock & Roll Hall of Fame. He died at age 21, under mysterious circumstances, of a gunshot wound at a seedy motel in Los Angeles.

Don Cornell (born April 21, 1919)

Famous EASY-POP hit single during the 50s: ***Hold My Hand*** 1954
Don Cornell also had hits with *I'm Yours* and *I'll Walk Alone* in 1952
and *The Bible Tells Me So* in 1955.
Recording career with hits on the charts: 1950-1957   Record Label: Coral

Popular singer-guitarist, Don Cornell, was born Luigi Francisco Valaro in the Bronx. The teenager entered the music world as a guitar player when he joined the band of famed trumpeter Red Nichols. He emerged as a singer and achieved his greatest success with Sammy Kaye's 'Swing and Sway' band. In 1949, he launched a solo career and recorded legendary standards *I'm Yours* and *I'll Walk Alone*. In 1954, his smash hit record *Hold My Hand* was featured in the Dick Powell/Debbie Reynolds film 'Susan Slept Here.' By this time, he had become the top recording artist in the nation with three of his recordings occupying the top-ten charts. Don Cornell earned a dozen gold record awards between 1950 and 1962 and played to record-breaking audiences in nightclubs—his appearance at the Palladium in London stopped traffic around Piccadilly. He died in 2004.

Bing Crosby (born May 3, 1903)

Famous EASY-POP hit single during the 50s: ***True Love*** 1953
Bing Crosby's other hits included: *Play a Simple Melody* (with son Gary) in 1950, *In the Cool, Cool, Cool of the Evening* (with Jane Wyman) in 1951, *Y'all Come* in 1954, and *Around the World* in 1957.
Recording career with hits on the charts: 1931-1962   Record Label: Decca

This influential media star was born Harry Lillis Crosby in Tacoma, Washington, the fourth of seven children. Bingo was a childhood nickname from one of his favorite comic strips 'The Bingville Bugle.' His friends and teachers shortened it to Bing. In 1920, he entered Gonzaga College in Spokane, Washington, with the intent of becoming a lawyer. During his fifty-year singing career he recorded more than 1700 songs. He earned 23 million-selling gold records. His persona represented the strong yet affable American everyman. *True Love,* a duet with Grace Kelly from the film 'High Society,' climbed to #3 on the charts. His 1942 recording of *White Christmas* was reissued every year during the fifties and became the best selling single of all time. He is often remembered for seven classic comedy 'Road to...' films with Bob Hope and Dorothy Lamour during the forties and fifties and Irving Berlin's 1954 film extravaganza 'White Christmas' with Danny Kaye and Rosemary Clooney. Bing Crosby died suddenly of a heart attack, on a Spanish golf course in 1977.

Vic Damone (born June 12, 1928)

Famous POP hit during the 50s: ***On the Street Where You Live*** 1956
Other hits included: *You're Breaking My Heart* in 1949,
April in Portugal in 1953, and *An Affair To Remember* in 1957.
Recording career with hits on the charts: 1947-1965 Record Labels: Mercury & Columbia

Born Vito Farinola in Brooklyn, but adopting his mother's maiden name, popular crooner Vic Damone was a prototypical Italian-American ballad singer. Perry Como heard him sing and encouraged him. They became good friends—Vic's son is named Perry and Perry Como is the boy's godfather. After winning a place on 'Arthur Godfrey's Talent Scouts' in 1947, he started singing regularly on the radio and in nightclubs, and signed with Mercury Records. He had a million-seller with *You're Breaking My Heart*, based on the turn-of-the-century ballad by Leoncavallo, composer of the opera 'I Pagliacci.' But it was his recording of *On the Street Where You Live* from Lerner and Loewe's Broadway show 'My Fair Lady' that put Vic Damone into super-star status. He had another hit in 1957 with his recording of *An Affair to Remember* from the Cary Grant, Deborah Kerr film. He starred in MGM musicals 'Rich, Young and Pretty,' 'Athena,' 'Kismet,' and 'Hit the Deck.' Frank Sinatra said that Vic Damone had "the best set of pipes in the business."

Bobby Darin (born May 14, 1936)

Famous EASY-POP hit single during the 50s: ***Dream Lover*** 1959
Bobbie Darin also had hits with *Splish Splash* in 1958,
Mack the Knife in 1959, and *Clementine* and *Beyond the Sea* in 1960.
Recording career with hits on the charts: 1958-1973 Record Label: Atco

Versatile vocalist Bobby Darin was born Walden Robert Cassotto in New York City. He went to Bronx High School of Science and received a scholarship to Hunter College. He began to write songs and taught himself to play the piano. He found fame at Atco Records in 1958 with his first hit records *Splish Splash* and *Dream Lover*, both of which he composed. Late in 1958, Bobby Darin recorded the album 'That's All' an LP of standards that contained his signature song *Mack the Knife*, which won the 1959 'Record of the Year' and Darin the 'Best New Artist' Grammy. *Mack the Knife* is one of the biggest selling records in history. He married actress Sandra Dee in 1960 and in 1963, received an Oscar nomination for his role as a drugged hospital patient in 'Captain Newman, MD.' His life was cut short in 1973 when, following his second open-heart surgery, he died at the young age of 37.

Johnny Desmond (born November 14, 1919)

Famous POP hit single during the 50s: *The Yellow Rose of Texas*   1955
Desmond also had hits with *Play Me Hearts and Flowers* in 1955 and
(The Gang that Sang) Heart of My Heart (with Don Cornell & Alan Dale) in 1953.
Recording career with hits on the charts: 1946-1957   Record Labels: MGM and Coral

Johnny Desmond was born Giovanni Alfredo De Simeone in Detroit. He worked at his father's grocery store and, in his teens, attended the Detroit Conservatory of Music. The composer and pianist formed his own singing group, working with Bob Crosby's big band, calling themselves the Bob-O-Links. Enlisting in the service, he was the vocalist with Glenn Miller's Army Air Force Band. After the war, he spent six years singing on the radio in Chicago on the national variety program 'The Breakfast Club.'   On Broadway he starred opposite Vivian Blaine in 1958's 'Say Darling.' Johnny Desmond's repertoire was extremely varied—light ballads, standards, and novelties. His version of *The Yellow Rose of Texas* almost outsold the original by Mitch Miller. He recorded the vocal versions of the theme from the movie *The High and The Mighty* and *Tara's Theme (My Own True Love)* from the classic 1939 film 'Gone with the Wind.' Johnny Desmond died of cancer in 1985.

Tommy Edwards (born February 17, 1922)

Famous EASY-POP hit single during the 50s: *It's All in the Game*   1958
Tommy Edwards also had a hit with *Morningside of the Mountain*
released for the first time in 1951 and released again in 1959
and *Please Mr. Sun* released in 1952 and released again in 1959.
Recording career with hits on the charts: 1951-1960   Record Label: MGM Records

Black singer, pianist, composer, Tommy Edwards was born in Richmond, Virginia. He began performing at age nine and at age 27 recorded for Top Records. He had his first hit in 1951 with *All Over Again*, a top-ten song on the R&B charts. *It's All in the Game*, a song that Tommy Edwards originally recorded in 1951 and re-recorded with a 'beat-ballad' arrangement, became his big #1 R&B and EASY-POP hit in 1958. It had only placed 18th in 1951. The song was composed by future U.S. Vice President Charles G. Dawes in 1912 as *Melody in A Major* with lyrics written in 1951 by Carl Sigman. His familiar *Please Love Me Forever* was the 'B' side of *It's All in the Game*. Tommy Edwards also re-worked his early fifties hits, *Morningside of the Mountain* and *Please Mr. Sun*, and re-released them successfully in 1959. His last chart tune was *My Melancholy Baby* in 1959. Tommy Edwards died of a brain aneurysm in 1969.

Eddie Fisher (born August 10, 1928)

Famous EASY-POP hit single during the 50s: *Any Time*   1951
Eddie Fisher also had hits with *Wish You Were Here* in 1952, *I'm Walking Behind You* and *Oh! My Papa* in 1953, *I Need You Now* in 1954, *Heart* and *Dungaree Doll* in 1955, and *Cindy, Oh Cindy* in 1956.
Recording career with hits on the charts: 1950-1967   Record Label: RCA Victor

Edwin Jack Fisher, born in 1928 in Philadelphia to Russian Jewish immigrants, was the #1 idol of bobbysoxers during the early 1950s. He appeared on Arthur Godfrey's 'Talent Scouts' and at age 18 was crooning with the bands of Buddy Morrow and Charlie Ventura. The next year he got his first nationwide exposure on Eddie Cantor's radio show where he was an instant hit and signed to a contract with RCA Victor. Drafted into the US Army in 1951, he served a year in Korea. After his discharge the melodious tenor became even more popular. He had twenty-one big hits in a row and hosted his own TV variety series 'Coke Time with Eddie Fisher.' Showman Mike Todd, who died in a plane crash in 1958, was his best friend and Eddie Fisher's affair and subsequent marriage to his friend's famous widow, Elizabeth Taylor, caused a show business scandal. He appeared in several 50s movies including a musical comedy 'Bundle of Joy' with first wife Debbie Reynolds and the serious drama 'Butterfield 8' with second wife Elizabeth Taylor.

Al Hibbler (born August 16, 1915)

Famous EASY-POP hit single during the 50s: *Unchained Melody*   1955
Al Hibbler also had hits with *He* in 1955 and
After The Lights Go Down Low in 1956.
Recording career with hits on the charts: 1955-1957   Record Label: Decca

Albert Hibbler was born in Tyro, Mississippi, and blind since birth. After moving to Little Rock, Arkansas, where he sang soprano in the choir of a school for the blind at the age of 12, he later studied voice at the Conservatory for the Blind in Little Rock. When his voice deepened, he began singing blues at area roadhouses. He first recorded with Jay McShann in 1942 and was a vocalist with Duke Ellington from 1943 to 1951. He also recorded with Harry Carney, Tab Smith, Mercer Ellington, and Billy Strayhorn. His strong masculine voice was emotive with a steady vibrato and he often employed a gravely, growling technique. In 1955, he signed a contract with Decca and hit the pop charts in a big way with two million-selling singles, *Unchained Melody* and *He*, spotlighting his deep tone and distinctive phrasing. Al Hibbler died in 2001.

Buddy Holly (born September 7, 1936)

Famous EASY-POP hit single during the 50s: *Everyday* 1957
Buddy Holly also had hits with *That'll Be the Day* and *Oh, Boy!* in 1957
and *It Doesn't Matter Any More* in 1959.
Recording career with hits on the charts: 1957-1959 Record Labels: Brunswick & Coral

Charles Hardin Holley, the youngest of four children, was born in Lubbock, Texas, where Buddy was a popular nickname for a male 'baby of the family.' By age 13, he and his friend Bob Montgomery were playing a kind of music they called 'Western Bop,' which they performed at local clubs. He added Larry Welborn and Jerry Allison to form 'The Crickets.' Bespectacled Buddy Holly was the guitarist and vocalist with a singing style that blends rockabilly irreverence with pop and rock 'n' roll. Among his Clovis, New Mexico, recordings were the western/bop/rock hit *Peggy Sue*, the hillbilly *That'll Be the Day*, and the 50s EASY-POP hit *Everyday* featuring Norman Petty on the celeste. The Crickets musical talent, together with Buddy Holly's unique 'excited' style of singing, quickly made them a success. He died in 1959 before his 23rd birthday. As part of a rock show, Buddy Holly toured with 'The Big Bopper' and Ritchie Valens. After a concert at the Surf Ballroom in Clear Lake, Iowa, their small chartered plane crashed and everyone on board was killed. His entire recording career lasted just 18 months.

Johnny Horton (born April 3, 1925)

Famous POP hit single during the 50s: ***The Battle of New Orleans*** 1959
He also had hits with *Sink the Bismarck* and *North to Alaska* in 1960.
Recording career with hits on the charts: 1959-1962 Record Label: Columbia

Johnny Horton recorded three top-ten songs before he was killed in a 1960 automobile accident in Milano, Texas. Born in Los Angeles, he was raised in Tyler, Texas, and worked in the fishing industry in Alaska. Singing country songs on the Cormac label in the early fifties, he picked up the nickname the 'Singing Fisherman.' He became a regular on the 'Louisiana Hayride' and married Billie Jean Jones, the widow of country music legend Hank Williams. In the late fifties he began to record a series of saga songs that crossed over to the pop charts. He covered Jimmy Driftwood's *The Battle Of New Orleans*, a tribute to the final battle of the War of 1812, and his #1 hit version was one of the top-ten hits of the decade. In 1960, he recorded *Sink The Bismarck*, suggested by the film 'Sink the Bismarck,' and then sang the title song for the John Wayne movie 'North To Alaska'—both made the top-ten.

Tab Hunter (born July 11, 1931)

Famous EASY-POP hit single during the 50s: *Young Love* 1957
This was the only top-ten hit recording for Tab Hunter.

Recording career with hits on the charts: 1957-1959 Record Labels: Dot & Warner

Born Arthur Andrew Kelm* in New York City, sportsman turned actor, Tab Hunter, became one of Hollywood's blond-haired, blue-eyed golden boys. His first starring role, at 19, was opposite Linda Darnell in the romantic South Seas adventure 'Island of Desire.' An instant success, he went on to star in over 50 films including 'Battle Cry,' 'The Pleasure of His Company,' 'Ride the Wild Surf,' and the Academy Award-nominated 'Damn Yankees.' His leading ladies included Sophia Loren, Natalie Wood, Gwen Verdon, Rita Hayworth, Lana Turner, and Debbie Reynolds. The popular film star appeared on hundreds of TV shows and starred on Broadway in Tennessee Williams's 'The Milk Train Doesn't Stop Here Anymore' with Tallulah Bankhead. Never really known as a singer, Tab Hunter's version of *Young Love* was a cover of the original by country singer/songwriter Sonny James. The song, also covered by the Crew-Cuts in 1957, became the only #1 hit for movie star Tab Hunter.

*His last name was changed to Gelien when his mother divorced.

Frankie Laine (born March 30, 1913)

Famous EASY-POP hit single during the 50s: *Jezebel* 1951
Frankie Laine also had hits with *The Cry of the Wild Goose* in 1950, *Jealousy* in 1951, *High Noon* in 1952, *I Believe* in 1953, *Moonlight Gambler* in 1956, and *Rawhide* (theme from the TV western) in 1959.

Recording career with hits on the charts: 1947-1969 Record Labels: Mercury & Columbia

Born Frank Paul LoVecchio in Chicago's Little Italy, Frankie Laine's swirling musical melodramas made him one of the top singing stars of the decade after World War II. At the age of 17, he left home to try his luck as a marathon dancer and with partner Ruth Smith, set the all-time marathon dance record in Atlantic City, New Jersey. They danced for 3,501 hours over 145 days and split a grand prize of $1,000. Singing at Billy Berg's jazz club on Vine Street in Hollywood, resulted in a recording contract with Mercury Records. In 1949, he had #1 hits with *That Lucky Old Sun* and *Mule Train*. His dynamic style and manly baritone on swinging standards as well as western movie themes found favor with white and black audiences and garnered 21 gold records. On television, Frankie Laine's singing of the *Rawhide* theme in 1959 has become one of the most popular TV theme songs of all time.

Mario Lanza (born January 31, 1921)

Famous EASY-POP hit single during the 50s: ***Be My Love*** 1950
Mario Lanza also had hits with *The Loveliest Night of the Year* in 1951
and *Because You're Mine* in 1952.
Recording career with hits on the charts: 1950-1954   Record Label: RCA Victor

Born Alfredo Arnold Cocozza in Philadelphia, Mario Lanza was the most spectacularly popular operatic tenor since Enrico Caruso, who died the same year Mario was born. As a teenager he studied to be a concert singer and gained fame while performing in the US Army for fellow infantrymen. MGM studio head Louis B. Mayer signed him to a seven-year contract and cast him in 'The Toast of New Orleans' opposite Kathryn Grayson, introducing his first million-selling hit *Be My Love* in 1950. The next year he starred as his idol, Enrico Caruso, in 'The Great Caruso,' featuring another million seller, *The Loveliest Night of the Year.* The Academy Award nominated title song from 1952's 'Because You're Mine' became his third and final million-seller. Beset with weight problems, alcohol, and tranquilizers, he became a recluse for several years. After moving to Italy, he made one more film 'Seven Hills of Rome' which included the song *Arrivederci Roma.* Mario Lanza died of a heart attack in 1959.

Julius LaRosa (born January 2, 1930)

Famous EASY-POP hit single during the 50s: ***Eh Cumpari*** 1953
Julius LaRosa also had hits with *Anywhere I Wander* in 1953
and *Domani (Tomorrow)* in 1955.
Recording career with hits on the charts: 1953 - 1958   Record Labels: Cadence & RCA

This earnest Italian singer, was born in Brooklyn, sang with the US Navy Band, and was 'discovered' by Arthur Godfrey. For two years Julius La Rosa was a member of the immensely popular CBS TV variety series 'Arthur Godfrey and his Friends.' His first single release, *Anywhere I Wander* shot into the top-30, his third release, *Eh, Cumpari,* was a run-away hit, and he was named 'best new male vocalist' for 1953. That fall, Julius LaRosa was dismissed on-the-air after singing *Manhattan* because Arthur Godfrey said that he had "lost his humility." La Rosa thanked him for giving him his big break and left the show. Hearing the big-guy-hurt-the-little-guy, the public turned on Arthur Godfrey, whose TV image as a down-to-earth, plain-speaking Mr. Nice Guy, belied his actual tyrannical and judgmental nature. Julius LaRosa went on to well-publicized appearances on the Ed Sullivan Show and followed with several hit records. Arthur Godfrey's shows, and his career, went into a decline and never recovered.

Steve Lawrence (born July 8, 1935)

Famous EASY-POP hit single during the 50s: *Pretty Blue Eyes* 1959
Steve Lawrence also had hits with *Party Doll* in 1957, *Footsteps* in 1960,
Portrait of My Love in 1961, and *Go Away Little Girl* in 1962.
Recording career with hits on the charts: 1952 - 1972   Record Labels: Coral & ABC

Born Sidney Leibowitz, the son of a cantor in Brooklyn, New York, he studied piano and saxophone in high school. Taking the first names of two nephews, he won first prize on Arthur Godfrey's TV series 'Talent Scouts' in 1951. His vocal range and warmth earned him a place on Steve Allen's 'Tonight' TV show in 1953 where he met and performed with singer Eydie Gorme. They married in 1957 in Las Vegas and he began a two year stint in the US Army. He had two hits in 1957: *Banana Boat Song*, although calypso singer Harry Belafonte had the blockbuster version, and *Party Doll* even though the version by rockabilly Buddy Knox was the #1 hit. His hit singles were recorded between 1959 and 1962. He starred in the Broadway musical 'What Makes Sammy Run?' in 1964 and with wife, Eydie Gorme, in 'Golden Rainbow' in 1968. Steve and Eydie, as they are always billed, continue to perform as a duet.

Dean Martin (born June 7, 1917)

Famous EASY-POP hit during the 50s: *That's Amore* 1953
Dean Martin also had hits with *Memories Are Made of This* in 1955 and
Return to Me and *Volare* in 1958.
Recording career with hits on the charts: 1948-1969   Record Label: Capitol

Born Dino Crocetti in Steubenville, Ohio, Dean Martin, in the late forties, formed a fast friendship with comic Jerry Lewis. They participated in each other's acts and began performing together in nightclubs. They appeared on television and eventually hosted their own rotating series 'The Colgate Comedy Hour.' Their phenomenally successful partnership broke up in 1956 after 16 hit films and hundreds of television and club appearances. The eternal essence of cool—detached, serene, and cavalier—the ballad singer had a low, sweet sound and a loose-limbed sense of his own laid-back persona. In the late 50s he appeared as a member of Frank Sinatra's 'Rat Pack' that also included Sammy Davis Jr., Peter Lawford, and Joey Bishop. The group performed at the Sands Hotel on the Las Vegas strip and starred in seven films including 1960's 'Ocean's Eleven.' Dean Martin starred in his own enormously successful television series for nine seasons in the mid 1960s. Diagnosed with lung cancer, he died of respiratory failure at 78 on Christmas morning, 1995.

Tony Martin (born December 25, 1912)

Famous EASY-POP hit single during the 50s: *I Get Ideas* 1951
Martin also had hits with *Here* in 1954 and *Walk Hand in Hand* in 1956.
Recording career with hits on the charts: 1938-1957   Record Label: RCA Victor

Born Alvin Morris to a Jewish family in Oakland, California, Tony Martin, at grammar school, played saxophone and was a boy soprano in the glee club. Dubbed 'the Butterscotch Baritone' he was featured on the George Burns and Gracie Allen radio program. His 1946 million-selling recording of *To Each His Own* at Mercury, prompted RCA to offer him a long-term record contract in 1947. In the fifties he starred in a number of MGM film musicals including 'Two Tickets to Broadway' with Janet Leigh in 1951, singing his biggest hit song *There's No Tomorrow*, and he sang the title song in 'Easy to Love' with Esther Williams in 1953. His version of *Lover Come Back To Me* with Joan Weldon in 1954's 'Deep in My Heart' was a highlight of Hollywood musicals and in the 1955 musical 'Hit The Deck' he sang *More than You Know* to Ann Miller. Tony Martin has been married to dancer/singer/actress Cyd Charisse since 1948.

Al Martino (born October 7, 1927)

Famous EASY-POP hit single during the 50s: *Here in My Heart* 1952
Al Martino had hits in the sixties including *I Love You Because* in 1963,
I Love You More and More Everyday in 1964, and *Spanish Eyes* in 1965.
Recording career with hits on the charts: 1952-1977   Record Label: Capitol

The internationally popular Italian balladeer was born Alfred Cini in South Philadelphia where he worked as a bricklayer in the family's construction business and performed in neighborhood clubs in the evenings. Family friend and renowned Italian-American tenor, Mario Lanza, encouraged young Al Martino to pursue a musical career. By 1950, after winning first prize on Arthur Godfrey's 'Talent Scouts' TV show, he landed a much sought-after record deal with Capitol Records. His first recording, *Here In My Heart*, sold over one million copies in the United States and hit number one on the British 'singles' charts. After several more hits, his recording career was interrupted by gangster interference in the mid fifties that kept him out of the United States. He returned in 1958 and resumed recording. Ironically he is best remembered for his role as the Mafia-connected singer Johnny Fontane singing the love theme *Speak Softly Love* in Francis Ford Coppola's 1972 cinematic masterpiece 'The Godfather.'

Johnny Mathis (born September 30, 1935)

Famous EASY-POP hit single during the 50s: *Chances Are* 1957
Johnny Mathis also had hits with *It's Not for Me to Say* and
The Twelfth of Never in 1957 and *Misty* in 1959.
Recording career with hits on the charts: 1957-1984 Record Label: Columbia

The fourth of seven children, John Royce Mathis was born in Gilmer, Texas, and grew up in San Francisco. He was invited to attend the trials for the 1956 US Olympic track teams to compete in Melbourne, Australia that summer but Columbia Records requested that he come to New York for a recording session. He gave up his Olympic chance and went to New York to record two of his most popular hits: *It's Not For Me To Say* and *Wonderful, Wonderful*. In 1959, he recorded another song that became synonymous with the name of Johnny Mathis, the Erroll Garner composition, *Misty*. As a thirteen-year-old, he studied with an opera coach who influenced his style. Albums of his songs, like his singles, became immediate successes. 'Johnny Mathis's Greatest Hits' album, released in 1958, became one of the most popular albums of all time, spent ten years on the albums chart, and began a 'Greatest Hits' tradition copied by every artist and record company since. Having recorded more than 100 albums, he ranks with Elvis Presley and Frank Sinatra as a top album artist.

Guy Mitchell (born February 27, 1927)

Famous EASY-POP hit during the 50s: *Heartaches by the Number* 1959
Mitchell also had hits with *My Heart Cries for You* and *The Roving Kind*
in 1950, *My Truly, Truly Fair* in 1951, and *Singing the Blues* in 1956.
Recording career with hits on the charts: 1950-1960 Record Label: Columbia

Guy Mitchell was born Al Cernik into a Yugoslavian immigrant family in Detroit. As a teenager in the San Joachin Valley he worked as an apprentice saddle-maker, joined the Navy for two years, and in 1947 Al Cernik began singing with Carmen Cavellaro's orchestra. In 1948, he recorded songs at King Records as Al Grant and won first prize on Arthur Godfrey's 'Talents Scouts' radio program. In 1951, Columbia Record's A&R head Mitch Miller had set recording sessions for Frank Sinatra, when he declined, Guy Mitchell was brought to the studio and his recordings of *My Heart Cries for You* and *The Roving Kind* sold nearly two million copies. His first #1 hit, *Singing The Blues,* came in 1956 and in 1959, he had his second, *Heartaches By The Number*. He made movies with Teresa Brewer and Rosemary Clooney and he had his own television show in 1957. Guy Mitchell retired in the 1960s and he died in 1999.

Ricky Nelson (born May 8, 1940)

Famous EASY-POP hit single during the 50s: ***Poor Little Fool*** 1958
also *A Teenager's Romance, Be-Bop Baby*, and *Stood Up* in 1957,
Lonesome Town in 1958, and *Never Be Anyone Else But You* in 1959.
Recording career on the charts: 1957–1973   Record Labels: Verve & Imperial

The son of bandleader Ozzie Nelson and vocalist Harriet Hilliard, Eric Nelson was born in Teaneck, New Jersey. In 1949, 8-year-old 'Ricky' and brother David made their first appearance on the 'Adventures of Ozzie and Harriet,' a radio show centered on the real life of the couple. Initially, actors were hired to play the children but the boys pressured their parents to play themselves. On their TV show in 1957, Ricky debuted *I'm Walkin'* and *Be-Bop Baby* and each sold a million copies. Ozzie supervised the tight top-notch combo that backed his son—rockabilly whiz James Burton played lead guitar. His music crossed between 50s EASY-POP, rockabilly, and rock 'n' roll. On the big screen, he co-starred in John Wayne's western 'Rio Bravo' and the comedy 'The Wackiest Ship in the Navy' with Jack Lemmon. His self-composed last hit, *Garden Party*, in 1972 was a response to audiences wanting to hear only his old songs. Adult, Rick Nelson died in a New Year's Eve plane crash in Texas in 1985.

Elvis Presley (born January 8, 1935)

Famous EASY-POP hit during the 50s: ***Love Me Tender*** 1956
Heartbreak Hotel and *Don't Be Cruel* in 1956, *(Let Me Be Your)Teddy Bear,*
Too Much, Jailhouse Rock, and *Don't* in 1957, and *Stuck on You* in 1959.
Recording career with hits on the charts: 1957-1977   Record Label: RCA Victor

The King of Rock & Roll, Elvis Aaron Presley, was born in a two-room house in Tupelo, Mississippi; twin brother Jessie Garon was stillborn, leaving him to grow up as an only child. Influenced by the music he heard at all-night gospel sings in Memphis and the black R&B he absorbed on historic Beale Street, his recording career began in 1954 with Sun Records—a year later he moved to RCA Victor. With a unique sound and style, he ushered in a new era of American music. In addition to his rock 'n' roll hits: *Heartbreak Hotel* and *Jailhouse Rock*, he had EASY-POP hits: *Love Me Tender, Teddy Bear, It's Now or Never*, and *Loving You*. He made a huge impact on the Ed Sullivan TV program in 1956 and starred in more than thirty films beginning with 'Love Me Tender.' His Las Vegas performances and 1973 comeback concert in Hawaii are legendary. Globally, he sold over one billion records, more than any other artist. He died of drug-related heart failure in 1977 at his home, Graceland, in Memphis.

Lloyd Price (born March 9, 1933)

Famous POP hit single during the 50s: ***Personality***   1959
Lloyd Price also had a hit with *Stagger Lee* in 1958.
Recording career with hits on the charts: 1957-1964   Record Label: ABC-Paramount

Born in Kenner, Louisiana, Lloyd Price was a rhythm & blues vocalist, pianist, and composer. As a teenager, he and his brother Leo formed a rock band. His first recording on the Specialty label in 1952 was the #1 R&B hit *Lawdy Miss Clawdy*. After returning from his 1953-1956 tour of duty with the US Army in Korea he signed with ABC-Paramount Records. His 1958 hit rock recording of folk/blues standard *Stagger Lee* was raw and its lyrics had to be toned down for appearances on Dick Clark's squeaky-clean TV series 'American Bandstand,' but the sound on his 1959 hit recording *Personality* was more cosmopolitan, with massive horn sections and prominent pop background singers. In the early 60's he began recording less, opened a club in New York, produced records, and worked as a booking agent. In 1969, when his co-writing partner Harold Logan was murdered, he moved to Africa to get away from the music business. He returned to performing bouncy up-beat oldies in the 1980s and 1990s.

Johnnie Ray (born January 10, 1927)

Famous EASY-POP hit single during the 50s: ***Cry***   1951
Johnnie Ray also had hits with *The Little White Cloud that Cried* in 1951, *Please Mister Sun* in 1952, and *Just Walking in the Rain* in 1956.
Recording career with hits on the charts: 1951-1959   Record Label: Columbia

To overcome a hearing loss from a childhood accident, Johnnie Ray, born in Dallas, Oregon, wore a hearing aid all of his life. His distinctive style is attributed in part to over-enunciating words and phrases in his performances. Thought by radio audiences to be a black singer, he was actually a tall, fair complected, boyish looking man of 24. In 1951, he recorded two songs for Columbia Records, *Cry* and his own composition *Little White Cloud That Cried*. Mitch Miller produced the two-sided hit with backing vocals by the Four Lads. In March 1952, his songs accounted for half of the Top 6 positions on the charts. Number 1 that week was *Cry*, #3 was *Please Mr. Sun*, and #6 was *Little White Cloud That Cried*. His intense, emotional delivery and the power and clarity of his voice put 25 hits in the top-thirty. In 1954, he appeared in MGM's hit musical film 'There's No Business Like Show Business' also starring Marilyn Monroe. Johnnie Ray died of liver failure in 1990.

Jimmie Rodgers (born September 18, 1933)

Famous EASY-POP hit single during the 50s: ***Honeycomb*** 1957
Jimmie Rodgers also had hits with *Kisses Sweeter Than Wine* in 1957
and *Oh-Oh, I'm Falling in Love Again* and *Secretly* in 1958.
Recording career with hits on the charts: 1957-1967   Record Label: Roulette

Jimmie F. Rodgers, the ingratiating fifties singer (not to be confused with the 1920's legendary father-of-country music, Jimmie Rodgers, the 'Singing Brakeman') was an original. Born in Camas, Washington, this vocalist and acoustic guitarist, with a high, sweet voice, recorded hit versions of traditional folk songs with brisk tempos and muted rock arrangements. Taught music by his mother, he learned to play piano and guitar and he formed a band while serving in the US Air Force. Like a number of other entertainers of the era, he was one of the contestants on Arthur Godfrey's talent show on the radio. Roulette Records became aware of Jimmie Rodger's talent and signed him. In the summer of 1957, he recorded a song called *Honeycomb* which had been done by Bob Merrill three years earlier. It was his first big hit, reaching the top of the charts for four weeks. He had his own NBC-TV variety series in 1959, but his career was hampered following a mysterious assault on the San Diego Freeway in 1967 which left him with a fractured skull.

Frank Sinatra (born December 12, 1915)

Famous EASY-POP hit single during the 50s: ***Young At Heart*** 1954
also had hits with *Learnin' the Blues* and *Love and Marriage* in 1955,
Hey Jealous Lover in 1956, *All the Way* in 1957, and *Witchcraft* in 1958.
Recording career on the charts: 1942-1980   Record Labels: Columbia & Capitol

Francis Albert Sinatra, the greatest popular singer of the 20th century, was an only child, born in Hoboken, New Jersey. He dropped out of high school to follow in the footsteps of his idol, Bing Crosby. In 1935, he won first prize on a radio talent show, 'Major Bowes Amateur Hour.' Trumpeter Harry James discovered the youngster and a year later, with Tommy Dorsey's orchestra, the classic crooning began. Second wife, movie star, Ava Gardner helped secure her husband a role in 1953's 'From Here to Eternity.' He won the Best Supporting Actor Oscar. He gave a riveting performance in 'The Man With the Golden Arm' and again in the psychodrama 'The Manchurian Candidate' while appearing in light musical films like 'High Society,' 'Young at Heart,' and 'Pal Joey.' Frank Sinatra and his classy pals, Dean Martin, Sammy Davis, Jr., Peter Lawford, and Joey Bishop, often called the Rat Pack, performed together in Las

Vegas with a hip, relaxed humor. 'Old Blue Eyes' collaborations with arranger Nelson Riddle produced some of the most popular concept albums of the fifties—'Songs for Young Lovers,' 'A Swingin' Affair,' 'Come Fly With Me,' 'In the Wee Small Hours,' and 'Songs for Swingin' Lovers.' Frank Sinatra died in 1998 at age 82.

Andy Williams (born December 3, 1928)

Famous EASY-POP hit single during the 50s: *Canadian Sunset* 1956 also *Butterfly* and *I Like Your Kind of Love* in 1957, *Are You Sincere* in 1958, and *Lonely Street* and *The Village of St. Bernadette* in 1959.

Recording career with hits on the charts: 1956-1972   Record Label: Cadence

As a 7-year-old, Howard Andrew Williams, born in Wall Lake, Iowa, began singing with his three brothers. Their radio exposure caught the attention of Bing Crosby and the Williams Brothers recorded their first #1 hit song, *Swinging On a Star*, with him in 1944. Andy Williams began his solo career in 1952, appearing for three years as a regular with Eydie Gorme and Steve Lawrence on Steve Allen's 'Tonight Show.' In 1961, he married French singer/actress Claudine Longet and in 1962, he sang *Moon River* at the Oscar Awards—it won the Academy Award and became his theme song. He starred in his own highly successful, 9-year-running, NBC-TV series in the sixties. Andy Williams, one of America's great middle-of-the-road pop singers, frequently appeared at his own Moon River Theater in Branson, Missouri, into the 21st century.

Brief biographies of less well-known male singers Jerry Keller, Garry Mills, and Nick Noble are included in Chapter 9 'Fifty Fabulous, all-but-forgotten, EASY-POP Songs.'

References from Chapter 5:

Bogdanov, Vladimir, Woodstra, Chris and Erlewine, Stephen Thomas, editors. *All Music Guide: The Definitive Guide to Popular Music*. 4th Edition. San Francisco: Backbeat Books, 2001.

Larkin, Colin. *The Virgin Encyclopedia of Fifties Music*. Third Edition. London: Virgin Books Limited, 2002.

No pleasure endures unseasoned by variety.

Publilius Syrus

Chapter 6

Quintessential Singing Groups of the 50s
(Duets, Trios, and Quartets)

Chapter 3 presented the popular hit songs of the 50s, while chapters 4 and 5 described the girl and the guy singers. This chapter describes thirty-seven of the decade's most popular duets, trios, and quartets and their fifties-style EASY-POP hits.

The richness, breadth, and brilliance of American POP vocal group music is often overlooked. The group revival of the 50s was part of the post-war trend away from big bands. Vocal groups came in twos, threes, fours, and fives—the Everly Brothers, the McGuire Sisters, the Crew-Cuts, the Platters—all were effective singers, blending unique sounds and styles. Whatever their origins or musical backgrounds, the vocal groups brought bright, youthful melodies to their audiences.

A list of the 'Quintessential Singing Groups of the Fifties' along with their most memorable recording of the decade is shown in chart 6.1. Following the chart there are brief biographies of each of these legendary groups and an identification of some of their popular 50s EASY-POP standards.

Quintessential Singing Groups of the Fifties

Artists	Famous EASY-POP Hit Song in the fifties	year released
Ames Brothers[+]	*You, You, You*	1953
Andrews Sisters[+]	*I Wanna Be Loved*	1950
The Browns	*The Three Bells*	1959
Chordettes[+]	*Mr. Sandman*	1954
Crew-Cuts	*Sh-Boom**	1954
Crickets (see Buddy Holly, p. 111)		
Danny & the Juniors[+]	*At the Hop*	1957
DeCastro Sisters	*Teach Me Tonight*	1954
Dell-Vikings[+]	*Come Go with Me*	1957
Diamonds[+]	*Little Darlin'**	1957
Dion & the Belmonts[+]	*A Teenager in Love*	1959
Everly Brothers[+]	*Wake Up Little Susie*	1957
Fleetwoods[+]	*Come Softly to Me*	1959
Fontane Sisters	*Hearts of Stone**	1954
Four Aces[+]	*Love is a Many-Splendored Thing*	1955
Four Coins	*Shangri-La*	1957
Four Freshmen[+]	*Graduation Day*	1956
Four Knights[+]	*I Get So Lonely*	1954
Four Lads[+]	*Moments to Remember*	1955
Four Preps	*26 Miles (Santa Catalina)*	1958

Chart 6.1. Quintessential Singing Groups of the Fifties
(Chart continues on the next page)

Quintessential Singing Groups of the Fifties (continued)

Artists	Famous EASY-POP Hit Song in the fifties	year released
Gaylords	*The Little Shoemaker*	1954
Terry Gilkyson & the Easy Riders	*Marianne*	1957
Hilltoppers[+]	*P.S. I Love You*	1953
Impalas	*Sorry (I Ran All the Way Home)*	1959
Frankie Lymon & the Teenagers[+]	*Why Do Fools Fall in Love*	1956
McGuire Sisters[+]	*Sincerely**	1955
Mills Brothers[+]	*Glow-Worm*	1952
Patience & Prudence	*Tonight You Belong To Me*	1956
Les Paul & Mary Ford	*Vaya Con Dios*	1953
Penguins[+]	*Earth Angel*	1954
Platters[+]	*The Great Pretender*	1955
Poni-Tails	*Born Too Late*	1958
Tarriers	*Banana Boat Song (Day-O)*	1956
Teddy Bears	*To Know Him, is to Love Him*	1958
Teen Queens	*Eddie My Love*	1956
Tempos	*See You in September*	1959
Art & Dotty Todd	*Chanson d'Amour*	1958
Weavers[+]	*Goodnight, Irene*	1950

+ Vocal Group Hall of Fame Inductee
* These recordings were covers of recordings from the original artists

Chart 6.1. Quintessential Singing Groups of the Fifties

Ames Brothers
Ed Urick, lead, (b.1927), **Vic Urick,** first tenor, (b.1926),
Gene Urick, second tenor, (b.1925), **Joe Urick,** bass, (b.1924)

Famous EASY-POP hit single during the 50s: ***You, You, You***   1953
The Ames Brothers also had hits with *Rag Mop* in 1950, *Undecided* in
1951, *Naughty Lady of Shady Lane* in 1954, *Forever Darling* and *It
Only Hurts for a Little While* in 1956, and *Melodie D'Amour* in 1957.
Recording career with hits on the charts: 1948-1960   Record Labels: Coral & RCA

Four brothers from Malden, Massachusetts, whose actual family
name was Urick, formed a close-harmony vocal group in the late
1940s. After winning talent contests in their hometown, they began
performing in nightclubs around Boston as the 'Amory Brothers.'
Taking their act to New York they got a job with bandleader Art
Mooney. At the suggestion of playwright Abe Burroughs, they
shortened their name to the Ames Brothers and in 1949 were the first
artists to sign with Coral Records. The tight-knit quartet swept the
country with their first hit, *Rag Mop*. They made their debut on the
original Ed Sullivan television show when it was known as 'Toast of
the Town.' The group, known for their uncomplicated, bouncy songs
ended recording in 1959 but Ed Ames, who played Mingo on the
Daniel Boone TV series, became a solo star in the 1960s with hits
Try To Remember, My Cup Runneth Over, and *Who Will Answer.*

Andrews Sisters
Patty, lead singer, (b.1918),
Maxine, high harmony, (b.1916), **LaVerne,** contralto, (b.1911)

Famous EASY-POP hit single during the 50s: ***I Wanna Be Loved***   1950
The Andrews Sisters also had hits with *I Can Dream Can't I* in 1949
and *Quick Silver* in 1950 with Bing Crosby.
Recording career with hits on the charts: 1938-1951   Record Label: Decca

Born in Minnesota to a Greek immigrant father and a Norwegian
American mother, the Andrews Sisters started their career as imitators
of the singing group, the Boswell Sisters. After singing with dance
bands, their recordings and radio broadcasts brought them fame in the
forties. Their unmistakable close-harmony entertained troops during
World War II. The 1941 comedy film 'Buck Privates' with Abbott
and Costello introduced their best-known recording, *Boogie Woogie
Bugle Boy*. It won the Academy Award for best song and Bette Midler
made it popular again with her stage show in 1973. The sisters, who
recorded many hits with Bing Crosby, broke up in 1953 with Patti's
choice to go solo. During their career, they sold 75 million records.

The Browns
Maxine, (b.1932), **Jim Ed,** (b.1934), **Bonnie,** (b.1937)

Famous EASY-POP hit single during the 50s: ***The Three Bells*** 1959
Browns had one other hit song in the sixties, *The Old Lamplighter* in 1960.
Recording career with hits on the charts: 1959-1961   Record Label: RCA Victor

The Dixie-born brother and sister duo of Jim Ed Brown and Maxine Brown were joined by younger sister Bonnie in 1955 and performed in schools and on local radio and TV programs. By the end of 1955, the trio had a hit with *Here Today and Gone Tomorrow*, which was given a boost by their national appearances on 'The Ozark Jubilee.' By the late 50s, the Browns teamed with RCA's visionary producer Chet Atkins to create idealized songs of small-town life but their biggest hit was a song whose origin was not even American. *The Three Bells*, actually a translation of a 1952 song by French chanteuse Edith Piaf, spent weeks on the country charts in 1959 and #1 on the pop charts. Their polished country sound provided cross-over hits and the Browns appeared on TV with Ed Sullivan and Jimmy Dean.

The Chordettes
Janet Ertel, bass, (1913-1988), **Carol Bushman,** baritone,
Lynn Evans, lead, (replaced Dorothy Schwartz in 1952),
Margie Needham, tenor, (replaced Jinny Lockard [or Osborn] in 1953)

Famous EASY-POP hit single during the 50s: ***Mr. Sandman*** 1954
also had hits with *Born To Be With You* in 1956 and *Lollipop* in 1958.
Recording career with hits on the charts: 1954-1961   Record Label: Cadence

College friends, the Chordettes, organized in Sheboygan, Wisconsin, in 1946. Original members were Janet Ertel, her sister-in-law Carol Bushman, Dorothy Schwartz, and Jinny Lockard (1927-2003). Lynn Evans replaced Dorothy Schwartz and Margie Needham replaced Jinny Lockard (who was having a baby), though she later returned. Nancy Overton was also a member at a later time. Originally they sang folk music but changed to barbershop harmony and made regular appearances on Arthur Godfrey's TV series. Orchestra leader Archie Bleyer wanted the girls to move beyond traditional barbershop, so when he created Cadence Records, they signed with him and Janet Ertel married him. In 1954, the Chordettes *Mr. Sandman* rocketed to the top of the charts (the deep voiced "YES" was Archie Bleyer's). Their 1958 hit, *Lollipop*, was sparked by a chime introduction, a round-like arrangement, popping sounds, and the line, "Lollipop, lollipop, ooh lolli, lolli, lolli," that is instantly recognizable even today.

The Crew-Cuts
John Perkins, lead, (b.1931), **Ray Perkins,** bass. (b.1932),
Pat Barrett, first tenor, (b.1931), **Rudi Maugeri,** baritone, (b.1931)

Famous EASY-POP hit single during the 50s: ***Sh-Boom*** 1954
They also had hits with *Earth Angel*, *Ko Ko Mo (I Love You So)*,
Gum Drop, and *Angels In the Sky* in 1955 and *Young Love* in 1957.
Recording career with hits on the charts: 1954 - 1957   Record Label: Mercury

This wholesome vocal group from Toronto, Canada, was formed by
students at St. Michael's Cathedral Choir School, where they studied
arranging, harmony, and voice together. In 1952, they formed a
group, the 'Canadaires' and drove to New York to appear on Arthur
Godfrey's 'Talent Scouts,' where they came in second. Cleveland
disk jockey Bill Randle coined the name the, Crew-Cuts and arranged
for them to audition with Mercury Records, who signed the quartet.
They quickly became specialists in cover recordings of R&B songs—
11 of their first 22 sides were covers. Their recording of *Sh-Boom* hit
#1 on the charts in 1954 and by all objective standards it was the first
mass-appeal, rock and roll hit. Other hits followed. With their clean-
cut personas and glee-club harmony they gave their covers a pop
treatment that helped smuggle raunchy R&B sounds into established
radio formats and mainstream acceptance.

Danny and the Juniors
Danny Rapp, lead vocals, (1941-1983), **David White,** first tenor,
Frank Maffei, second tenor, **Joe Terranova,** baritone

Famous EASY-POP hit single during the 50s: ***At the Hop*** 1957
Danny and the Juniors also hit with *Rock and Roll is Here to Stay* in 1958.
Recording career with hits on the charts: 1957-1963   Record Label: ABC Paramount

High school friends, Danny & the Juniors, are recognized for their hit
single *At the Hop*. Formed in 1955 as 'The Juvenairs,' their song *Do
the Bop*, written by Dave White and his friend John Madara, came to
the attention of Dick Clark who suggested they rename it *At the Hop*.
The song transferred rock and roll energy into a catchy dance tune. It
quickly became a monumental hit on five continents, reaching #1 on
the pop, country, and R&B charts. It remains the #23 all-time biggest
record according to Billboard Magazine. They followed up with
another similar sounding Dave White and John Madara song, *Rock
And Roll Is Here To Stay*. Danny & the Juniors, one of the first acts
to interpret black music into white rock and roll, toured with Alan
Freed's rock-and-roll shows and were featured more than fifty times
on 'American Bandstand.' Danny Rapp committed suicide in 1983.

The DeCastro Sisters
Peggy DeCastro, (1922-2004), **Cherie DeCastro,**
Babette DeCastro, (replaced by cousin Olgita DeCastro in 1958)

Famous EASY-POP hit single during the 50s: ***Teach Me Tonight*** 1954
The DeCastro Sisters also had a hit with *Boom Boom Boomerang* in 1955.
Recording career with hits on the charts: 1954-1959   Record Label: Abbott

The three sisters first gained attention in Cuba for their flamboyant nightclub act. In 1945, the DeCastro family moved from their sugar plantation in Cuba to Miami. The sisters became protégées of Brazilian singer and film star Carmen Miranda, who had a huge hit in 1948 with *Cuanto La Gusta.* She helped include them in the film, 'Copacabana.' The DeCastro Sisters performed their three-part harmony on the first live broadcast of Los Angeles television station KTLA, following an introduction by Bob Hope. They hit the big time when their 1954 song *Teach Me Tonight* sold more than 5 million copies. Their singing style was reminiscent of the popular Andrews Sisters, but with a Latin flavor and flair. They provided bird and animal voices in Walt Disney's 'Song of the South,' and became a popular singing act in Las Vegas nightclubs and hotels.

The Dell-Vikings
Norman Wright, lead tenor, replaced original member Bernard Robertson,
Clarence Quick, bass, **Corinthian (Kripp) Johnson,** first tenor,
Don Jackson, second tenor, later replaced by **Gus Backus,**
David Lerchy, baritone, replaced original member Samuel Paterson

Famous EASY-POP hit single during the 50s: ***Come Go With Me*** 1957
The Dell-Vikings also had a hit with *Whispering Bells* in 1957.
Recording career with hits on the charts: 1956-1958   Record Label: Dot

Notable for being one of the few racially integrated musical groups to attain success in the 1950s, The Dell-Vikings, were an American doo-wop musical group who recorded several hit singles. (They were also known as The Del-Vikings (without the double 'l') and with and without the hyphen). The group was formed in 1955 by members of the US Air Force stationed in Pittsburgh, Pennsylvania. Their first hit came in 1956 when the Norman Wright-led *Come Go With Me*, with its simple, swinging verse and punchy bridge, propelled into the top-ten. *Whispering Bells* with Clarence Quick on lead and Norman Wright doing bass, was recorded and released before the group split. In the sixties, after they all had completed their Air Force service, they reunited and toured widely.

The Diamonds
Dave Somerville, lead, **Ted Kowalski,** tenor, replaced by John Felton in 1959, **Phil Levitt,** baritone, replaced by Michael Douglas in 1958, **Bill Reed,** bass, replaced by Evan Fisher in 1959

Famous POP hit single during the 50s: *Little Darlin'* 1957
The Diamonds also had hits with *Silhouettes* and *The Stroll* in 1958.
Recording career with hits on the charts: 1956-1961   Record Label: Mercury

In 1953, Dave Somerville, an engineer for the Canadian Broadcasting Corporation in Toronto, met his future partners practicing for a talent show. He became their manager and then the lead singer of the group—The Diamonds. After an appearance on Arthur Godfrey's 'Talent Scouts,' Mercury Records signed the group to expand their radio audience—they needed white artists to cover the recordings of black artists whose records were not played on white radio stations. The Diamonds' first recording was *Why Do Fools Fall in Love*, a cover of The Teenagers' original. Their smash hit *Little Darlin'* with castanets, Spanish guitar, piano, and cowbells was originally recorded by The Gladiolas. An original song by Clyde Otis and Nancy Lee, *The Stroll*, was an exuberant song and photogenic dance, perfect for TV and it aired repeatedly on American Bandstand. By 1961, all original members of the group had been replaced.

Dion and the Belmonts
Dion DiMucci, lead vocals, **Angelo D'Aleo,** first tenor, **Freddie Milano,** second tenor, **Carlo Mastrangelo,** bass

Famous EASY-POP hit single during the 50s: *A Teenager in Love* 1959
also had hits with *I Wonder Why* in 1958 and *Where or When* in 1959.
Recording career with hits on the charts: 1958-1960   Record Label: Laurie

Born and raised in the Bronx, Dion DiMucci, began singing at five and playing guitar a few years later. He found the three best Italian street singers he knew and formed a group named after Belmont Avenue. Their first hit was *I Wonder Why* in 1958 earning them a reputation for creating vital and exciting doo-wop music. Their biggest hits came in 1959 with *A Teenager in Love* and *Where or When*. On tour in 1959, Dion declined a ride on the plane that crashed, killing Buddy Holly, Ritchie Valens, and the Big Bopper. By the early '60s Dion's heroin habit, nurtured since he was sixteen, broke up the Belmonts. As a solo artist in 1960, Dion racked up #1 hits including *Runaround Sue* and *The Wanderer*. In 1968, a more contemplative Dion shot up the charts again as songwriter and singer with *Abraham, Martin and John* and began recording gospel albums.

The Everly Brothers
Donald Everly, (b.1937), **Philip Everly,** (b.1939)

Famous POP hit single during the 50s: *Wake Up Little Susie* 1957
also had hits with *Bye, Bye Love* in 1957, *All I Have To Do Is Dream* in
1958, *('Til) I Kissed You* in 1959, and *Cathy's Clown* in 1960.
Recording career with hits on the charts: 1957 - 1967   Record Label: Cadence

Isaac Donald Everly, was born in Brownie, Kentucky, and younger
brother, Phillip in Chicago. The boys grew up in Iowa, and at ages 8
and 6 began to perform on their parents' live radio shows. Their dad
encouraged them to sing and taught them to play guitar. By 1950, the
radio show had become known as 'The Everly Family Show.' The
Everly Brothers compelling melodies mixed early rock 'n' roll
elements with country and pop music and a close two-part harmony.
The duo enjoyed support from guitarist Chet Atkins and producer
Archie Bleyer. The Everly Brothers discovered a hit formula with
Bye Bye Love: Boudleaux Bryant's rhythms, Felice Bryant's lyrics,
Don's guitar introductions, and Phil's harmony. Their next hit, *Wake
Up Little Susie*, again written by husband and wife songwriters,
Boudleaux and Felice Bryant, became their second million seller. *Bye
Bye Love* began a string of 26 top-forty singles for The Everly
Brothers whose worldwide record sales topped 40 million.

The Fleetwoods
Gretchen Diane Christopher, lead, (b.1940)
Barbara Ellis, harmony, (b.1940), **Gary Troxel,** doo-wop scat, (b.1939)

Famous Doo-Wop hit single during the 50s: *Come Softly To Me* 1959
Fleetwoods also had hits with *Graduation's Here* and *Mr. Blue* in 1959.
Recording career with hits on the charts: 1959-1963   Record Label: Dolphin/Dolton

Gretchen Christopher, Barbara Ellis, and Gary Troxel attended
Olympia High School in Washington. Gretchen Christopher and
former-fellow-cheerleader Barbara Ellis composed *Come Softly* for
the Senior Class Talent Assembly. The trio combined it with a hook
that trumpet player Gary Troxel had written that went "mmm-do-be-
do dum-dim-dum do-dum." They put it all together and *Come Softly
To Me* and 'The Fleetwoods' were an overnight sensation. For their
Senior Class Party, Gretchen Christopher and Barbara Ellis wrote
Graduation's Here. It became their second top-forty hit. Their third
release, *Mr. Blue*, also turned to gold and in 1961 they had a hit with
Tragedy. One of the few white vocal groups to enjoy success on both
the Pop and R&B charts, their smooth, dreamy, ethereal harmonies
were a welcome counterpoint to rock's frenzy in the late fifties.

Fontane Sisters
Marge Rosse, lead, **Geri Rosse,** harmony, **Bea Rosse,** low harmony

Famous EASY-POP hit single during the 50s: ***Hearts Of Stone*** 1954
The Fontane Sisters also had hits with *Seventeen* in 1955, *Eddie My Love*
in 1956, and *Chanson d'Amour (Song of Love)* in 1958.
Recording career with hits on the charts: 1951-1958   Record Labels: RCA & Dot

The three sisters, Marge, Geri, and Bea Rosse were born in New Milford, New Jersey, and their mom was their vocal teacher. Before World War II they became the Fontane Sisters and were joined by brother Frank on guitar until he was killed in World War II. They were featured on Perry Como's radio shows and later on his TV programs. In 1949, they were signed by RCA Records, and did some recordings as backup to Perry Como, including the #1 hits *A You're Adorable* and *Hoop Dee Doo*. In 1951, they had a minor hit with *The Tennessee Waltz*, but Patti Page had the more popular version. Beginning in 1954, with arrangements by Dot Record's A&R man Billy Vaughn, they charted more than a dozen hits including their #1 smash *Hearts of Stone* and follow-ups *Rollin' Stone* and *Seventeen*, as well as their version of the holiday novelty *Nuttin' For Christmas*.

The Four Aces
Al Alberts, (originally Albertini), lead singer, (replaced by Fred Diodati in 1956),
Dave Mahoney, tenor, **Rosario 'Sol' Voccaro,** baritone, **Lou Silvestri,** bass

Famous EASY-POP hit in the 50s: ***Love is a Many-Splendored Thing*** 1955
also *Heart and Soul* in 1952, *Stranger in Paradise* in 1953, *Three Coins in the Fountain* in 1954, and *A Woman in Love* and *Melody of Love* in 1955.
Recording career with hits on the charts: 1951-1959   Record Label: Decca

Returning to civilian life from Navy duty in Newfoundland, Al Alberts began singing (backed by Dave Mahoney playing tenor sax) and later the act added Sol Vaccaro on trumpet and Lou Silvestri on drums. With their unusual style of harmony, they discovered they were even better vocalists than musicians. The Four Aces started their own record label when they could not find a distributor to release their first recording, *(It's No) Sin*. It sold a million copies and Decca Records signed the group, billing them as The Four Aces featuring Al Alberts. Their 1952 recording of *Heart and Soul* is a classic. A change of orchestra from Owen Bradley to Jack Pleis brought further successes with *Heart of My Heart*, their first American No.1 hit, and several movie title songs including the million-selling *Three Coins in the Fountain*, and *Love is a Many-Splendored Thing*. In 1956, Fred Diodati, replaced Al Alberts as lead.

The Four Coins
George Mahramas, lead, **Michael Mahramas**, tenor,
George Mantalis, tenor, **James Gregorakis**, baritone

Famous EASY-POP hit single during the 50s: ***Shangri-La*** 1957
The Four Coins also had hits with *Memories of You* in 1955
and *The World Outside* in 1958.
Recording career with hits on the charts: 1954-1959   Record Label: Epic

The Four Coins were a strong-voiced vocal group from Cannonsburg, Pennsylvania. George Mantalis, Jimmy Gregorakis, and brothers Michael and George Mahramas were all of Greek heritage. Local orchestra leader, Lee Barrett, took them to an audition in Cincinnati, Ohio, where they recorded several songs and began singing on television. The Four Coins powerful recording of *Shangri-La* sold over a million copies. They appeared in the film 'Disc Jockey Jamboree' and recorded the song *Memories of You* from the 1955 film 'The Benny Goodman Story.' Their 1958 recording of *The World Outside* was originally introduced in the 1942 film 'Suicide Squadron.' In 1970, they left show business to tend to family obligations.

The Four Freshmen
Bob Flanigan, (b.1926), **Ross Barbour,** (b.1928),
Don Barbour, (b.1929), **Ken Errair,** (b.1930) replaced
original member **Hal Kratzsch,** (b.1929) in 1953

Famous EASY-POP hit single during the 50s: ***Graduation Day*** 1956
also had hits with *It's a Blue World* in 1952 and *Charmaine* in 1955.
Recording career with hits on the charts: 1952-1956   Record Label: Capitol

Brothers Ross and Don Barbour and cousin Bob Flanigan formed a jazz-styled instrumental and vocal group in 1948 at the Arthur Jordan Conservatory of Music in Indianapolis. A fourth member, Hal Kratzsch was replaced by Ken Errair in 1953. They were influenced by Glenn Miller's 'Modernaires' and Mel Torme's 'Mel-Tones' but began to show signs of a unique style of free improvisational vocal group harmony, highly touted by jazz legends like Dizzy Gillespie and clarinetist, Woody Herman. Bandleader, Stan Kenton saw them in concert in Dayton, Ohio, and arranged for an audition with Capitol Records. In 1952, they released their first hit single *It's a Blue World*, which brought them instant recognition with mainstream audiences. The Four Freshmen recorded *Graduation Day* four years later and another version was released the same summer by the Canadian group The Rover Boys, both placed in the top-twenty in 1956.

The Four Knights
Gene Alford, lead tenor, **Oscar Broadway,** bass,
Clarence Dixon, baritone, **John Wallace,** second tenor and guitar

Famous EASY-POP hit single during the 50s: *I Get So Lonely* 1954
The Four Knights also had hits with *I Love the Sunshine of Your Smile*
in 1951 and *Oh, Happy Day* in 1953.
Recording career with hits on the charts: 1951-1959   Record Label: Capitol

Best-known for their refined pop ballad recordings, the Four Knights performed a mix of gospel and secular material. The quartet, first known as the Southland Jubilee Singers, formed in 1943 in Charlotte, North Carolina. In 1945, they changed their name to the Four Knights, to reflect pop rather than gospel, and appeared on Arthur Godfrey's radio program. Their polished style and soft harmony suited TV and they appeared on Red Skelton's show and The Ed Sullivan Show. The Four Knights' biggest hit came in 1954 with *(Oh Baby Mine) I Get So Lonely (when I think about you)* which made it to the #2 spot on the pop charts and was a smash in England, tough for a black American group in the fifties. They also appeared on several records backing up Capitol Records' superstar Nat King Cole.

The Four Lads
John Bernard 'Bernie' Toorish, lead, **James 'Jimmy' Arnold,** tenor,
Frank Busseri, baritone, **Corrado 'Connie' Codarini,** bass

Famous POP hit single during the 50s: *Moments to Remember*   1955
They also had hits with *Istanbul* in 1953, *Skokiaan* in 1954, *No, Not
Much* and *Standing on the Corner* in 1956, *Who Needs You* and *Put A
Light in the Window* in 1957, and *There's Only One Of You* in 1958.
Recording career with hits on the charts: 1952-1959   Record Label: Columbia

Choirboys growing up together in Canada, the Four Lads, arrived in the US in 1950 with influence from St. Michael's Cathedral Choir School in Toronto where they learned to sing. Connie Codarini and Bernie Toorish sang earlier with two other St. Michael's students, Rudi Maugeri and John Perkins—who founded The Crew-Cuts. The Four Lads worked at New York's fashionable Le Ruban Bleu where arranger Mitch Miller, then new at Columbia records, took an instant liking to them and utilized them as back-up singers at Columbia Records where they backed Johnnie Ray on his #1 million-selling hits *Cry* and *The Little White Cloud That Cried*. After that, the Four Lads were signed to their own recording contract, receiving their first Gold Record in 1953 for *Istanbul*, which launched them to stardom. Their sound was classic, clean-cut, polished and crisp, group harmony.

Four Preps
Bruce Belland, lead, (b.1936), **Glen Larson,** tenor, (b.1937),
Ed Cobb, bass, **Marvin Inabnett** (later changed to Ingraham), high tenor
(for a short time **Don Clarke** replaced Marvin Inabnett)

Famous POP hit single during the 50s: *26 Miles (Santa Catalina)* 1958
The Four Preps also had a hit with *Big Man* in 1958.

Recording career with hits on the charts: 1956 - 1964   Record Label: Capitol

This wholesome, preppy West Coast-based vocal group was formed while the four teenagers, influenced by the Mills Brothers, the Four Aces, and the Four Freshmen, were students at Hollywood High School. Mel Shauer, manager of Les Paul and Mary Ford, was so impressed with their demo tape that he took the group under his wing. Shortly after performing in a Hollywood High School talent show in 1956, they were signed by Capital Records' A&R executive Nik Venet. The eighteen-year-olds' biggest hit was *26 Miles (Santa Catalina)*, which was written by Belland and Larson and reached #2. Those two members of the group also wrote *Big Man*, with its heavy piano chords and strong harmonies (which reached #3) and the re-written camp song, *Down by the Station,* another lesser hit for the quartet. The collegiate group with their button-up sweaters, crew cuts, and four-part harmonies, were quintessential fifties. In 1959, the group played themselves in the movie, 'Gidget.'

The Gaylords
Ronnie Gaylord (Fredianelli), **Burt Holiday** (Bonaldi), **Don Rea**

Famous EASY-POP hit single during the 50s: *The Little Shoemaker* 1954
The Gaylords also had hits with *Tell Me You're Mine* in 1952 and
From the Vine Came the Grape and *The Isle of Capri* in 1954.

Recording career with hits on the charts: 1952 - 1958   Record Label: Mercury

Italian duo Ronnie Fredianelli and Burt Bonaldi added vocalist and pianist Don Rea to accompany them while they were students at the University of Detroit. The vocal group specialized in rapturous Italian-derived love songs and infectious novelty recordings. Their debut outing, *Tell Me You're Mine* hit #2 in 1952 and the trio signed with Mercury. In the same year, Ronnie Fredianelli was drafted into the Army, changed his name to Ronnie Gaylord, and began recording as a solo vocalist but continued making records as a member of the Gaylords. Soloist, Ronnie Gaylord had a hit of his own, *Cuddle Me,* in 1954. On some recordings, Billy Christ sang tenor in place of Ronnie Gaylord. The Gaylord's clean execution and unreserved sentiment keeps their songs popular today.

Terry Gilkyson and the Easy Riders
Terry Gilkyson, baritone, **Richard Dehr**, lead, **Frank Miller**, tenor

Famous Folk-POP hit single during the 50s: *Marianne* 1957
This was the only top-ten hit recording for Terry Gilkyson and the Easy Riders.
Recording career with hits on the charts: 1957   Record Label: Columbia

Hamilton Henry Gilkyson was born in Phoenixville, Pennsylvania, and attended the University of Pennsylvania, majoring in music. In 1949, he recorded *Cry Of The Wild Goose*, but Frankie Laine recorded a version and had the number one hit with it. In the early fifties, Richard Dehr and Frank Miller, calling themselves 'The Easy Riders' were performing folk songs while Terry Gilkyson performed with the folk group 'The Weavers'. The talents of the threesome as singers and songwriters complemented each other and they became a group, with Richard Dehr performing most of the lead vocals. Early in 1956, the three wrote the #1 song *Memories Are Made Of This* recorded by Dean Martin with the 'The Easy Riders' trio providing background. In 1957, they wrote and recorded their own song about a sand-sifter, it was based on a Bahamian folk tune, and their version of the toe-tapping *Marianne* became a top-ten hit and a million seller.

The Hilltoppers
Jimmy Sacca, lead, (b.1929), **Billy Vaughn**, baritone, (b.1919),
Seymour Spiegelman, tenor, (b.1930), **Don McGuire**, bass, (b.1931)

Famous EASY-POP hit during the 50s: *P.S. I Love You* 1953
The Hilltoppers also had hits with *Trying* in 1952,
I'd Rather Die Young in 1953, *Only You* in 1955, and *Marianne* in 1957.
Recording career with hits on the charts: 1952-1957   Record Label: Dot

Originally a trio formed at Western Kentucky State College (now Western Kentucky University), in Bowling Green, the original members were students, Jimmy Sacca, born in Lockport, New York, Don McGuire born in Hazard, Kentucky, and Seymour Spiegelman born in Seneca Falls, New York. 'Hilltoppers' was the nickname of Western Kentucky's athletic teams. They added a pianist, Billy Vaughn, who became the fourth member of the singing group. Born in Glasgow, Kentucky, he became music director for Dot, came up with the hit *Melody of Love*, and he was the arranger/conductor for many of the records released on the Dot label. In 1952, the Hilltoppers recorded *Trying*, written by Billy Vaughn. It became a top-ten hit and they recorded 17 more hit songs from 1952 to 1957, the biggest was *P.S. I Love You*. A popular act in their college sweaters and beanies, they frequently appeared on TV including Ed Sullivan's Show.

The Impalas
Joe 'Speedo' Frazier, lead singer,
Tony Carlucci, first tenor,   Lenny Renda, second tenor,
Richard Wagner, baritone

Famous Doo-Wop hit in the 50s: *Sorry (I Ran All the Way Home)* 1959
This was the only 50s top-ten hit recording for the Impalas.
Recording career with hits on the charts: 1959-1961   Record Label: Cub

This pop vocal quartet was unusual in that it was a racially integrated foursome. Sweet-voiced lead singer Joe 'Speedo' Frazier, the only black member of the Impalas, was from New York City, Richard Wagner, Lenny Renda, and Tony Calouchi were from the Carnesie section of Brooklyn. They were discovered by disc jockey Alan Freed and Artie Zwirn, who co-wrote the bright, brash novelty tune with Gino Giosasi (of the Gino and Gina vocal duo). Cub Records, an MGM subsidiary, signed them and in 1959 they had an overnight success with their first record *(Sorry) I Ran All The Way Home*. Leroy Holms conducted the orchestra on the Impalas' recordings. The follow-up, *Oh What A Fool* was a smaller hit. They made a few later recordings before disbanding in 1961.

Frankie Lymon and the Teenagers
Frankie Lymon, lead singer, (b.1942),
Joe Negroni, baritone, (b.1940), Herman Santiago, tenor, (b.1941),
Jimmy Merchant, tenor, (b.1940), Sherman Garnes, bass, (b.1940)

Famous Doo-Wop hit single in the 50s: *Why Do Fools Fall In Love* 1956
also *I Want You To Be My Girl* in 1956 and *Goody, Goody* in 1957.
Recording career with hits on the charts: 1956-1960   Record Label: Gee

The doo-wop group consisted of three black and two Hispanic teen-age singers from New York City, but centered around the extraordinary talent of 13-year-old Frankie Lymon, the first black teen pop star. Their first top-ten hit, the up-tempo *Why Do Fools Fall in Love* was also a top-ten 'cover' hit for Gale Storm and for the Diamonds. The enthusiastic young teens' high tenor, deep bass, and soprano, created a distinctive sound. They appeared in two films, Alan Freed's classic 'Rock, Rock, Rock' and 'Mister Rock 'n' Roll,' but by the summer of 1957 Frankie Lymon split from the group and all of their careers plummeted. A victim of the excesses of stardom—drinking, three marriages, and drugs, he entered a rehabilitation program for heroin addiction. In 1968, the twenty-five-year-old died in his grandmother's New York apartment of a drug overdose.

The McGuire Sisters
Phyllis, (b.1931), **Dorothy,** (b.1930), **Christine,** (b.1929)

Famous EASY-POP hit single during the 50s: *Sincerely*   1955
They also had hits with *Muskrat Ramble* in 1954, *Something's Gotta
Give* in 1955, *Sugartime* in 1957, and *May You Always* in 1959.
Recording career with hits on the charts: 1954 - 1961   Record Label: Coral

The McGuire Sisters of Middletown, Ohio, started singing in their
mother's church before they were ten years old. At an early age they
had an uncanny ability to harmonize. Musician Jerry Herman called it
instant harmony—Phyllis could start singing in any key while Dot
and Chris would immediately pick up the appropriate part and chime
in. They appeared at clubs, on TV, did eight weeks on Kate Smith's
radio show in 1952, and were winners on Arthur Godfrey's 'Talent
Scouts' where they replaced the Chordettes. At Coral Records
producer Bob Thiele got them the best instrumental talent—arranger
Neal Hefti (who was doing arrangements for Count Basie) and
bandleader Dick Jacobs. In 1957, Bob Thiele brought them
Sugartime, a quasi-novelty tune from Norman Petty's Clovis, New
Mexico studio, where Buddy Holly was recording. It earned the sisters
a gold record. Few groups approached their level of excellence.

The Mills Brothers
John Jr. bass, (b.1911), replaced in 1936 by **John Sr.** baritone, (b.1882)
Herbert, tenor, (b.1912), **Harry,** baritone, (b.1913),
Donald, lead tenor, (b.1915)

Famous EASY-POP hit single during the 50s: *Glow-Worm*   1952
They also had hits with *Say "Si Si"* in 1953 and *Get a Job* in 1958.
Recording career with hits on the charts: 1931-1968   Record Labels: Decca & Dot

The four young Mills brothers from Piqua, Ohio, were proficient at
imitating musical instruments. John would imitate the tuba and Harry
the trumpet. Herbert became second trumpet and Donald trombone.
They entertained on the Midwest theater circuit with their amazing
ability to harmonize. The quartet achieved fame in vaudeville, radio,
and film. In 1930, broadcast executive William Paley at CBS radio,
heard their audition and they became the first African-Americans to
have a network show on radio. John Jr. died in 1936 and the brothers
considered breaking up the quartet but their father, John Sr. replaced
the deceased brother—as a tribute to their brother they retained the
name The Mills Brothers. Their 1943 hit *Paper Doll* was #1 for three
months and sold six million copies. In 1952, *Glow Worm* jumped to
number one on the pop charts.

Patience & Prudence
Patience McIntyre, (b.1945), Prudence McIntyre, (b.1942)

Famous POP hit single during the 50s: *Tonight You Belong to Me* 1956
This was the only top-ten hit recording for Patience and Prudence.
Recording career with hits on the charts: 1956 - 1957   Record Label: Liberty

A Los Angeles sister duo, Patience and older sister Prudence McIntyre, were 11 and 14 when they released all three of their recordings in 1956. Their father, orchestra leader Mark 'Mack' McIntyre, was a well known piano player and songwriter. When he heard his daughters sing *Tonight You Belong to Me*, that they learned at summer camp, he had them prepare a demo of the 1927 Gene Austin hit (words and music by Billy Rose & Lee David) for Liberty Records. Patience and Prudence recorded the bouncy song, that was intended for cabaret singer Lisa Kirk, and it became a top-five hit. Their follow-up single, *Gonna Get Along Without Ya Now*, was a second popular recording for them. In spite of a recording legacy consisting of little more than a few singles, their innocence and harmonies were among the most bewitching of the era.

Les Paul and Mary Ford
Les Paul, (b.1915), Mary Ford, (b.1928)

Famous POP hit during the 50s: *Vaya Con Dios (May God Be With You)* 1953
Les Paul & Mary Ford also had hits with *Mockin' Bird Hill,*
How High the Moon and *The World is Waiting for the Sunrise* in 1951,
Bye Bye Blues in 1953, and *Hummingbird* in 1955.
Recording career with hits on the charts: 1946-1961   Record Label: Capitol

Les Paul, born Lester Polfus, played the guitar for dance band Fred Waring's Pennsylvanians and accompanied Bing Crosby on his 1945 hit *It's Been a Long Long Time*. In the late forties he designed the first solid-body amplified electric guitar and developed the multi-track, sound-on-sound technique, now called over-dubbing. A combination of his guitar and electronic talents with the vocals of his wife Mary Ford, resulted in two million-selling records in 1951: *Mockin' Bird Hill* and *How High the Moon*. They recorded their biggest hit *Vaya Con Dios* in 1953. She was born Iris Colleen Summers in Pasadena, California. The pair met in the late 40s (while Mary Ford was a country singer) and married in 1949. From 1953 through 1960, they hosted, 'The Les Paul and Mary Ford at Home Show,' and they continued to record together until they divorced in 1964. In the 1960s Paul retired from performing. Mary Ford died in 1977.

The Penguins
Cleveland 'Cleve' Duncan, lead singer, (b. 1935),
Curtis Williams, bass, (replaced by **Randy Jones** in 1957), **Dexter Tisby,**
tenor, **Bruce Tate,** baritone, (replaced by **Teddy Harper** in 1957)

Famous Doo-Wop hit single during the 50s: *Earth Angel* 1954
This was the only top-ten hit recording for the Penguins.
Recording career with hits on the charts: 1954-1955   Record Label: DooTone

The Penguins *Earth Angel (Will You Be Mine),* often called the first
Doo-Wop recording, was an all-time best seller. Cleve Duncan was
singing at a talent show in Los Angeles when Curtis Williams came
up and wanted to form a group. Curtis Williams got Bruce Tate from
his high school, Jefferson, and Cleve Duncan got Dexter Tisby from
his high school, Fremont. 'Willie the Penguin,' a cartoon character in
Kool mentholated cigarette ads, inspired their name. *Earth Angel*
evolved through several Los Angeles artists before The Penguins
finally taped it in a garage studio in South Los Angeles. By
December 1954, *Earth Angel,* one of the first R&B hits to cross over,
was #8 on the Pop charts while a cover version by the Crew-Cuts hit
#3 and Gloria Mann's recording rose to #18. The Penguins couldn't
come up with a successful follow-up and broke up in 1959.

The Platters
Tony Williams, lead vocalist, (b.1928), **David Lynch,** tenor, (b.1929)
Paul Robi, baritone, (b.1931), **Herb Reed,** bass, (b.1931),
Zola Taylor, contralto, (b.1938)

Famous EASY-POP hit single during the 50s: *The Great Pretender*   1955
They also had hits with *Only You (And You Alone)* in 1955, *The Magic
Touch* and *My Prayer* in 1956, and *Smoke Gets in Your Eyes* in 1958.
Recording career with hits on the charts: 1955 - 1967   Record Label: Mercury

This successful Los Angeles R&B quintet, with rich sweet tenor Tony
Williams, was managed by talent agent Buck Ram who made two
changes to the original quartet: he replaced Alex Hodge with Paul
Robi and he added a female singer, seventeen-year-old Zola Taylor.
Buck Ram took a song that he had written, *Only You,* had the revised
quintet record it, and it rose to the top-ten in 1955. They followed
with another Buck Ram song, *The Great Pretender.* It was their first
#1 record. The 1956 film 'Rock Around The Clock,' included
performances by the Platters of both *Only You* and *The Great
Pretender.* That same year they reached the top-ten again with *The
Magic Touch.* They went on to record 33 pop hits. By the early
sixties most original members of The Platters had left the group.

The Poni-Tails

Toni Cistone, lead vocals, **LaVerne Novak,** high harmony,
Patti McCabe, low harmony (replaced **Karen Topinka** in 1957)

Famous EASY-POP hit single during the 50s: ***Born Too Late*** 1958
This was the only top-ten hit recording for the Poni-Tails.
Recording career with hits on the charts: 1958-1959   Record Label: ABC Paramount

The wispy pop female trio of Toni Cistone, LaVerne Novak, and
Karen Topinka were students at Brush High School in Lynhurst,
Ohio, near Cleveland, when they started singing together in 1956.
Point Records issued their first single *Your Wild Heart* in 1957.
Unfortunately, a cover became a hit for Mercury artist Joy Layne.
ABC Records' Don Costa was interested in the group and released
their *It's Just My Luck To Be 15* in 1957. *It's Just My Luck To Be 15*
spawned the similarly themed *Born Too Late*, but before the Poni-
Tails recorded their classic hit, Karen Topinka was replaced by
Regina High School student, Patti McCabe. The song was actually
the 'B' side of their *Come on Joey, Dance With Me*, but DJs favored
Born Too Late and it rose to #7 on the charts. They were unable to
recapture their magic in future recordings and, turning down an ABC
contract extension, the Poni-Tails decided to settle into family life.

The Tarriers

Alan Arkin, (b. 1934), **Bob Carey, Erik Darling,** (b. 1933)

Famous EASY-POP hit single in the 50s: ***Banana Boat Song (Day-O)*** 1956
This was the only top-ten hit recording for the Tarriers.
Recording career with hits on the charts: 1956 - 1957   Record Label: Glory

In 1950, teenage Erik Darling became fascinated with folk musicians
who gathered on Sunday in Manhattan's Washington Square. He met
Bob Carey, an 18-year-old Brooklyn College student, and the trio was
completed with Alan Arkin. Glory Records signed them to back
balladeer Vince Martin on *Cindy, Oh Cindy*, it was a hit and so was a
cover by Eddie Fisher. In 1956, the Tarriers recorded *The Banana
Boat Song*, a fusion of two Jamaican folk songs that they had heard
Bob Gibson perform in Washington Square. It became such a hit that
RCA Victor capitalized, releasing Harry Belafonte's single of *Day-O*
from his 'Calypso' album. In 1957, Alan Arkin left the group to
pursue acting, won a Tony award for 'Enter Laughing' and remains a
well-known character actor. Erik Darling performed with the
Weavers and the Rooftop Singers and charted another pop hit, *Walk
Right In*. Bob Carey's personal problems led to a physical decline and
in the seventies his body was found on a Central Park West bench.

Teddy Bears
Phil Spector, tenor, **Carol Connors,** lead, **Marshall Leib**, tenor,
Harvey Goldstone, bass

Famous POP hit during the 50s: ***To Know Him Is to Love Him*** 1958
This was the only top-ten hit recording for the Teddy Bears.
Recording career with hits on the charts: 1958 - 1959   Record Label: Dore

Following his graduation from Fairfax High School in Los Angeles, Phil Spector put together his first pop trio with lead singer Carol Connors (born Annette Kleinbard) and Marshall Leib. Phil Spector, a songwriter, guitarist, and back up singer was born in 1940 in the Bronx, New York. *To Know Him Is To Love Him* was his first recorded composition—written as a tribute to his father who committed suicide during his childhood—his grave marker read 'To Know Him Was to Love Him.' After a hasty audition, the trio recorded the song at Gold Star Studios (Bass Harvey Goldstone was serving in the Army Reserve during the recording). Released on ERA's Dore label, in two months *To Know Him Is To Love Him* began its rise to #1. At age seventeen, Phil Spector had written, arranged, played, sung, and produced the best-selling record in the country. Subsequent releases by the Teddy Bears did not sell and within a year they disbanded. Phil Spector though would produce dozens of hits in the sixties and beyond.

Teen Queens
Betty Collins, (b. 1939), **Rosie Collins**, (b. 1941)

Famous EASY-POP hit single during the 50s: ***Eddie My Love*** 1956
This was the only top-ten hit recording for the Teen Queens.
Recording career with hits on the charts: 1956   Record Label: RPM Records

Betty and Rosie Collins formed the Teen Queens in Los Angeles in 1955. Their brother, Aaron Collins, sang with the R&B quintet The Jacks in 1955 and The Cadets in 1956 on RPM Records and helped his sisters sign with his label. Their only recording, *Eddie My Love* rose to #14 on the pop charts, despite covers by the Fontane Sisters with a #11 version and the Chordettes with a #14 version. It was an unusual situation that three versions of the same song cracked the pop top-twenty in the spring of 1956. They were never again able to achieve the commercial success of *Eddie My Love*. The Teen Queens broke up in 1961. It was a tragic story, Rosie and Betty Collins were nationally famous as The Teen Queens during their adolescence, consigned as has-beens before they were 18, and drug casualties before their deaths in their early thirties.

The Tempos
Mike Lazo, lead singer, Gene Schacter, Jim Drake, Tom Monito

Famous EASY-POP hit single during the 50s: *See You in September* 1959
This was the only top-ten hit recording for the Tempos.
Recording career with hits on the charts: 1958 - 1959   Record Label: Climax

Lead singer Mickey Lazo and Gene Schachter met while in the Army in Korea, appearing in a number of U.S.O. shows. After completing their service, they returned to their hometown, Pittsburgh, where they expanded their act to a quartet by adding Tom Monito, who hailed from neighboring Cannonburg, Pennsylvania, and then in 1959, adding Jim Drake. Producer Jack Gold gave them the name The Tempos. The quartet recorded *Bless You My Love* and *See You In September*. Initially, *Bless You My Love* was the record's 'A' side, but public opinion changed that and ultimately *See You In September* became the 'A' side. It was featured in the acclaimed 'American Graffiti' movie and its soundtrack album. The Tempos' version of *See You In September* has been 'covered' by a wide array of artists, instrumentals, and vocals including Shelley Fabares' 1962 recording and The Happenings #3 hit record in 1966.

Art and Dotty Todd
Art Todd, (b.1920), Dotty Todd, (b.1923)

Famous POP hit during the 50s: *Chanson d'Amour (Song of Love)* 1958
This was the only top-ten hit recording for Art and Dotty Todd.
Recording career with hits on the charts: 1958   Record Label: Era Records

Arthur W. Todd and Dotty Todd were a husband-and-wife singing duo from Elizabeth, New Jersey. Art and Dotty Todd were married in 1941, had their own CBS radio show in the 1950s, and were regular performers in Las Vegas. Their recording of *Chanson d'Amour* raced to #6 on the pop charts and sixth-most-played by the disc jockeys in the spring of 1958—surprising for a first release from a small record company. The song was covered by the Fontane Sisters with a version that reached #12 on the charts. Art and Dotty Todd have the unusual distinction of being regarded as one hit wonders in both the United Kingdom and in the United States, but with different songs: *Broken Wings* in the UK and *Chanson d'Amour (Song Of Love)* in the US. They did not have any other recordings that appear on the charts. They retired to Honolulu, Hawaii, in 1980 and opened a nightclub. Dotty Todd died in 2000 at the age of 87.

The Weavers
Fred Hellerman, (b.1927), Lee Hays, (b.1914),
Ronnie Gilbert, (b.1926), Pete Seeger, (b.1919)

Famous Folk-POP hit during the 50s: *Goodnight, Irene*   1950
The Weavers also had hits with *Tzena, Tzena, Tzena* in 1950 and
So Long (It's Been Good To Know Ya) and *On Top of Old Smoky* in 1951.
Recording career with hits on the charts: 1950-1954   Record Label: Decca Records

In many ways, The Weavers resemble an earlier group—the Almanac Singers. In 1940, Pete Seeger and Lee Hays who were part of the Almanac Singers with Woody Guthrie, formed a similar ensemble including Brooklyn-born Fred Hellerman and New York-born songstress Ronnie Gilbert. The Weavers performed at New York's Village Vanguard and audiences loved their simple, unaffected enthusiasm. Bandleader/arranger, Gordon Jenkins, brought them to Decca Records where they recorded *Tzena, Tzena, Tzena* and *Goodnight, Irene*, selling two million copies as a double-sided hit. Gordon Jenkins added string arrangements and brass but kept their sound intact. Decca teamed The Weavers with Terry Gilkyson, a baritone folk singer, on *On Top of Old Smoky*. Anti-Communist political blacklisting denounced Pete Seeger as subversive and the group was placed under FBI surveillance, cutting short their recording career, but a 1955 reunion concert at Carnegie Hall was a sellout.

Brief biographies of less well-known groups the Jamies, the Kalin Twins, and the Play-Mates are included in Chapter 9 'Fifty Fabulous, all-but-forgotten, EASY-POP Songs.'

References from Chapter 6:

Bogdanov, Vladimir, Woodstra, Chris and Erlewine, Stephen Thomas, editors. *All Music Guide: The Definitive Guide to Popular Music*. 4th Edition. San Francisco: Backbeat Books, 2001.

Larkin, Colin. *The Virgin Encyclopedia of Fifties Music*. Third Edition. London: Virgin Books Limited, 2002.

Ginger Rogers did everything that Fred Astaire did. She just did it backwards and in high heels.

Variously attributed to Linda Ellerbee and others

Chapter 7

Fifties Songs from Movies, TV, and Broadway

One reason that the fabric of fifties music is so varied is that 50s POP songs came from a wide variety of sources. In addition to music written directly for the recording industry, hundreds of songs were written for films, television, and the musical theater. The impact of the visual/musical/popular arts on the record buying public was greater in the fifties than during any other period in recorded music history. Movies, television programs, and Broadway shows were a dominant influence on popular taste and a major source for new sounds in recorded music.

Movies

Dozens of EASY-POP songs of the fifties were written for the movies and the record-buying public liked what they saw on the screen. Then the disc jockeys picked up the songs and played them repeatedly on the radio. Seeing the singers perform their songs was an early precursor to the MTV generation.

The Academy of Motion Picture Arts and Sciences began presenting awards for outstanding achievement in film in 1929. Five years later a 'best original song' category was added to the 'Oscar' awards. Several of the award winners during the thirties and forties have become classic standards: *The Continental* in 1934, *Lullaby of Broadway* in 1935, *Thanks for the Memory* in 1938, *Over the Rainbow* in 1939, *The Last Time I Saw Paris* in 1941, *White Christmas* in 1942, *It Might as Well Be Spring* in 1945, and *Buttons and Bows* in 1948.

During the fifties, every academy-award-winning 'best original song' became a huge EASY-POP hit recording—though not necessarily for the vocalist who performed it in the movie. Frankie Laine's version of *High Noon* reached #5 on the charts, while the version that was heard in the film, by Tex Ritter, only placed twelfth. Doris Day had big hit records with two academy award winning songs that she introduced on the screen: *Secret Love* and *(Que Sera, Sera) Whatever Will Be, Will Be* (see chart 7.1). Frank Sinatra also had hit recordings with two 'Oscar' songs

---

Academy Award Winning Songs of the 50s

Mona Lisa from the film 'Captain Carey, U.S.A.' 1950
Music & lyrics by Ray Evans & Jay Livingston.
More than a dozen orchestras and singers recorded versions of *Mona Lisa*, but Nat King Cole had the #1 hit.
also nominated: *Be My Love, Bibbidy-Bobbidi-Boo, Mule Train, Wilhelmina*

In the Cool, Cool, Cool of the Evening
from the film 'Here Comes the Groom' 1951
Music by Hoagy Carmichael, lyrics by Johnny Mercer.
Performed in the romantic comedy film by Bing Crosby and Jane Wyman.
also nominated: *A Kiss to Build a Dream On, Never, Too Late Now, Wonder Why*

High Noon *(Do Not Forsake Me, Oh My Darlin')*
from the film 'High Noon' 1952
Music by Dimitri Tiomkin, lyrics by Ned Washington.
Sung in the film by Tex Ritter over drama-building pre-action sequences.
also nominated: *Am I in Love, Because You're Mine, Thumbelina, Zing a Little Zong*

Secret Love *from the film* 'Calamity Jane' 1953
Music by Sammy Fain, lyrics by Paul Francis Webster.
Performed in the film by Doris Day. One of her biggest hit songs.
also nominated: *The Moon Is Blue, My Flaming Heart, Sadie Thompson's Song, That's Amore*

Chart 7.1. Academy Award Winning Songs of the 50s
(Chart continues on the next page)

Academy Award Winning Songs of the 50s (continued)

Three Coins in the Fountain
from the film 'Three Coins in the Fountain'   1954
Music by Jule Styne, lyrics by Sammy Cahn.
Sung by the Four Aces over the opening titles at the beginning of the film.
also nominated: *Count Your Blessings, The High and the Mighty, Hold My Hand, The Man That Got Away*

Love is a Many-Splendored Thing
from the film 'Love Is a Many-Splendored Thing'   1955
Music by Sammy Fain, lyrics by Paul Francis Webster.
The Four Aces set the scene during the opening credits with this title song.
also nominated: *I'll Never Stop Loving You, Something's Gotta Give, The Tender Trap, Unchained Melody*

Whatever Will Be, Will Be *(Que Sera, Sera)*
from the film 'The Man Who Knew Too Much'   1956
Music & lyrics by Jay Livingston & Ray Evans.
Performed by Doris Day early in the film and reprised at the climax.
also nominated: *Friendly Persuasion, Julie, True Love, Written on the Wind*

All the Way   from the film 'The Joker Is Wild'   1957
Music by Jimmy Van Heusen, lyrics by Sammy Cahn.
Performed in the dramatic film by Frank Sinatra. It became one of his most popular hit recordings.
also nominated: *An Affair to Remember, April Love, Tammy, Wild is the Wind*

Gigi   from the film 'Gigi'   1958
Music by Frederick Loewe, lyrics by Alan Jay Lerner.
Performed in the film by Louis Jourdan during an extended plot twist.
also nominated: *Almost in Your Arms, A Certain Smile, To Love and Be Loved, A Very Precious Love*

High Hopes   from the film 'Hole in the Head'   1959
Music by Jimmy Van Heusen, lyrics by Sammy Cahn.
Performed by Frank Sinatra, with a group of children, in this light comedy film.
also nominated: *The Best of Everything, The Five Pennies, The Hanging Tree, Strange Are the Ways of Love*

Chart 7.1.   Academy Award Winning Songs of the 50s

he performed in films: *All the Way* and *High Hopes*. Both of the Four Aces' number one hit recordings, *Three Coins in the Fountain* and *Love is a Many-Splendored Thing*, won academy awards. Nat King Cole's biggest hit recording was 'Oscar' winner *Mona Lisa* and Vic Damone had a hit recording with *Gigi*. The Bing Crosby and Jane Wyman duet *In the Cool, Cool, Cool of the Evening* was also a hit recording for Frankie Laine and Jo Stafford.

In addition to the ten 'Oscar' winning songs during the fifties, another forty songs received nominations during the decade but did not win the 'Oscar.' Three female singers of the fifties had big hit recordings with runner-up songs that they performed in musical films: Debbie Reynold's recorded her memorable hit, *Tammy;* Judy Garland's biggest hit of the fifties was *The Man That Got Away*; and Doris Day scored with both *I'll Never Stop Loving You* and *Julie*, all written for the silver screen.

Male singers charted big hits with nominated songs that they introduced in films too: Dean Martin's *That's Amore*, Don Cornell's *Hold My Hand*, Frank Sinatra's *The Tender Trap*, Mario Lanza's most popular recording, *Be My Love*, Pat Boone's *Friendly Persuasion* and *April Love* were all 'Oscar' losers. Dozens of crooners had big hits on records with nominated songs: Frankie Laine's *Mule Train*, Louis Armstrong's *A Kiss to Build a Dream On*, Eddie Fisher's *Count Your Blessings Instead of Sheep*, Vic Damone's *An Affair to Remember*, Al Hibbler's *Unchained Melody*, and Johnny Mathis' *A Certain Smile* all came from movies.

In addition to the soloists, Bing Crosby and Grace Kelly's duet *True Love* was a huge hit; the McGuire Sisters' scored with *Something's Gotta Give*, and the Ames Brothers' had success with *A Very Precious Love*. Les Baxter and his orchestra had an instrumental hit with the theme from *The High and the Mighty*.

Music was an important element to set-the-stage for both dramatic and comedy films in the fifties. Often, an EASY-POP composition, commissioned just for the movie, played during the opening credits, setting the mood for the film. Several artists including the Four Aces became popular for their recordings of these 'opening title' songs.

The impact of academy-award winning songs on popular music began to fade as the decade progressed. By the seventies, the winners were often raw and more reflective of the changes in music—*Shaft*, the 1971 award winner suggested the more liberated cinematic times. Many of the winners were quickly forgotten. Who remembers *Last Dance* from 1978's 'Thank God It's Friday'? By the end of the decade the award was frequently given to a song from an animated children's movie, rarely heard outside of the film. 'Oscar' winners were no longer popular top-ten recordings.

The Hollywood Musical

Movie musicals hit the peak of their popularity in the fifties and many popular songs came from these films. During the early and mid-fifties more than two dozen musical movies were turned out by the major studios each year. A new musical was released every two weeks!

In the first half of the fifties, movie studios created an active production schedule for musicals. MGM was the most productive and innovative in story, music, and dance and their 1952 'Singing in the Rain' is considered the quintessential Hollywood musical movie. The sparkling 1958 'Gigi' was the last hurrah for MGM musical movies although 'The Sound of Music' from 20th Century Fox would light up screens in 1965.

The musical, more than any other type of film, depended on the 'studio system' to assemble the necessary cadre of musical specialists required to create the expensive Hollywood musical movies. The major studios kept the musicals alive and the musicals kept the studios alive during the post-war years. In 1950, the United States Department of Justice decided to break-up the movie studio's monopoly on distributing the films that they produced in the movie palaces that they owned. The decision required movie studios to divest themselves of their movie theaters and the 'studio system' began to unravel.

Even with the addition of technical innovations like wide-screen Cinemascope, multi-speaker Stereophonic sound, and 3-D, the number of Hollywood musicals had dropped to just a dozen released annually by 1958 and 1959 and the number continued to decline. Although musical movies continued to be produced after 1959, the peak of the genre had passed (see chart 7.2).

In addition to the mainstream, traditional Hollywood musicals, there were several, hard-to-classify, 'films-with-music' in the fifties. The famous series of spontaneously zany 'road' pictures with Bing Crosby, Bob Hope, and Dorothy Lamour, continued with the 5th film in the series

---

Popular Movie Musicals of the 50s
Film title, studio, musical composer, year released, stars, and popular musical numbers

Annie Get Your Gun MGM   Music & lyrics by Irving Berlin   1950
Betty Hutton, Howard Keel, Keenan Wynn, Louis Calhern
There's No Business Like Show Business (Hutton, Keel, Wynn, Calhern).

Summer Stock MGM
Music & lyrics by Harry Warren, Jack Brooks, and Saul Chaplin   1950
Judy Garland, Gene Kelly, Phil Silvers, Gloria De Haven, Eddie Bracken
Get Happy, written by Harold Arlen & Ted Koehler (Garland); *If You Feel Like Singing, Sing* (Garland).

On the Town MGM
Music by Leonard Bernstein, lyrics by Betty Comden & Adolph Green   1950
Gene Kelly, Frank Sinatra, Jules Munshin, Vera-Ellen, Ann Miller, Betty Garrett
New York, New York (Kelly, Sinatra, Munshin).

Three Little Words MGM   Music & lyrics by Bert Kalmar & Harry Ruby 1950
Fred Astaire, Red Skelton, Vera-Ellen, Phil Regan, Debbie Reynolds
Three Little Words (Astaire, Skelton, Vera-Ellen); *You are My Lucky Star* (Regan);
I Wanna Be Loved By You Boop-Boop-a-Doop (Reynolds dubbed by Helen Kane).

The Toast of New Orleans MGM   (operatic standards)   1950
Mario Lanza, Kathryn Grayson, David Niven, James Mitchell, Rita Moreno
Be My Love, written by Nicholas Brodszky & Sammy Cahn (Lanza, Grayson).

Young Man with a Horn Warner Brothers   (1920's and 1930's music)   1950
Kirk Douglas (with trumpet dubbed by Harry James), Doris Day, Lauren Bacall
Lullaby of Broadway, Too Marvelous for Words, I Only Have Eyes for You (Day).

Show Boat MGM   Music & lyrics by Jerome Kern & Oscar Hammerstein II   1951
Kathryn Grayson, Howard Keel, Ava Gardner, Marge & Gower Champion
Make Believe (Keel, Grayson); *Old Man River* (William Warfield).

An American in Paris MGM   Music & lyrics by George & Ira Gershwin 1951
Gene Kelly, Leslie Caron, Oscar Levant, Georges Guetary
I Got Rhythm (Kelly); *American in Paris* (ballet – Kelly, Caron).

Royal Wedding MGM   Music & lyrics by Alan Jay Lerner & Burton Lane   1951
Fred Astaire, Jane Powell, Peter Lawford, Sarah Churchill
Too Late Now (Powell); *You're All The World To Me* (Astaire, dancing on the walls and ceiling).

On Moonlight Bay Warner Brothers   (period music standards)   1951
Doris Day, Gordon MacRae, Leon Ames, Rosemary De Camp, Mary Wickes
On Moonlight Bay, written by Percy Wenrich & Edward Madden (Day, MacRae).

Chart 7.2. Popular Movie Musicals of the 50s
(Chart continues on the next page)

Popular Movie Musicals of the 50s (continued)

The Great Caruso MGM (various operatic extracts) 1951
Mario Lanza, Ann Blythe, Dorothy Kirsten,
The Loveliest Night of the Year, adapted from Juventino Rosas' *Over the Waves,* lyrics by Paul Francis Webster.

Here Comes the Groom Paramount
Music & lyrics by Johnny Mercer & Hoagy Carmichael 1951
Bing Crosby, Jane Wyman, Anna Maria Alberghetti, Dorothy Lamour, Phil Harris
In the Cool, Cool, Cool of the Evening (Crosby, Wyman).

With a Song in My Heart 20th Century Fox (Jane Froman Standards) 1952
Susan Hayward (vocals dubbed by Jane Froman herself), David Wayne, Rory Calhoun
With a Song in My Heart, Blue Moon, Tea for Two (Hayward dubbed by Froman).

Singin' in the Rain MGM
Music & lyrics by Arthur Freed & Nacio Herb Brown 1952
Gene Kelly, Debbie Reynolds, Donald O'Connor, Cyd Charisse, Jean Hagen
Singin' in the Rain (Kelly); *Good Morning* (Kelly, Reynolds, O'Connor); *Make 'Em Laugh* (O'Connor).

Hans Christian Andersen RKO Music & lyrics by Frank Loesser 1952
Danny Kaye, Jeanmaire, Joey Walsh, Farley Granger, Roland Petit
Anywhere I Wander, No Two People, Thumbelina, The Ugly Duckling (Kaye).

Stars and Stripes Forever 20th Century Fox (John Phillip Sousa music) 1952
Clifton Webb, Robert Wagner, Debra Paget
Stars and Strips Forever, El Capitan, Washington Post March, King Cotton.

Call Me Madam 20th Century Fox Music & lyrics by Irving Berlin 1953
Ethel Merman, Donald O'Connor, Vera-Ellen, George Sanders, Billy De Wolfe
Hostess With the Mostest (Merman); *You're Just in Love* (Merman, O'Connor).

Calamity Jane Warner Bros
Music & lyrics by Sammy Fain & Paul Francis Webster 1953
Doris Day, Howard Keel, Allyn McLerie, Philip Carey
Secret Love (Day); *The Deadwood Stage* (Day); *Black Hills of Dakota* (Day).

Kiss Me Kate MGM (in 3D) Music & lyrics by Cole Porter 1953
Kathryn Grayson, Howard Keel, Ann Miller, Keenan Wynn, Bobby Van
So In Love (Grayson, Keel); *Wunderbar* (Grayson, Keel); *Too Darn Hot* (Miller).

The Band Wagon MGM Music & lyrics by Howard Dietz & Arthur Schwartz 1953
Fred Astaire, Cyd Charisse, Jack Buchanan, Nanette Fabray, Oscar Levant
That's Entertainment (entire cast); *Dancing in the Dark* (Astaire, Charisse, dubbed by India Adams).

By the Light of the Silvery Moon Warner Bros. (period music standards) 1953
Doris Day, Gordon MacRae, Leon Ames, Rosemary De Camp, Mary Wickes
By the Light of the Silvery Moon, Ain't We Got Fun (Day, MacRae).

Chart 7.2. Popular Movie Musicals of the 50s
(Chart continues on the next page)

Popular Movie Musicals of the 50s (continued)

Gentlemen Prefer Blondes 20th Century Fox
Music & lyrics by Jule Styne & Leo Robin   1953
Marilyn Monroe, Jane Russell, Elliot Reid, Tommy Noonan, Charles Coburn
Diamonds are a Girl's Best Friend (Monroe); *Little Girl from Little Rock* (Monroe, Russell).

White Christmas Paramount (in VistaVision)   Music & lyrics by Irving Berlin 1954
Bing Crosby, Danny Kaye, Rosemary Clooney, Vera-Ellen
White Christmas (Crosby, Kaye, Clooney, Vera-Ellen); *Sisters* (Clooney, Vera-Ellen).

The Glenn Miller Story Universal International   (Big Band era music)   1954
Jimmy Stewart, June Allyson, Louis Armstrong, Gene Krupa, Francis Langford
Moonlight Serenade, written by Mitchell Parish & Glenn Miller; *In the Mood,* written by Andy Razaf & Joe Garland.

Seven Brides for Seven Brothers MGM
Music & lyrics by Gene DePaul & Johnny Mercer   1954
Jane Powell, Howard Keel, Russ Tamblyn, Julie Newmar, Virginia Gibson
Goin' Courtin' (Powell and the brothers); *Lonesome Polecat* (the brothers); *Wonderful Day* (Powell).

A Star is Born Warner Bros. Music & lyrics by Harold Arlen & Ira Gershwin 1954
Judy Garland, James Mason, Charles Bickford, Tom Noonan
The Man That Got Away (Garland); *Born in a Trunk* (Garland).

There's No Business Like Show Business 20th Century Fox
Music & lyrics by Irving Berlin   1954
Dan Daily, Ethel Merman, Marilyn Monroe, Donald O'Connor,
Mitzi Gaynor, Johnnie Ray
There's No Business Like Show Business (entire cast); *Heat Wave* (Monroe).

Young At Heart Warner Brothers   music & lyrics from various writers   1955
Doris Day, Frank Sinatra, Gig Young, Dorothy Malone, Ethel Barrymore
Young at Heart, written by Johnny Richards & Carolyn Leigh (Sinatra); *Ready, Willing and Able,* written by Floyd Huddleston & Al Rinker (Day); *One for My Baby,* written by Harold Arlen & Johnny Mercer (Sinatra).

Guys And Dolls Samuel Goldwyn
Music & lyrics by Jo Swerling, Abe Burrows, & Frank Loesser   1955
Marlon Brando, Frank Sinatra, Jean Simmons, Vivian Blaine, Stubby Kaye
Luck Be a Lady (Brando); *Guys and Dolls* (Brando, Sinatra); *Sit Down You're Rockin' the Boat* (Kaye).

Kismet MGM   Music & lyrics by Bob Wright and Chet Forrest   1955
Howard Keel, Ann Blyth, Vic Damone, Delores Gray, Sebastian Cabot
Stranger in Paradise (Damone, Blyth); *Baubles, Bangles, and Beads* (Chorus).

Oklahoma 20th Century Fox
Music & lyrics by Richard Rodgers & Oscar Hammerstein II   1955
Gordon MacRae, Shirley Jones, Gene Nelson, Gloria Graham
Oh What a Beautiful Morning (MacRae); *I Cain't Say No* (Graham).

Chart 7.2. Popular Movie Musicals of the 50s

(Chart continues on the next page)

Popular Movie Musicals of the 50s (continued)

Love Me or Leave Me MGM (Singer Ruth Etting's 20s and 30s music standards) 1955
Doris Day, James Cagney, Cameron Mitchell
Love Me or Leave Me (Day); *I'll Never Stop Loving You*, written by Nicholas Brodszky & Sammy Cahn (Day).

The King and I 20ᵗʰ Century Fox
Music & lyrics by Richard Rodgers & Oscar Hammerstein II 1956
Yul Brynner, Deborah Kerr (vocals dubbed by Marni Nixon), Rita Moreno
Getting to Know You (Kerr, dubbed by Nixon); *Shall We Dance* (Brynner, Kerr, dubbed by Nixon).

High Society MGM Music & lyrics by Cole Porter 1956
Bing Crosby, Frank Sinatra, Grace Kelley, Louis Armstrong, Celeste Holm
True Love (Crosby, Kelly); *Now You Has Jazz* (Crosby, Armstrong);
Well Did You Evah (Crosby, Sinatra).

Bundle of Joy RKO Music & lyrics by Josef Myrow & Mack Gordon 1956
Eddie Fisher, Debbie Reynolds, Nita Talbot, Tommy Noonan
Lullaby in Blue (Fisher, Reynolds); *All About Love* (Fisher); *Someday Soon* (Fisher).

Carousel 20ᵗʰ Century Fox
Music & lyrics by Richard Rodgers & Oscar Hammerstein II 1956
Gordon MacRae, Shirley Jones, Barbara Ruick, Claramae Turner
You'll Never Walk Alone (Turner); *Soliloquy* (MacRae); *If I Loved You* (Jones, MacRae).

Pal Joey Columbia Music & lyrics by Richard Rodgers & Lorenz Hart 1957
Frank Sinatra, Rita Hayworth (vocals dubbed by Lu Ann Greer), Kim Novak
Bewitched, Bothered and Bewildered (Sinatra, Hayworth, dubbed by Greer); *The Lady is a Tramp* (Sinatra).

Jailhouse Rock MGM Music & lyrics by Jerry Lieber & Mike Stoller 1957
Elvis Presley, Judy Tyler, Mickey Shaughnessy
Jailhouse Rock (Presley); *Treat Me Nice* (Presley); *You're So Square* (Presley).

South Pacific 20ᵗʰ Century Fox
Music & lyrics by Richard Rodgers & Oscar Hammerstein II 1958
Mitzi Gaynor, Rossano Brazzi (vocals dubbed by Giorgio Tozzi), Ray Walston,
Juanita Hall (vocals dubbed by Muriel Smith), John Kerr (vocals dubbed by Bill Lee)
Some Enchanted Evening (Gaynor, Brazzi/Tozzi); *Younger Than Springtime* (Kerr/Lee);
Bali Ha'i (Hall/Smith); *There is Nothing Like a Dame* (Walston and sailors).

Gigi MGM Music & lyrics by Alan Jay Learner & Frederick Lowe 1958
Leslie Caron, Louis Jourdan, Maurice Chevalier, Hermione Gingold, Isobel Jeans
Gigi (Jourdan); *I Remember It Well* (Chevalier, Gingold).

Porgy and Bess Samuel Goldwyn Music & lyrics by George & Ira Gershwin 1959
Sidney Poitier, Dorothy Dandridge, Brock Peters, Sammy Davis Jr.,
Diahann Carroll, Pearl Bailey
I Got Plenty O' Nuthin' (Poitier); *It Ain't Necessarily So* (Davis).

Chart 7.2. Popular Movie Musicals of the 50s

'Road to Bali' in 1953. There were seventeen Dean Martin & Jerry Lewis movies-with-songs including 'Jumping Jacks' in 1952, 'Scared Stiff' and 'The Caddy' (that introduced Dean Martin's hit song *That's Amore*) in 1953, 'Living It Up' in 1954, 'Artists and Models' in 1955, and finally their 17th and last film together 'Hollywood or Bust' in 1956.

Walt Disney studios created memorable full-length animated musical films during the fifties: 'Cinderella' in 1950, 'Alice in Wonderland' in 1951, 'Peter Pan' in 1953, 'Lady and the Tramp' in 1954, and 'Sleeping Beauty' in 1959. *You Can Fly, A Dream is a Wish Your Heart Makes* and the spaghetti-sharing *Bella Notte* were all introduced in Disney films. Peggy Lee recorded the memorable *He's a Tramp* from 'Lady and the Tramp.' The catchy tune *Bibbidi-Bobbidi Boo* from 'Cinderella' was a hit recording for Jo Stafford & Gordon MacRae and for Perry Como and for Dinah Shore. In addition to their animated films, Disney studio's introduced the unforgettable children's favorite *The Mickey Mouse March (M-I-C, K-E-Y, M-O-U-S-E)* on their daily television series 'The Mickey Mouse Club' and their Sunday evening 'Disneyland' TV series introduced *The Ballad of Davy Crockett* in 1955. Bill Hayes, Tennessee Ernie Ford, and Fess Parker (who originated the title role) all had top-ten hit recordings.

Musicals targeted for teenagers—capitalizing on the popularity of young performers—have been popular since Judy Garland and Mickey Rooney starred in several in the thirties and forties. During the mid-fifties, studios featured teen favorites in movies like Elvis Presley's 'Love Me Tender' in 1956, 'Loving You' and 'Jailhouse Rock' in 1957, and 'King Creole' in 1958. Pat Boone starred in 'April Love' in 1957 and 'Mardi Gras' in 1958. Not quite as successful were Tommy Sands' 'Sing Boy Sing' in 1958, Fabian's 'Hound Dog Man' in 1959, and Louis Prima and Keely Smith in 'Hey Boy, Hey Girl' in 1959. These musicals did help establish a younger-generation genre to appeal to the teenage moviegoer.

The growing generational conflict of the time was the subject of a serious, landmark, dramatic film in 1955, 'Rebel Without a Cause.' According to rock historian Charlie Gillett: James Dean, Natalie Wood, and Sal Mineo provided figures with whom the new teenagers could identify; figures whose style of dress, speech, movement, facial expressions, and attitudes helped give shape and justification to unrealized feelings in the audience. The integrity of James Dean was simultaneously a reflection of, and a model for, large segments of the audience. (Gillett, 1972, p.24)

At the other end of the dramatic spectrum, and perhaps the most unbelievable movie phenomenon in the fifties, was the success of Olympic swimmer Esther Williams and her musical 'water' spectaculars. Her fifties films included: 'Pagan Love Song' in 1950, 'Million Dollar Mermaid' and 'Skirts Ahoy!' in 1952, 'Dangerous When Wet' and 'Easy To Love' in 1953, and 'Jupiter's Darling' in 1955.

Hundreds of 50s EASY-POP songs originated in fifties movies. The musical tastes in film influenced a wide variety of audiences—in big city movie palaces, small town theaters, and outdoor drive-ins. But movies were not the only influence—the arrival of television at the beginning of the decade would precipitate another huge influence on fifties pop music.

Television

The arrival, acceptance, and then dominance of television in the 1950s was phenomenal. Commercial television broadcasting, initiated in 1947 in the United States, signaled that a new medium would influence popular music. In 1948, only New York, Washington, and Philadelphia were networked to receive live television, by 1949, the east and midwest were joined, and in 1951, the link was completed to the west coast.

The growth in the purchase of television sets was unprecedented. In 1948, fewer than 2% of US homes had a TV set. (Brooks & Marsh, 1995, p.xv) Television became a household staple faster than any appliance had done previously—by the end of the decade nearly 90% of homes in the United States had a TV set. (Croteau & Hoynes, 2001, p.54) The fifties, often called the 'golden age of television,' presented live drama, live comedy, live music, and live variety offerings to an eager audience.

Ed Sullivan's variety show 'Toast of the Town' debuted in 1949 and ran in the same 8pm EDT Sunday time slot on CBS for 23 years. Most Americans got their first glimpse of Elvis Presley and the Beatles from this series. Television was important to the recording industry and many singers appeared on TV to perform their popular hit songs (see chart 7.3). They wanted to promote the sale of their records while television producers wanted to showcase the singers to get the high ratings that came with presenting popular performers. Audiences, even before MTV, liked to see the singers perform the songs that were hits on the radio and records.

TV series of the 50s that featured EASY-POP Singers
(Evening broadcast times listed are Eastern Time, programs aired one hour earlier in the Midwest)

All Star Review
Wednesdays 8:00-9:00 (NBC) 1950-1951; Saturdays 8:00-9:00 (NBC) 1951-1953
A vaudeville-flavored program with popular comedians and singers.

American Bandstand
Ninety minutes every weekday afternoon (ABC) 1957-1963
Live from Philadelphia, host Dick Clark presented guest artists and also played
dozens of current hit recordings while the teenage studio audience danced.

Arthur Godfrey and His Friends   Wednesdays 8:00-9:00 (CBS) 1949-57
A blend of musical numbers and relaxed comedy with friends including singers
Anita Bryant, the Chordettes, Pat Boone, the McGuire Sisters, Julius LaRosa,
Haleloke, Johnny Nash, LuAnn Simms, and the Mariners.

Arthur Murray Dance Party
Appeared on all four networks at various times between 1950 and 1960. Dance
teacher Arthur Murray and wife, Kathryn, hosted singing and dancing guest stars.

The Big Record   Wednesdays 8:00-9:00 (CBS) 1957-1958
Hostess Patti Page introduced popular singers who performed their hits songs.

Colgate Comedy Hour   Sundays 8:00-9:00 (NBC) 1950-1955
This top-rated variety hour featured comedians and popular singers. Dean Martin
& Jerry Lewis, Bob Hope, Donald O'Connor, Abbott & Costello, and Jimmy
Durante hosted frequently.

The Dick Clark Saturday Night Beechnut Show
Saturdays 7:30-8:00 (ABC) 1958-1960
Each week several 'Top Forty' recording artists performed their hit songs.

Dick Clark's World of Talent   Sundays 10:30-11:00 (ABC) 1959
A celebrity panel rated aspiring performers. Singers appearing on the series
included Don Cornell, Della Reese, Alan Dale, and the Four Aces.

Ed Sullivan Show (Toast of the Town)
Sundays 8:00-9:00 (CBS) 1948-1971
Nearly every popular singer and comedian appeared over twenty-three years on
this syndicated newspaper columnist's variety program including early career
appearances by Dean Martin & Jerry Lewis, Elvis Presley, and the Beatles.

Chart 7.3. Network TV series of the 50s that featured EASY-POP Singers
(Chart continues on the next page)

TV series of the 50s that featured EASY-POP Singers

(continued)

George Gobel Show

Saturdays 10:00-10:30 (NBC) 1954-1957; Tuesdays 8:00-9:00 (NBC) 1957-1959
Low-key comedian's variety show included regular singers Peggy King and
Anita Bryant plus John Scott Trotter's band and the Johnny Mann Singers.

Jukebox Jury
Sundays 9:30-10:30 (ABC) 1953-1954
Peter Potter played new records for a celebrity panel on this game show and
queried, "Will it be a hit (bong!) or a miss (clunk!)?"

Lawrence Welk Show
Saturdays 9:00-10:00 (ABC) 1955-1971
Melodic 'Champagne Music' hour with Alice Lon and the Lennon Sisters.

Perry Presents
Wednesdays 8:00-9:00 (CBS) Summer 1959
Musical series featured Teresa Brewer, Tony Bennett, the Four Lads, Jaye P.
Morgan, and the Modernaires.

Stop the Music
Thurs 8:00-9:00 (ABC) 1949-52; Tues 10:30-11:00 (ABC) 1954-56
Game show host Bert Parks had members of the studio audience and home
viewers identify songs by vocalists including Kay Armen, Jimmy Blaine, Betty
Ann Grove, Jaye P. Morgan, and June Valli.

TV's Top Tunes
Mondays/Wednesdays/Fridays 7:45-8:00 (CBS) 1957-58
Summer series featured Peggy Lee, the Fontane Sisters, Helen O'Connell, Bob
Eberly, Julius LaRosa, and the Mitchell Ayres Orchestra.

Ted Mack's Original Amateur Hour
Tues 10:00-11:00 (NBC) 1949-1954
Each week amateur performers displayed their talents and the viewing audience
was invited to vote—by postcard—for their favorite act.

Talent Scouts
Tuesdays 8:30-9:00 (CBS) 1948-1958
Host Arthur Godfrey and celebrity guests introduced new talent. Aspiring singers
on the series included: June Valli, Pat Boone, Johnny Nash, the McGuire Sisters,
Edie Adams, and Shari Lewis.

Tonight Show (with Steve Allen)
weeknights 11:30pm-1:00am (NBC) 1954-1957
Host Steve Allen featured regular singers Steve Lawrence, Eydie Gorme, Pat
Marshall, and Andy Williams.

Your Hit Parade
Saturdays 10:30-11:00 (NBC) 1950-1958
The top seven most popular songs of the week were performed by regular cast:
Dorothy Collins, Eileen Wilson, Snooky Lanson, Sue Bennett, Russell Arms,
June Valli, and Gisele MacKenzie.

Chart 7.3. Network TV series of the 50s that featured EASY-POP Singers

Comedy/variety shows that were hosted by comedians were very popular and often included musical performers as part of the cast. Vaudeville comedian, Milton Berle's 'Texaco Star Theater' was a frantic and highly visual hour that garnered huge ratings. It is often credited with spurring the sales of television sets and earning him the label 'Mr. Television.' 'Your Show of Shows' with Sid Caesar and Imogene Coca featured ninety-minutes of outrageous comedy sketches and live musical production numbers every Saturday night.

Music programs were a staple of television programming in the 1950s. During the first half of the decade network broadcasts in the early evening typically included a fifteen-minute national newscast followed by a fifteen-minute light entertainment program, usually a musical show, each weekday. CBS had Perry Como, Jane Froman, and Jo Stafford, while NBC had Dinah Shore, Eddie Fisher, and Tony Martin. Later in the fifties, local and national news programs expanded and began to dominate the early evening schedule and the music shows were extended to a half-hour, moved to prime time, and garnered even larger audiences. By the mid-fifties, top rated musical/variety shows were hosted by popular vocalists like Dinah Shore and Perry Como (see chart 7.4).

Popular 50s Singers with their own Network TV Series
(Evening broadcast times listed are Eastern Time, programs aired one hour earlier in the Midwest)

Andy Williams Show	Thursdays 9:00-9:30 (ABC) 1958
	Tuesdays 10:00-11:00 (CBS) 1959
Dinah Shore Show and	Tues & Thurs 7:30-7:45 (NBC) 1951-1957
Dinah Shore Chevy Show	Sundays 9:00-10:00 (NBC) 1957-1962
Coke Time with Eddie Fisher	Wed & Fri 7:30-7:45 (NBC) 1953-1957
and **Eddie Fisher Show**	Tuesdays 8:00-9:00 (NBC) 1957-1959
Frank Sinatra Show	Tuesdays 8:00-9:00 (CBS) 1950-1952
	Fridays 9:00-9:30 (ABC) 1957-1958
Frankie Laine Time	Wednesdays 8:00-9:00 (CBS) 1955-1956
Georgia Gibbs Million Record Show	Mondays 7:30-7:45 (NBC) 1957
Gordon MacRae Show	Mondays 7:30-7:45 (NBC) 1956
Guy Mitchell Show	Mondays 8:00-8:30 (ABC) 1957-1958

Chart 7.4. Popular 50s Singers with their own Network TV Series
(Chart continues on the next page)

Popular 50s Singers with their own Network TV Series
(continued)

Helen O'Connell Show	Wednesdays & Fridays 7:30-7:45 (NBC) 1957
Jane Froman's USA Canteen	Tues & Thursdays 7:45-8:00 (CBS) 1952-1955
Jaye P. Morgan Show	Wednesdays & Fridays 7:30-7:45 (NBC) 1956
Jo Stafford Show	Tuesdays 7:45-8:00 (CBS) 1954-1955
Jimmie Rodgers Show	Tuesdays 8:30-9:00 (NBC) 1959
Julius LaRosa Show	Mon, Wed, & Fri 7:45-8:00 (CBS) 1955 Saturdays 8:00-9:00 (NBC) 1956-57
June Valli/Andy Williams Show	Tues & Thurs 7:30-7:45 (NBC) 1957
Kate Smith Evening Hour	Wednesdays 8:00-9:00 (NBC) 1951-1952 (also had a daytime show on (NBC) 1950-1954)
Nat King Cole Show	Mondays 7:30-7:45 (NBC) 1956 Tuesdays 10:00-10:30 (NBC) 1957
Pat Boone – **Chevy Showroom**	Thursdays 9:00-9:30 (ABC) 1957-1960
Patti Page Show and **Patti Page Olds Show**	Saturdays 8:00-9:00 (NBC) 1956 and Wednesdays 9:30-10:00 (ABC) 1958-1959
Perry Como Show	Mon, Wed, Fri 7:45-8:00 (CBS) 1950-1955 Wednesdays 9:00-10:00 (NBC) 1955-1963
Polly Bergen Show	Saturdays 9:00-9:30 (NBC) 1957-1958
Rosemary Clooney (The Lux Show)	Tuesdays 10:00-10:30 (NBC) 1957-58
Steve Allen Presents the **Steve Lawrence - Eydie Gorme Show**	Sundays 8:00-9:00 (NBC) 1958
Tony Bennett Show	Wednesdays 9:00-10:00 (NBC) summer 1956 & 59
Tony Martin Show	Mondays 7:30-7:45 (NBC) 1954-1956
Vaughn Monroe Show	Tues & Thurs 7:30-7:45 (NBC) summer 1954 & 55
Vic Damone Show	Mondays 9:30-10:00 (CBS) 1956 Wednesdays 8:00-9:00 (CBS) 1957

Chart 7.4. Popular 50s Singers with their own Network TV Series

In addition to the weekly television series featuring popular singers, the networks created one-time musical specials starring the legendary performers of the decade (see chart 7.5). These exciting, top-notch productions garnered huge ratings for the television networks.

Performers Starring in Network TV Specials in the 50s

The Bing Crosby Show   (CBS)   January 3, 1954
Bing Crosby's first variety special featured guest star Jack Benny.

The Judy Garland Show   (CBS)   September 24, 1955
Judy Garland made her TV debut on this 'Ford Star Jubilee' musical variety special.

The Maurice Chevalier Show   (NBC)   December 4, 1955
Maurice Chevalier's variety special with Marcel Marceau, Jeannie Carson, Pat Carroll.

The Victor Borge Show   (CBS)   December 11, 1956
A one-man show by the Danish pianist/humorist.

Ginger Rogers   (CBS)   October 15, 1958
Film star Ginger Rogers' variety special with Ray Bolger and the Ritz Brothers.

An Evening with Fred Astaire   (NBC)   October 17, 1958
Fred Astaire's first variety special, choreographed by Hermes Pan, featured guest Barrrie Chase.

Magic with Mary Martin /
Music with Mary Martin   (NBC)   Mar. 29, 1959
Two Mary Martin Easter Sunday specials—one in the afternoon, a second in prime time.

The Gene Kelly Show   (CBS)   April 24, 1959
Gene Kelly's music/dance special with Liza Minnelli (then age 13) and Carl Sandburg.

Tonight with Belafonte   (CBS)   December 10, 1959
Music variety special with popular singer Harry Belafonte.

Chart 7.5. Performers starring in Network TV Specials in the 50s

Occasionally, television dramatic programs introduced new songs that would become top-ten hit recordings. In November 1954, the critically acclaimed television dramatic series 'Studio One' featured the song *Let Me Go, Lover*. Overnight, record companies rushed their top singers into the studios to record *Let Me Go, Lover*. Joan Weber's version was the biggest hit (and the only hit of her career) while Teresa Brewer, Patti Page, Sunny Gale, and Peggy Lee all scored with the song, and even Hank Snow's version went high on the country charts.

Gisele McKenzie, one of the stars of the popular TV series 'Your Hit Parade,' had only one top-ten hit recording in her career, *Hard To Get*. She introduced the song on NBCs long-running, hard-hitting anthology series 'Armstrong Circle Theater' in 1955 when she appeared as a struggling new singer in a gritty dramatic production titled 'Sound of Violence.' It gave her the only opportunity she had during the run of 'Your Hit Parade' to perform one of her own hit records.

Betty Johnson's only top-ten hit recording, *I Dreamed,* was introduced in 1956 on NBC-TV's weekday series 'Modern Romances' where host Martha Scott introduced a new five-part story each week. Popular singer Jill Corey had hits from two different TV dramatic programs in 1957: *Let It Be Me* was from the CBS TV series 'Climax,' and her more popular recording the same year, *Love Me To Pieces*, was from the CBS TV show 'Studio One, Summer Theater.' In the same year, teen star Tommy Sands introduced himself and his top hit song *Teenage Crush* on the 1957 TV play 'The Singing Idol.'

In the 1950s the television networks mounted impressive musical reviews with classy production values and top musical performers. These musical tributes saluted composers, music genres, and the recording industry itself (see chart 7.6). Major advertisers were anxious to celebrate their anniversaries with lavish musical telecasts.

In 1954, film actress Betty Hutton made television history in producer Max Liebman's lavish color musical spectacular 'Satins and Spurs.' It was the first full-scale musical written especially for television (see chart 7.7). The title song, *Satins and Spurs*, and *Back Home*, both written by Jay Livingston and Ray Evans, were released by this singer-actress on Capitol records.

In 1956, the CBS anthology 'Ford Star Jubilee' presented a musical adaptation of Maxwell Anderson's 1937 stage play 'High Tor' starring Bing Crosby, Nancy Olson, Everett Sloane, and Julie Andrews—before she became a Broadway superstar in 'My Fair Lady.' The 90-minute color production of 'High Tor" was one of the first filmed productions made especially for TV. Original songs included W*hen You're in Love* and *Once Upon a Long Ago* with lyrics by Maxwell Anderson and music by veteran Broadway and Hollywood tunesmith Arthur Schwartz.

Kay Starr was featured in the 1956 'Producer's Showcase Production' of 'The Lord Don't Play Favorites.' In this made-for-television musical drama, she introduced two songs *The Good Book* and *The Things I Never Had*, written by Hal Stanley and Irving Taylor—both became hits for her that year.

Throughout the fifties television viewership grew and the four TV networks, ABC, CBS, Dumont, and NBC provided the only program options available. With the arrival of cable TV in the eighties and new TV networks in the nineties, audiences fragmented and the percentage of

Lavish Network TV Musical Celebrations during the 50s

Richard Rodgers Jubilee Show   (NBC)   March 4, 1951
Music tribute with Mary Martin, Celeste Holm, and Patrice Munsel.

Irving Berlin: Salute to America   (NBC)   September 12, 1951
Music with Irving Berlin and guests Tony Martin, Dinah Shore, and Margaret Truman.

Ford Fiftieth Anniversary Show   (CBS and NBC)   June 15, 1953
Variety celebration, with appearances by Marian Anderson, Eddie Fisher, Frank Sinatra, and Rudy Vallee, highlighted by a Mary Martin and Ethel Merman duet.

General Foods Anniversary Show   (all 4 networks) March 28, 1954
Musical special featuring Mary Martin, Jack Benny, Ezio Pinza, John Raitt, Groucho Marx, Tony Martin, Rosemary Clooney, Yul Brynner, and Gordon MacRae.

Sunday In Town   (NBC)   October 10, 1954
Musical review with Judy Holiday, Steve Allen, and Dick Shawn.

Three For Tonight   (CBS)   June 22, 1955
Musical review with Harry Belafonte and Marge and Gower Champion.

Rock 'n' Roll Show   (ABC) May 4 and May 11, 1957
Alan Freed's special with Sal Mineo, Guy Mitchell, June Valli, Martha Carson, the Clovers, Screamin' Jay Hawkins, and the Dell-Vikings.

Holiday In Las Vegas   (NBC)   November 16, 1957
Variety show with Jayne Mansfield, Sammy Davis, Jr., Tony Randall, and Vic Damone.

General Motors Fiftieth Anniversary Show (NBC) Nov 17, 1957
Music/variety celebration with Kirk Douglas, Cyril Ritchard, Helen Hays, Pat Boone, Dean Martin, Carol Burnett, June Allyson, and Steve Lawrence.

All Star Jazz   (CBS)   November 10, 1958
Music with Louis Armstrong, Gene Krupa, Lionel Hampton, and Jane Morgan.

Accent on Love   (NBC)   February 28, 1958
Musical revue with Ginger Rogers, Louis Jourdan, Mike Nichols and Elaine May, Marge and Gower Champion, and Jaye P. Morgan.

The Golden Age of Jazz   (CBS)   January 7, 1959
Music with Louis Armstrong, Duke Ellington, Dizzy Gillespie, and Gene Krupa.

The Record Years   (NBC)   June 28, 1959
Dick Clark's tribute to the recording industry with guests Johnny Mathis, Fabian, the McGuire Sisters, Les Paul and Mary Ford, Fats Domino, and Stan Freberg.

Chart 7.6. Lavish Network TV Musical Celebrations during the 50s

Original Made-for-TV Musical Productions of the 50s

Amahl and the Night Visitors Chet Allen, Rosemary Kuhlmann (NBC) Dec. 24, 1951
Score and libretto by Gian Carlo Menotti for the first production of this Christmas Opera.

Satins and Spurs Betty Hutton, Kevin McCarthy (NBC) September 12, 1954
Jay Livingston and Jay Evans wrote the lively score for this first TV spectacular.

Svengali and the Blonde Carol Channing, Basil Rathbone (NBC) Aug 22. 1955
Charles Gaynor and Alan Handley wrote the score for this spoof of DuMaurier's classic.

Our Town Frank Sinatra, Paul Newman, Eva Marie Saint (NBC) Sept. 19, 1955
Sammy Cahn and James Van Heusen created this musical version of Thornton Wilder's play that included the popular song *Love and Marriage*.

High Tor Bing Crosby, Julie Andrews, Nancy Olsen (CBS) March 10, 1956
With music by Arthur Schwartz and lyrics by Maxwell Anderson (based on his 1937 play) this musical fantasy, the first on film, included songs *When You're in Love* and *Once Upon a Long Ago*.

The Lord Don't Play Favorites Kay Starr (CBS) September 17, 1956
This musical drama with score by Hal Stanley & Irving Taylor introduced the song *The Good Book*.

A Bell for Adano Anna Maria Alberghetti, Barry Sullivan (CBS) June 2, 1956
Musical based on John Hersey's novel with music by Arthur Schwartz and lyrics by Howard Dietz.

Marco Polo Alfred Drake, Doretta Morrow, Beatrice Kraft (NBC) Apr 14, 1956
Original musical based on themes by Rimsky-Korsakov, story co-written by Neil Simon.

The Bachelor Hal March, Jayne Mansfield, Carol Haney (NBC) July 15, 1956
Original music and lyrics by Steve Allen in this made-for-TV musical.

Ruggles of Red Gap Michael Redgrave, Jane Powell (NBC) February 3, 1957
Music by Jule Styne and lyrics by Leo Robin included the song *A Ride on a Rainbow*.

Cinderella Julie Andrews, Edie Adams, Jon Cypher (CBS) Live Telecast Mar 31, 1957
Richard Rodgers and Oscar Hammerstein II created this television musical including songs *In My Own Little Corner, Ten Minutes Ago,* and *Do I Love You (Because You're Beautiful)*.

Pinocchio Mickey Rooney, Fran Allison, Stubby Kaye (NBC) Oct 13, 1957
Music by Alec Wilder and lyrics by William Engvick. Songs included *Listen to Your Heart*.

The Pied Piper of Hamelin Van Johnson, Kay Starr (NBC) Nov 26, 1957
Songs by Hal Stanley and Irving Taylor adapted from classical Edward Grieg melodies.

Hans Brinker and the Silver Skates Tab Hunter, Peggy King (NBC) Feb. 9 1958
Music and lyrics by Hugh Martin. Cast included Olympic ice champion Dick Button.

Aladdin Cyril Ritchard, Sal Mineo, Anna Marie Alberghetti (CBS) Feb. 21, 1958
Music and lyrics by Cole Porter—it was the last musical score Cole Porter wrote.

The Gift of the Magi Gordon MacRae, Sally Ann Howes (CBS) Dec. 9. 1958
Music and lyrics by Richard Adler based on the O. Henry tale.

No Man Can Tame Me Gisele MacKenzie, John Raitt (CBS) Feb 1. 1959
Music by Jay Livingston and Ray Evans.

Chart 7.7. Original Made-for-TV Musical Productions of the 50s

Americans watching any one individual TV program was never as high as it was in the fifties. By 2000, the top rated TV shows were considered extraordinarily successful if the ratings reached 20% of the viewing audience, by contrast 'I Love Lucy' ratings on CBS in the mid fifties often reached above 67% of the viewing audience, (Brooks & Marsh, 1995, p.1259) and in its early years Milton Berle's 'Texaco Star Theater' on NBC exceeded 94%. (Halberstam, 1993, p.186)

Broadway

By 1950, the American musical theater had just witnessed one of the greatest seasons in Broadway history. The 76 productions of the 1948-49 theater season included landmark musicals 'Kiss Me Kate' and 'South Pacific' as well as groundbreaking dramatic plays 'Death of a Salesman,' 'Anne of the Thousand Days,' and 'The Madwoman of Chaillot.' It was the best year on Broadway since the heyday of live theater in the 1920s but sustaining that level of success was too much to expect.

Production costs were soaring and competition, especially from television, negatively impacted the chances for investors to recoup the increasing costs to mount a Broadway musical. Once viewers had purchased their TV set, they could sit comfortably at home and watch a variety of entertainment at virtually no expense. Moreover, television and movies continued to drain away creative talent from live theater.

In the 1950s musical theater began a slow decline in quantity even though there were some outstanding productions. By the 1951-52 season only nine new musicals opened on Broadway and that pattern continued through most of the fifties. With only eight musicals opening in the 1955-56 season, it would have been a very depressing year except for the arrival of 'My Fair Lady.' The Learner and Lowe musical version of George Bernard Shaw's 'Pygmalion' starring Rex Harrison and Julie Andrews represented the glorious fruition of the contemporary school of musical plays with its aim of cohesiveness and tonal integrity. It ran for more than 2,500 performances and the original cast LP became the biggest selling show album in history at the time. (Boardman, 1992, p.598) The fifties did introduce some highly entertaining Broadway musicals. Not all were as fully achieved as 'My Fair Lady' but many of them contained outstanding musical numbers that pleased audiences (see chart 7.8).

Popular Live Broadway Musical Productions of the 50s

Call Me Madam   Music & lyrics by Irving Berlin
opened at the Imperial Theater, October 12, 1950, ran for 644 performances
Ethel Merman, Russell Nype, Paul Lucas, Galina Talva
You're Just in Love (Merman, Nype); *It's a Lovely Day Today* (Nype);
The Best Thing for You (Merman).

Guys and Dolls   Music & lyrics by Frank Loesser
opened at the 46th Street Theater, November 24, 1950, ran for 1,200 performances
Robert Alda, Vivian Blaine, Sam Levene, Isabel Bigley, Stubby Kaye
A Bushel and a Peck (Blaine); *Luck Be a Lady* (Alda); *Guys and Dolls* (Kaye, Johnny
Silver); *If I Were a Bell* (Bigley); *Sit Down You're Rockin' the Boat* (Kaye).

The King and I   Music by Richard Rodgers,
lyrics by Oscar Hammerstein II
opened at the St. James Theater, March 29, 1951, ran for 1,246 performances
Gertrude Lawrence, Yul Brenner, Doretta Morrow, Dorothy Sarnoff
Getting to Know You (Lawrence); *Shall We Dance* (Lawrence, Brenner);
Hello Young Lovers (Lawrence).

Paint Your Wagon Music by Frederick Loewe,
lyrics by Alan Jay Lerner
opened at the Shubert Theater, November 12, 1951, ran for 289 performances
James Barton, Olga San Juan, Tony Bavaar
I Talk to the Trees (Bavaar); *Wand'rin' Star* (Barton);
They Call the Wind Maria (chorus).

Wish You Were Here   Music & lyrics by Harold Rome
opened at the Imperial Theater, June 25, 1952, ran for nearly 600 performances
Jack Cassidy, Patricia Marand, Harry Clark, Sidney Armus, Paul Valentine
Wish You Were Here (Cassidy); *Where Did the Night Go* (Cassidy).

Wonderful Town   Music by Leonard Bernstein,
lyrics by Betty Comden and Adolph Green
opened at the Winter Garden Theater, Feb. 25, 1953, for more than 500 performances
Rosalind Russell and Edith Adams
(Why, Oh Why, Oh Why O, Did I Ever Leave) Ohio (Russell and Adams).

Can-Can   Music & lyrics by Cole Porter
opened at the Shubert Theater, May 7, 1953, ran for nearly 900 performances
Lilo, Peter Cookson, Hans Conried, Gwen Verdon, Erik Rhode
Allez-Vous En, Go Away (Lilo); *C'est Magnifique* (Lilo); *I Love Paris* (Lilo).

Chart 7.8. Popular Live Broadway Musical Productions of the 50s

(Chart continues on the next page)

Popular Live Broadway Musical Productions of the 50s
(continued)

Kismet   Original music composed in the 19th century by Aleksandr Borodin,
   Musical adaptation & lyrics by Robert Wright and George Forrest
opened at the Ziegfeld Theater, Dec. 3, 1953, and ran for nearly 600 performances
   Alfred Drake, Doretta Morrow, Joan Diener, Henry Calvin, Richard Kiley
   Stranger in Paradise (Morrow, Kiley); *Baubles, Bangles & Beads* (Morrow).

Pajama Game   Music & lyrics by Richard Adler & Jerry Ross
opened at the St. James Theater, May 13, 1954, for more than 1,000 performances
   John Raitt, Janis Paige, Eddie Foy Jr., Carol Haney, Reta Shaw
   Hey There (Raitt); *I'm Not At All In Love* (Paige); *Steam Heat* (Haney).

Peter Pan   Music by Mark Charlop (additional music by Jule Styne),
   lyrics by Carolyn Leigh (additional lyrics by Betty Comden & Adolph Green)
opened at the Winter Garden Theater, Oct. 20, 1954, for just over 150 performances
   Mary Martin and Cyril Ritchard
   I'm Flying (Martin); *I've Gotta Crow* (Martin).

Silk Stockings   Music & lyrics by Cole Porter
opened at the Imperial Theater, February 24, 1955, ran for nearly 500 performances
   Don Ameche, Hildegarde Neff, Gretchen Wyler
   All of You (Ameche); *Stereophonic Sound* (Wyler).

Damn Yankees   Music & lyrics by Richard Adler & Jerry Ross
opened at the 46th Street Theater, May 5, 1955, for more than 1,000 performances
   Gwen Verdon, Russ Brown, Steven Douglas, Ray Walston
Heart (Brown); *Whatever Lola Wants* (Verdon); *Two Lost Souls* (Verdon, Douglas).

My Fair Lady   Music by Frederick Loewe, lyrics by Alan Jay Lerner
opened at the Mark Hellinger Theater, March 15, 1956, ran for 2,717 performances
   Rex Harrison, Julie Andrews, Stanley Holloway, Robert Coote, Leonard Weir
   I Could Have Danced All Night (Andrews); *On the Street Where You Live* (Weir).

Mr. Wonderful   Music & lyrics by Jerry Bock,
                              Larry Holofcener, & George Weiss
opened at the Broadway Theater, March 22, 1956, ran for 383 performances
   Sammy Davis Jr., Olga James, Jack Carter, Will Mastin Trio
   Too Close for Comfort (Davis); *Mr. Wonderful* (James).

Most Happy Fella   Music & lyrics by Frank Loesser
opened at the Imperial Theater, May 3, 1956, ran for 676 performances
   Robert Weede, Art Lund, Jo Sullivan, Susan Johnson, Shorty Long
Standing On The Corner and *Big 'D'* (Chorus); *Somebody, Somewhere* (Sullivan).

Chart 7.8.   Popular Live Broadway Musical Productions of the 50s
(Chart continues on the next page)

Popular Live Broadway Musical Productions of the 50s

(continued)

Bells are Ringing   Music by Jule Styne,
lyrics by Betty Comden & Adolph Green
opened at the Shubert Theater, November 29, 1956, ran for 925 performances
Judy Holiday, Sydney Chaplin, Jean Stapleton, Eddie Lawrence
Just in Time (Holiday, Chaplin); *The Party's Over* (Holiday).

Happy Hunting   Music by Harold Karr, lyrics by Matt Dubey
opened at the Majestic Theater, December 6, 1956, ran for 412 performances
Ethel Merman, Fernando Lamas, Virginia Gibson, Gordon Polk
Mutual Admiration Society (Merman, Gibson); *If'n* (Gibson, Polk).

West Side Story   Music by Leonard Bernstein,
lyrics by Stephen Sondheim
opened at the Winter Garden Theater, September 26, 1957, ran for 981 performances
Carol Lawrence, Larry Kert, Chita Rivera, Art Smith
Somewhere (Kert); *Maria* (Kert); *Tonight* (Kert, Lawrence); *America* (Rivera).

Music Man   Music & lyrics by Meredith Willson
opened at the Majestic Theater, December 19, 1957, ran for 1,375 performances
Robert Preston, Barbara Cook, David Burns, Pert Kelton
Seventy-Six Trombones (Preston); *Till There Was You* (Cook).

Flower Drum Song   Music by Richard Rodgers,
lyrics by Oscar Hammerstein II
opened at the St. James Theater, December 1, 1958, ran for 600 performances
Pat Suzuki, Miyoshi Umeki, Larry Blyden, Juanita Hall
I Enjoy Being a Girl (Suzuki); *Love Look Away* (Hong).

Once Upon a Mattress   Music by Mary Rodgers,
lyrics by Marshall Barer
opened at the Phoenix Theater, May 11, 1959, ran for 460 performances
Carol Burnett, Joe Bova, Jack Gilford, Jane White, Allen Case, Anne Jones
Shy (Burnett); *Man To Man Talk* (Bova, Gilford).

Gypsy   Music by Jule Styne, lyrics by Stephen Sondheim
opened at the Broadway Theater, May 21, 1959, ran for 700 performances
Ethel Merman, Jack Klugman, Sandra Church
Together Wherever We Go (Merman); *Everything's Coming Up Roses* (Merman).

The Sound of Music   Music by Richard Rodgers,
lyrics by Oscar Hammerstein II
opened at the Lunt-Fontanne Theater, November 16, 1959, for 1,443 performances
Mary Martin, Theodore Bikel, Patricia Neway, Kurt Kasznar
Sound of Music (Martin); *My Favorite Things* (Martin); *Climb Ev'ry Mountain* (Neway).

Chart 7.8. Popular Live Broadway Musical Productions of the 50s

While dozens of 50s EASY-POP songs were introduced in movies, dozens more were written for Broadway musicals. It is interesting to note that artists who popularized songs in the movies—Frank Sinatra, Bing Crosby, Doris Day, and Debbie Reynolds—were very often the artists who had the popular hit version of the song on records. On the contrary, when songs originated from Broadway musicals, the singers who introduced the songs and performed them on stage—Ethel Merman, Mary Martin, Larry Kert, John Raitt, and Richard Kiley—were never the singers who had popular success with the song. These 'show tunes' were recorded by established vocalists, similar to the way popular singers recorded 'covers' of little-known R&B artists.

EASY-POP singers in the fifties often struck gold recording songs that were originally introduced in Broadway musicals. Vic Damone's biggest hit *On the Street Where You Live* was from 'My Fair Lady.' Rosemary Clooney's classic *Hey There* was a showstopper in 'Pajama Game' and Perry Como's *Hello, Young Lovers* was from 'The King and I.' Tony Bennett had the top rated version of *Stranger in Paradise* from 'Kismet,' but Tony Martin and the Four Aces also released top-ten versions and Gordon MacRae recorded it too. All of the songs from 'Kismet" were adapted by Robert Wright and George Forrest from the 'Polovetsian Dances' in Aleksandr Borodin's 1888 opera 'Prince Igor.'

The baseball-themed Broadway musical 'Damn Yankees' introduced three EASY-POP singles: *Heart*, a top-ten hit record for Eddie Fisher, *Whatever Lola Wants*, one of Sarah Vaughan's biggest singles, and *Two Lost Souls,* a hit duet for Jaye P. Morgan and Perry Como. Other EASY-POP songs from Broadway included Doris Day's *It's a Lovely Day Today* from 'Call Me Madam,' Kay Starr's *Allez-Vous-En* from 'Can-Can,' Patti Page's hit *Steam Heat* from 'Pajama Game,' Peggy Lee's *Joey, Joey, Joey* from 'Most Happy Fella,' and the Margaret Whiting/Jimmy Wakely duet *A Bushel and a Peck* from 'Guys and Dolls.'

Well-known Broadway musicals produced popular hit songs, but long-forgotten shows and off-Broadway shows produced their share of hits too. *Wish You Were Here* was a memorable hit for Eddie Fisher, but the show 'Wish You Were Here' was forgettable. Judy Garland's *Make Someone Happy* was from the barely-remembered 'Do Re Me,' Doris Day's ballad *Love in a Home* was introduced by comic-strip-character, Daisy Mae, played by Edie Adams, in 'Li'l Abner,' and the Four Lads' *Standing on the Corner* was from composer Frank Loesser's extended musical comedy 'Most Happy Fella.' Off-Broadway, in the long running show 'The Fantastics' at the minuscule Sullivan Street Theater, Jerry Orbach introduced *Try To Remember* that became a hit single for Ed Ames.

Two of the most successful writers ever to collaborate in American musical theater, Richard Rodgers and Oscar Hammerstein II, created the hit shows 'Oklahoma,' 'South Pacific,' 'Carousel,' 'The King and I,' and 'The Sound of Music.' These shows are Broadway and movie classics, however two musicals they created in the fifties, 'Pipe Dream' and 'Me and Juliet' were neither commercial nor critical successes. But even their failures produced fifties EASY-POP record hits. Eddie Fisher's *Everybody's Got a Home but Me* and Perry Como's *All At Once You Love Her* are both from 'Pipe Dream' and another Perry Como hit *No Other Love* was introduced in 'Me and Juliet,' even though Richard Rodgers originally composed the melody for the television naval series 'Victory at Sea.'

Sarah Vaughan's *Mr. Wonderful* and Eydie Gorme's *Too Close for Comfort* were both introduced in the Sammy Davis Jr. nightclub-act-on-Broadway, 'Mr. Wonderful.' Dinah Shore's *Nobody's Chasing Me* was from 'Out of This World' and her *Salomee* as well as Eddie Fisher's *How Do You Speak to an Angel* came from 'Hazel Flagg.' The Four Aces' *It's Good to be Alive* was first heard in 'New Girl in Town,' Jaye P. Morgan and Eddy Arnold's duet *Mutual Admiration Society* was a showstopper in 'Happy Hunting,' and Eydie Gorme's *Guess Who I Saw Today* came from 'New Faces of 1952.' The irony of Joannie Sommers' EASY-POP hit single *One Boy*, is that it was intended to poke fun at the pop genre in the rock 'n' roll spoof, 'Bye Bye Birdie.'

In addition to EASY-POP songs, classic 'show tunes' came from the musical theater in the fifties. There were three standards, *Shall We Dance, Getting to Know You,* and *We Kiss in a Shadow* from 'The King and I' and three more, *I've Never Been in Love Before, Luck Be a Lady,* and *I'll Know* from 'Guys and Dolls.'

Other standards including *Just in Time* came from 'Bells Are Ringing,' *I Love Paris* from 'Can-Can,' *Make the Man Love Me* from 'A Tree Grows in Brooklyn,' *From This Moment On* from 'Out of This World,' and both *They Call the Wind Maria* and *I Talk to the Trees* from 'Paint Your Wagon.' The popular and often recorded *Young and Foolish* came from the Amish-based musical 'Plain and Fancy.'

The counter-point duet *You're Just in Love* that features the lyric "I hear singing and there's no one there" while the partner sings "You don't need analyzing, it's not so surprising" was introduced in 1950 by brassy Ethel Merman performing with nebbish Russell Nype in 'Call Me Madam.' The popular two-part standard was recorded by dozens of vocalists, paired just for this duet, but Ethel Merman and Russell Nype who stopped the show with it at every performance on Broadway never recorded it. RCA issued an 'original cast' album with the entire cast, but with Dinah Shore substituting for Ethel Merman, who was under contract to Decca Records. Decca released their own 'original cast' album with Ethel Merman, but using their own singers to replace the rest of the cast.

Soundtrack albums from musical films, recordings for television productions, and Original Cast albums from Broadway shows provided some of the most popular applications for the new $33\frac{1}{3}$ rpm records.* The soundtrack recording from the 1950 Warner Brothers film 'Young Man With a Horn' starring Doris Day and Kirk Douglas with Harry James dubbing on the trumpet was one of the first top-selling soundtrack albums. The original cast recordings from Broadway shows 'Oklahoma' and 'South Pacific' were so successful that record companies rushed to release albums from dozens of Broadway musicals.

These LPs (long-playing) 12" discs could capture about an hour's worth of music (thirty minutes on each side) which matched the requirements of the songs from movie musicals and Broadway shows. (The best selling movie musical Soundtrack albums are listed in chart 7.9; Albums from original TV productions are shown in chart 7.10; and the best selling Broadway Original Cast albums are listed in chart 7.11).

By the end of the century, Broadway 'show tunes' were no longer able to appeal to a popular music audience. Music from the American musical theater would never again provide top hit songs the way it did in the fifties.

---

* Recording formats during the 1950s evolved from 78rpm records to $33\frac{1}{3}$rpm LP albums and 45rpm singles. For a detailed look at the twentieth century developments in recording and playback technology including the evolution of the multi-song, long-playing album see chapter 10.

Best Selling 50s Musical Movie Soundtrack Albums

#1 **Oklahoma**   Gordon MacRae, Shirley Jones, Gene Nelson   1955

#2 **The King & I** Yul Brenner, Deborah Kerr (voice dubbed by Marni Nixon) 1956

#3 **South Pacific** Mitzi Gaynor, Rossano Brazzi (dubbed by Giorgio Tozzi) 1958

#4 **Gigi**   Leslie Caron, Louis Jourdan, Maurice Chevalier   1958

#5 **Porgy & Bess** Sidney Poitier, Dorothy Dandridge, Brock Peters,
Sammy Davis Jr., Diahann Carroll, Pearl Bailey   1959

#6 **Show Boat**   Howard Keel, Kathryn Grayson   1951

#7 **An American in Paris**   Gene Kelly, Leslie Caron   1951

#8 **Carousel**   Gordon MacRae, Shirley Jones, Barbara Ruick   1956

#9 **Young Man with a Horn**   Doris Day (Harry James dubbed the trumpet) 1950

#10 **The Great Caruso**   Mario Lanza, Ann Blyth, Dorothy Kirsten 1951

Chart 7.9.   Best Selling 50s Musical Movie Soundtrack Albums

Albums from Original TV Musical Productions of the 50s

Cinderella   Julie Andrews, Edie Adams, Jon Cypher

Amahl and the **Night Visitors**   Chet Allen, Rosemary Kuhlmann

Our Town   Frank Sinatra, Paul Newman, Eva Marie Saint

The Ford Fiftieth Anniversary Show   Mary Martin & Ethel Merman

High Tor   Bing Crosby, Julie Andrews

Satins and Spurs   Betty Hutton, Kevin McCarthy

Ruggles of Red Gap   Michael Redgrave, Jane Powell

Chart 7.10.   Albums from Original TV Musical Productions of the 50s

Best Selling Broadway Original Cast Albums of the 50s

#1 **My Fair Lady**   Rex Harrison, Julie Andrews, Stanley Holloway   1957

#2 **South Pacific**   Mary Martin, Ezio Pinza   1949

#3 **The Sound of Music**   Mary Martin, Theodore Bikel, Patricia Neway   1959

#4 **The Music Man**   Robert Preston, Barbara Cook   1957

#5 **West Side Story**   Carol Lawrence, Larry Kert, Chita Rivera   1958

#6 **Flower Drum Song**   Pat Suzuki, Miyoshe Umeki, Larry Blyden   1958

#7 **Gypsy**   Ethel Merman, Jack Klugman, Sandra Church   1959

#8 **The King & I**   Gertrude Lawrence, Yul Brenner   1951

#9 **Guys and Dolls**   Robert Alda, Vivian Blaine   1950

#10 **Pajama Game**   John Raitt, Janis Paige, Eddie Foy Jr.   1954

Chart 7.11.   Best Selling Broadway Original Cast Albums of the 50s

References from Chapter 7:

Bordman, Gerald. *American Musical Theater*. Second Edition. New York: Oxford University Press, 1992.

Brooks, Tim and Marsh, Earle. *The Complete Directory to Prime Time Network and Cable TV Shows*. New York: Ballantine Books, 1995.

Croteau, David and Hoynes, William. *The Business of Media*. Thousand Oaks, California: Pine Forge Press, 2001

Gillett, Charlie. *The Sound of the City – The Rise of Rock 'n' Roll*. New York: Dell Publishing, 1970.

Halberstam, David. *The Fifties*. New York: Random House Publishing Group, 1993.

Kenrick, John. Musicals on Television. www.musicals101.com

McNeil, Alex. *Total Television*. New York: Viking Penguin Inc., 1984.

Internet Broadway Database. www.ibdb.com

Whitburn, Joel. *Pop Hits, Singles & Albums 1940-1954*. New York: Billboard Books, 2002.

Whitburn, Joel. *Top Pop Albums 1955-1996*. New York: Billboard Books, 1996.

Without music life would be a mistake.

German philosopher Friedrich Nietzsche (1844-1900)

Chapter 8

Christmas Songs, Novelty Songs, Spoken Word Recordings, and Instrumental Hits

Earlier chapters have described quintessential 50s EASY-POP hit songs and singers. This chapter will look at four variations of EASY-POP music that the post-war era produced: classic Christmas songs; nonsense novelty songs; spoken word, voice-over-music 'talk' songs; and instrumental hits.

Christmas Songs

No musical era produced the quantity of memorable Christmas-season classics as the post-war years and these songs wait to be re-discovered each winter. The idealistic lyrics, upbeat arrangements, and familiar vocalists in the fifties, uniquely suited the holidays. Maybe the only time it is considered fashionable today to listen to 'old-fashioned' fifties music is during the magical Christmas season.

Holiday songs are an essential part of the season's magic. It's impossible to imagine the Christmas holidays without *Rudolph the Red Nosed Reindeer* and *Frosty the Snowman*. Perry Como's folksy *It's Beginning to Look a Lot Like Christmas, There's No Christmas Like a Home Christmas* and *(There's No Place Like) Home for the Holidays* conjure up fond Norman Rockwell style images. *Jingle Bells* and *Sleigh Ride* recall images of a cold starry night (see descriptions of post war Christmas songs in chart 8.1).

Popular Christmas Recordings of the Post-War Era

All I Want for Christmas is My Two Front Teeth
Recorded by Spike Jones and his City Slickers in 1949
Music and lyrics by Don Gardner

The lyrics of this novelty Christmas song, supposedly sung by a lisping child, initially delighted the audience on Perry Como's radio show and that led to a smash record by musical madcap Spike Jones. The song still generates smiles today.

Blue Christmas
Recorded by Elvis Presley in 1957 & 1964
Music and lyrics by Bill Hayes and Jay Johnson

Unrequited love is a familiar theme to country fans and Christmas gives it a poignant twist. *Blue Christmas* was written in 1948 and country singer Ernest Tubb made it a hit that year. Elvis Presley, the Browns, and Hugo Winterhalter had popular fifties versions.

The Chipmunk Song – Christmas Don't Be Late
Recorded by David Seville (Ross Bagdasarian) and the Chipmunks in 1958
Music and lyrics by Ross Bagdasarian

Armenian-American actor, Ross Bagdasarian, calling himself David Seville created the three 'Chipmunks' named for Liberty Records executives Alvin Bennett, Simon Waronker, and Theodore Keep. Recording voices at slow speed and playing them back at higher speed gave the chipmunks their sound.

The Christmas Song (Chestnuts Roasting on an Open Fire)
Recorded by Nat King Cole in 1956
Music and lyrics by Mel Torme and Robert Wells

Mel Torme, the supper-club singer known as 'the Velvet Fog,' co-wrote the classic Yuletide season song with roasting chestnuts, carolers, a nipping Jack Frost, and people dressed like Eskimos. Mel Torme recorded the song in 1946 and Nat King Cole recorded an even more successful version a decade later.

The Christmas Waltz
Recorded by Frank Sinatra in 1957
Music and lyrics by Sammy Cahn and Jule Styne

Frank Sinatra approached the successful songwriting team of Sammy Cahn and Jule Styne to write a song for his Christmas album with Gordon Jenkins Orchestra. Although reluctant to create another holiday song they imagined a gliding waltz of 'frosted window panes' and 'gleaming candles' in ¾ time. Doris Day also recorded a memorable version.

Chart 8.1. Popular Christmas Recordings of the Post-War Era

(Chart continues on the next page)

Popular Christmas Recordings of the Post-War Era
(continued)

Do You Hear What I Hear
Recorded by Bing Crosby and by the Harry Simeone Chorale in 1962
Music by Gloria Shayne, lyrics by Noel Regney

Noel Regney, a resistance fighter in France, wrote a poem about the first Christmas, he gave it to his wife Gloria Shayne, who had written the 1961 James Darren hit *Goodbye Cruel World*, to create a contemporary melody. Harry Simeone arranged the music.

Frosty the Snowman
Recorded by Gene Autry in 1950
Music and lyrics by Steven Nelson and Jack Rollins

These songwriters had already created the Easter character Peter Cottontail before they imagined Frosty's hat, corncob pipe, and button nose. Nat King Cole, Jimmy Durante, and others recorded versions, but cowboy movie star Gene Autry's was the million-seller.

Happy Holiday
Recorded by Bing Crosby and Marjorie Reynolds in 1942
Music and lyrics by Irving Berlin

While the classic *White Christmas* is the best-known yuletide song from the film 'Holiday Inn,' Irving Berlin also wrote *Happy Holiday* for the film. Jo Stafford had a hit recording of the song in the late forties and Peggy Lee had a hit in the early sixties.

Have Yourself a Merry Little Christmas
Recorded by Judy Garland in 1944
Music and lyrics by Hugh Martin and Ralph Blane

The original musical score for 'Meet Me in St. Louis' included the *Trolley Song* and this haunting little Christmas song that liquid-eyed Judy Garland, with a quiver in her lips, sang to Margaret O'Brien. It is one of the saddest Christmas songs of the century.

Here Comes Santa Claus (Right Down Santa Claus Lane)
Recorded by Gene Autry in 1947
Music and lyrics by Gene Autry and Oakley Haldeman

Another Christmas song that contributed to Gene Autry's fame was written by 'The Singing Cowboy' himself. This was his and Oakley Haldeman's salute to the holiday season and Santa Claus in 1947. His recording of the song was a huge hit, as was the recording by Bing Crosby and the Andrews Sisters.

A Holly Jolly Christmas
Recorded by Burl Ives in 1962
Music and lyrics by Johnny Marks

While this effervescent song was popularized by Burl Ives, portraying the narrator, Sam the Snowman, in the animated television classic 'Rudolph the Red-Nosed Reindeer,' it had been recorded earlier in the year by the six Quinto Sisters.

Chart 8.1. Popular Christmas Recordings of the Post-War Era
(Chart continues on the next page)

Popular Christmas Recordings of the Post-War Era
(continued)

(There's No Place Like) Home for the Holidays
Recorded by Perry Como in 1955
Music by Robert Allen, lyrics by Al Stillman
Well known for writing ballads like *Chances Are* for Johnny Mathis and *Moments to Remember* for the Four Lads, Al Stillman and Robert Allen turned their attention to Christmas for this Perry Como hit. You can't beat home for the holidays.

I Heard The Bells on Christmas Day
Recorded by Harry Belafonte in 1958
Music by Johnny Marks, words by Henry Wadsworth Longfellow
Sitting at his desk after his wife's tragic death, listening to church bells peal, librarian Henry Longfellow recognized the promise of Christmas. Johnny Marks adapted the poet's words of hope and provided the modern musical setting. In addition to Harry Belafonte's hit, Bing Crosby, Kate Smith, and Frank Sinatra recorded versions.

I Saw Mommy Kissing Santa Claus
Recorded by Jimmy Boyd in 1952
Music and lyrics by Thomas P. 'Tommie' Connor
Fathers have dressed up for years in white beards and red suits at Christmas to make their children think that the real Santa Claus has arrived. Twelve-year-old Jimmy Boyd recorded a version of this catchy little song of naiveté that sold nearly 2 million copies the first year. Zany Spike Jones recorded a popular version too.

I'll Be Home for Christmas
Recorded by Bing Crosby in 1943
Music by Walter Kent, lyrics by Kim Gannon
During World War II, many Americans spent Christmas away from loved ones—this is their wish for a reunion. Bing Crosby's 1943 record, with John Scott Trotter's Orchestra, was a million-seller. Frank Sinatra and Elvis Presley had hit recordings in the fifties.

It's Beginning to Look Like Christmas
Recorded by Perry Como and the Fontane Sisters in 1952
Music and lyrics by Meredith Willson
Meredith Willson is better know as the composer of the 1957 Broadway hit 'The Music Man.' Before that, however, he wrote the warmly melodic song *It's Beginning to Look Like Christmas*, with toys in stores, candy canes, and holly on doors.

It's The Most Wonderful Time of the Year
Recorded by Andy Williams in 1963
Music and lyrics by George Wyle and Eddie Pola
Joy explodes in Andy William's exuberant *It's The Most Wonderful Time of the Year.* The anticipation and excitement of Christmas is captured with kids jingle belling, hearts glowing, and loved ones near. An easygoing style and creamy delivery convey a holiday greeting in the happiest season of all.

Chart 8.1. Popular Christmas Recordings of the Post-War Era
(Chart continues on the next page)

Popular Christmas Recordings of the Post-War Era

(continued)

Jingle Bell Rock
Recorded by Bobby Helms in 1957
Music and lyrics by Joseph Beal and James Boothe

Jingle Bell Rock was written one hundred years after James Pierpont's 1857 *Jingle Bells*. New England public relations man, Joe Beal, and Texas advertising writer, Jim Boothe, collaborated on this unique best-seller for 21-year-old rockabilly singer Bobby Helms.

Let It Snow! Let It Snow! Let It Snow!
Recorded by Vaughn Monroe in 1945
Music and lyrics by Sammy Cahn and Jule Styne

The cozy classic, *Let It Snow! Let It Snow! Let It Snow!*, was written by Broadway's famed songwriters, Sammy Cahn and Jule Styne. The Norton Sisters backed big-voiced baritone/bandleader, Vaughn Monroe, on the popular version of this hit.

Little Drummer Boy
Recorded by the Harry Simeone Chorale in 1958
Music and lyrics by Katherine Davis, Henry Onorati, and Harry Simeone

Fred Waring's conductor-assistant, Harry Simeone, co-wrote *The Little Drummer Boy*. A poor shepherd boy makes his way to the manger in Bethlehem to present his simple song as a gift to the infant. The gentle boy's drumbeat accompanies the whole touching carol.

Marshmallow World
Recorded by Bing Crosby in 1951 and by Johnny Mathis in 1963
Music by Peter De Rose, lyrics by Carl Sigman

Peter De Rose, who also wrote the lushly romantic *Deep Purple,* created the sparkling melody for *A Marshmallow World.* Carl Sigman contributed a delicious lyric about marshmallows, whipped cream, and a blanket of snow for Christmas. Recordings by Bing Crosby and Johnny Mathis were the most successful of several contenders.

Mary's Boy Child
Recorded by Harry Belafonte in 1956
Music and lyrics by Jester Hairston

Folksinger Harry Belafonte popularized *Mary's Boy Child,* written by his friend Jester Hairston in the idiom of the West Indies. Based on Afro-American spirituals and folk material, *Mary's Boy Child*, is the story of Jesus' birth made vivid in its calypso rhythm. The pop group, Boney M, released a rousing version of *Mary's Boy Child/Oh My Lord* in 1978.

Mistletoe & Holly
Recorded by Frank Sinatra in 1957
Music and lyrics by Frank Sinatra, Henry Sanicola, and Dok Stanford

Frank Sinatra co-wrote *Mistletoe & Holly.* The charming holiday song, with the Ralph Brewster Singers and orchestra conducted by Gordon Jenkins, was co-authored with Dok Stanford and Hank Sanicola, with whom Frank Sinatra collaborated on other songs.

Chart 8.1. Popular Christmas Recordings of the Post-War Era

(Chart continues on the next page)

Popular Christmas Recordings of the Post-War Era

(continued)

Pretty Paper
Recorded by Roy Orbison in 1963
Music and lyrics by Willie Nelson

Versatile performer and songwriter Willie Nelson's compassion for the downtrodden and disadvantaged is clear in this moving Christmas song. Happy busy shoppers rush by the pauper selling pencils, ribbons, and *Pretty Paper*. Texas rockabilly singer, Roy Orbison, recorded the best-selling hit, but composer Willie Nelson released a touching version too.

Rockin' Around the Christmas Tree
Recorded by Brenda Lee in 1958
Music and lyrics by Johnny Marks

Rockin' Around the Christmas Tree is another Johnny Marks holiday favorite. In 1958, rock 'n' roll was affecting even Christmas—in a "new old-fashioned way"—and Brenda Lee's joyful, catchy recording was a top-twenty hit for 'Little Miss Dynamite.'

Rudolph the Red-Nosed Reindeer
Recorded by Gene Autry in 1949
Music and lyrics by Johnny Marks and Robert May

Rudolph was born as a promotion gimmick for Montgomery Ward department stores. Copywriter Robert May wrote the original poem and along with his brother-in-law, veteran composer Johnny Marks, they came up with the jaunty, jingle-like tune. Gene Autry's version is the second biggest-selling record after Bing Crosby's *White Christmas*.

Santa Baby
Recorded by Eartha Kitt in 1953
Music and lyrics by Joan Javits, Phil Springer, and Tony Springer

Sultry siren Eartha Kitt purred her sensual, materialistic Christmas wish list to a sugar-daddy *Santa Baby*. With orchestral backing by Henri Rene, it was a top-five hit in 1953 and it was the biggest hit in the career of this bluesy American-born singer.

Santa Claus is Coming To Town
Recorded by Bing Crosby and the Andrews Sisters in 1947
Music and lyrics by J. Fred (John Frederick) Coots and Henry Gillespie

The opening line, "You better watch out," is the attention-getting promise of a coming Christmas visit. Eddie Cantor originally preformed the bouncy and catchy melody on his radio show in 1934. It was one of the first pop hit Christmas songs and dozens of artists have recorded it.

Santo Natale
Recorded by David Whitfield in 1954
Music and lyrics by Dick Manning, Belle Nardone, and Al Hoffman

Popular British tenor David Whitfield had a top-ten hit recording with *Cara Mia* and a top-twenty hit with this Merry Christmas song in 1954. The accompaniment was by Stanley Black and his Orchestra. Patti Page also had a popular recording of the song.

Chart 8.1. Popular Christmas Recordings of the Post-War Era

(Chart continues on the next page)

Popular Christmas Recordings of the Post-War Era

(continued)

Silver Bells

Recorded by Bing Crosby and Carol Richards in 1953

Music and lyrics by Jay Livingston and Raymond Evans

Silver Bells was introduced by curvaceous Marilyn Maxwell and Bob Hope in the 1951 film 'The Lemon Drop Kid.' You can just visualize "shoppers rushing home with their treasures" on Bing Crosby's recording—he's teamed with Carol Richards, best known for dubbing vocals for MGM movie stars, like Cyd Charisse, in 1950s musical films.

Sleigh Ride

Recorded by the Boston Pops in 1949

Music by Leroy Anderson, lyrics by Mitchell Parish

Leroy Anderson's *Sleigh Ride* is a brisk Christmastime classic. Arthur Fiedler and the Boston Pops Orchestra, for whom Anderson was an arranger, first performed the song, delighting the audience recreating clip-clops, bells, and horse whinnies. Mitchell Parish provided the charming, homey, celebratory lyrics.

There's No Christmas Like a Home Christmas

Recorded by Perry Como in 1950 and again in 1968

Music and lyrics by Carl Sigman and Mickey J. Addy

Carl Sigman, who wrote the lyrics for *Marshmallow World*, describes the Yuletide spirit—Christmas bells ringing and roads leading home when you've been away. The record was the 'B' side of Perry Como's *It's Beginning to Look a Lot Like Christmas* with the Fontane Sisters. He re-recorded it in 1968, backed by the Ray Charles Singers.

White Christmas

Recorded by Bing Crosby in 1942

Music and lyrics by Irving Berlin

Every Christmas, Bing Crosby is heard singing *White Christmas*, the best selling record of all time. Written in 1942 for the film 'Holiday Inn' during World War II, *White Christmas* was so popular that it reappeared on the pop charts every December throughout the 1950s and sold more than 30 million copies.

White World of Winter

Recorded by Bing Crosby in 1964

Music and lyrics by Hoagy Carmichael and Mitchell Parish

Backed by Sonny Burke's orchestra, *White World of Winter* was one of Bing Crosby's last, one of his best, and most overlooked holiday recordings. He's having a wonderful time squeezin' in a toboggan, skating on Lake Happy, and skiing down Old Baldy. Writers Hoagy Carmichael and Mitchell Parish are best known for their classic *Stardust*.

Winter Wonderland

Recorded by Johnny Mathis in 1958

Music and lyrics by Felix Bernard and Richard B. Smith

Regarded as a Christmas song due to its seasonal theme, the holiday itself is never mentioned in the lyrics written in 1934 when parsons often traveled to small towns to perform wedding ceremonies. Guy Lombardo and Johnny Mercer also had hit records.

Chart 8.1. Popular Christmas Recordings of the Post-War Era

The best selling record of all time, *White Christmas*, first topped the charts in 1942. Bing Crosby introduced it in the film 'Holiday Inn.' His recording was so popular that it reappeared on the charts every December for twenty years. Its popularity was renewed when Bing Crosby, along with Danny Kaye, Rosemary Clooney, and Vera-Ellen reprised it in the 1955 musical 'White Christmas.' Not only did Bing Crosby's *White Christmas* top the charts each holiday season, so did his optimistic soldier boy lament *I'll Be Home for Christmas*.

Cowboy singer Gene Autry recorded the best-known version of *Here Comes Santa Claus* where he etched his own folksy, down-home pronunciation of 'Sanny Claus' in our minds. What is not so well known is that he also wrote the song. We don't think of Frank Sinatra as a songwriter either. "Yes, by gosh, by golly—it's time for mistletoe and holly" are the lyrics we remember from Frank Sinatra's recording of *Mistletoe and Holly* but we forget that he wrote the song as well.

Most prolific of post-war Christmas-song writers was Johnny Marks. He collaborated with his brother-in-law to create *Rudolph the Red-Nosed Reindeer* and went on to write *Rockin' Around the Christmas Tree, I Heard the Bells on Christmas Day,* and *Holly, Jolly Christmas.*

In 1952, Buddy Pepper and Inez James wrote the peppy Christmas song *Ol' Saint Nicholas* for Doris Day to sing at a Christmas family gathering in the Doris Day/Ronald Reagan baseball biopic 'The Winning Team.' Then, on her 1959 Christmas album, Doris Day released what many critics call the very best Christmas recording from the fifties, her gentle, dreamy *Toyland* from Victor Herbert's operetta 'Babes in Toyland.'

Record companies, capitalizing on the 33 $\frac{1}{3}$ rpm record format, had their singers assemble a dozen holiday favorites on a long-playing disc. Harry Belafonte, Tony Bennett, Rosemary Clooney, Nat King Cole, Connie Francis, Joni James, Dean Martin, Johnny Mathis, Patti Page, Elvis Presley, Frank Sinatra, and Andy Williams all recorded Christmas albums.

Dozens of post-war holiday songs are immediately recognizable but even more are nearly forgotten. English tenor David Whitfield and Patti Page both recorded *Santo Natale*. Irish tenor Dennis Day as well as Percy Faith's Orchestra with the Shillelagh Singers both recorded *Christmas in Killarney*. All four were successful in the fifties but rarely heard today. *You're All I Want for Christmas* was a top-twenty hit for Frankie Laine in 1948 and for Eddie Fisher in 1953—his version even prompted Betty Johnson's 1954 response record *I Want Eddie Fisher for Christmas*!

Some fifties Christmas recordings have virtually disappeared including Eddie Fisher's *Christmas Day*, the DeCastro Sisters' *Snowbound for Christmas*, Jimmy Dean's *Little Sandy Sleighfoot*, Jimmie Rodgers' *It's Christmas Once Again*, and the song *Christmas Alphabet* recorded by the McGuire Sisters and by Dickie Valentine in 1955. Still more obscure are Tommy Edwards' *Kris Kringle*, Ruby Wright's *Let's Light the Christmas Tree*, and Patti Page's *Where Did My Snowman Go*? Even Rosemary Clooney couldn't create a holiday classic with her recording of *Suzy Snowflake* nor with her version of the official 1954 Christmas Seal song *Happy Christmas Little Friend* written by Rodgers & Hammerstein.

The light-hearted fun of the Christmas season lent itself to the recording of several novelty tunes. In 1958, Liberty Records released *The Chipmunk Song – Christmas Don't Be Late* by David Seville and the Chipmunks. He had used the technique of recording voices at a slow speed and playing back at a higher speed in his novelty recording *Witch Doctor* the year before. In 1959, Dancer, Prancer, and Nervous released the similarly themed novelty record *Happy Reindeer*.

Earlier in the decade, eleven-year-old Gayla Peevey's *I Want a Hippopotamus for Christmas* made the top-twenty in 1953 and seven-year-old Barry Gordon sold two million copies of his top-ten hit *Nuttin for Christmas* in 1955. Harry Stewart called himself Yogi Yorgesson to record his top hits *I Yust Go Nuts at Christmas* and *Yingle Bells*.

Stan Freberg's bitingly satirical *Green Chritma*, was a merciless attack on merchandising. The parody of Dickens's 'A Christmas Carol,' had Scrooge as the head of a Madison Avenue advertising agency. Although tame today, at the time it was extremely controversial.

EASY-POP holiday songs continued to be popular well into the 1960s. Bing Crosby recorded *Do You Hear What I Hear* in 1963 and released *The White World of Winter* in 1965. Johnny Mathis recorded *Sounds of Christmas*, Andy Williams released *It's The Most Wonderful Time of the Year*, and Willie Nelson wrote and recorded the Christmas/country EASY-POP song *Pretty Paper* in the sixties. Jonathan Cain wrote *If Every Day Was Like Christmas* for his daughter's school Christmas play and Elvis Presley had a hit with it in 1966. Popular song writing team Sammy Cahn and Jule Styne wrote the graceful and sophisticated *Christmas Waltz* in the fifties, several singers recorded it during that decade, but they had to wait until Harry Connick Jr. released it in 2004 for it to be a top hit. While new holiday songs continue to be written and recorded, the Christmas season often revives the memorable and popular post-war hits.

Novelty Songs

Novelty songs were not limited to the holidays—any number of topics would lend themselves to novelty recordings during the fifties. It is difficult to provide a specific definition for a novelty song. The category includes songs that depend on nonsense syllables, plays-on-words, or unexpected misunderstandings of lyrics. Novelties can also include songs about imaginary creatures and childish human attributes to animals. The label 'novelty song' is a bit pejorative, it suggests music that amuses for just a moment and is then discarded. But memorable novelty recordings express a comic point of view with a longer lasting, universal appeal (see chart 8.2).

Novelty songs were not new in the fifties, they were just as popular, maybe more so, in the forties with: *Woody Woodpecker; Mairzy Doats; Jingle, Jangle, Jingle; I'm My Own Grandpa; Chickery Chick; 'A' You're Adorable; Huggin' and Chalkin'*; and *I'm a Lonely Little Petunia (in an onion patch)*. Zany Spike Jones and his City Slickers displayed their eccentric, eclectic style with hits including parodies of pop ballads *Cocktails for Two* and *Holiday for Strings* and, taking aim at Adolph Hitler, their clever, satirical *Der Fuehrer's Face*.

Novelty songs continued to be popular throughout the fifties, often resulting in a top-ten hit song. The Ames Brothers recording of *Naughty Lady of Shady Lane* leads the listener to believe that the song is about a 'loose woman' with phrases like "see the things they try to pin on her" and "she just needs someone to change her" when, in the last sentence of the song, it is revealed that they have been singing about a newborn baby.

Brilliant satirist Stan Freberg created several hit novelty records during the fifties including *John and Marsha* (a satirical look at radio soap operas); *St. George and the Dragonet* (based on the popular 'Dragnet' TV show); *The Yellow Rose of Texas* (a satire on Mitch Miller's hit recording, with a confounding snare drummer drowning out the chorus); *Banana Boat* (a take on Harry Belafonte's calypso hit *Day-O*); and *Wun'erful, Wun'erful* (a parody of popular bandleader Lawrence Welk).

Perry Como's *Delaware*, set to a martial beat and sounding like a marching song, is a clever use of the names of states asking questions like:

Popular Novelty Recordings of the 50s

Title	Artist	Year released	Highest chart rank
Rag Mop	Ames Brothers	1950	#1
(The) Thing	Phil Harris	1950	#1
If I knew You Were Comin'	Eileen Barton	1950	#1
I'd've Baked a Cake	Georgia Gibbs	1950	#5
Orange Colored Sky	Nat King Cole	1950	#5
Come On-A My House	Rosemary Clooney	1951	#1
Sweet Violets	Dinah Shore	1951	#3
John and Marsha	Stan Freberg	1951	#21
It's In the Book	Johnny Standley	1952	#1
(The) Doggie in the Window	Patti Page	1953	#1
St. George & the Dragonet	Stan Freberg	1953	#1
Purple Cow	Doris Day	1953	#25
This Ole House	Rosemary Clooney	1954	#1
Mr. Sandman	Chordettes	1954	#1
Somebody Bad Stole de Wedding	Eartha Kitt	1954	#16
Bell (Who's Got de Ding-Dong)	Georgia Gibbs	1954	#18
What It Was, Was Football	Andy Griffith	1954	#9
(The) Yellow Rose of Texas	Mitch Miller	1955	#1
(The) Yellow Rose of Texas (Parody)	Stan Freberg	1955	#16
Sixteen Tons (Work song)	Tennessee Ernie Ford	1955	#1
Naughty Lady of Shady Lane	Ames Brothers	1955	#3
Hot Diggity (Dog Ziggity Boom)	Perry Como	1956	#1
Witch Doctor	David Seville	1958	#1
(The) Purple People Eater	Sheb Wooley	1958	#1
Beep Beep	The Play-Mates	1958	#4
(The) Little Blue Man	Betty Johnson	1958	#17
Short Shorts	The Royal Teens	1958	#3
(The) Three Bells	The Browns	1959	#1
Mr. Custer	Larry Verne	1960	#1
Delaware	Perry Como	1960	#22

Chart 8.2. Popular Novelty Recordings of the 50s

What did Della wear? (She wore a brand New Jersey); and What did Misa sip? (She sipped a Minni soda). It was written by tunesmith Irving Gordon, who wrote the Abbott and Costello comedy routine 'Who's on First?' decades earlier. Doris Day's *I Said My Pajamas and I Put on My Prayers* was another song based on a play-on-words.

Both Eartha Kitt and Georgia Gibbs had a top-twenty hit with the same novelty song *Somebody Bad Stole de Wedding Bell (Who's Got de Ding Dong)* in 1954. Extraterrestrials, popular in films and TV shows in the fifties, were also the subject of several novelty songs including *The Thing, The Little Blue Man,* and *The Purple People Eater.* All three recordings made the top-twenty during the decade.

Spoken Word Recordings

In addition to the novelty records there were a series of 'talking' or 'spoken word' recordings released during the fifties. In this genre, the artist would deliver the lyrics/dialog in a speaking voice, backed by an appropriate orchestral arrangement and chorus. While novelty songs tend to be light, amusing, and irreverent, spoken word recordings tend to be more serious, personal, and sentimental (see chart 8.3).

Shifting, Whispering Sands was so successful in 1955 that two different versions made the top-five. Searching for the secrets of the settlers and miners in the desert, it tells of the mystery known only to the shifting, whispering sands. If you want to know the secret—listen to the sands. Country singer, Rusty Draper's version climbed to #3 on the charts and Billy Vaughn and his orchestra with narration by Ken Nordine, the 'guru of word jazz,' reached #5 in the same year.

The Three Stars was a tribute to the three young singers, Buddy Holly, Richie Valens, and the Big Bopper who were killed in a tragic plane accident near Mason City, Iowa on February 3, 1959. *The Three Stars* was released a month later. The most popular version had narration by Tommy Dee and singing by Carol Kay and the Teen-Aires.

Old Rivers was a huge hit for veteran film character actor, Walter Brennen. The three-time Academy Award winner appeared in more than 100 motion pictures. On the TV show 'The Real McCoys' (1957-1963), he

Popular Spoken Word Recordings of the 50s and 60s

Title	Artist	Year released	Highest chart rank
Shifting, Whispering Sands	Rusty Draper	1955	#3
Shifting, Whispering Sands	Billy Vaughn's orchestra Narration: Ken Nordine	1955	#5
What Is a Wife	Steve Allen	1955	#56
(The) **Ship That Never Sailed**	David Carroll	1957	#65
(The) **Ship That Never Sailed**	Billy Vaughn's orchestra Narration: Ken Nordine	1957	#95
What Is a Teenage Girl?	Tom Edwards	1957	#57
What Is a Teenage Boy?	Tom Edwards	1957	#96
Ten Commandments of Love	Harvey & the Moonglows	1958	#22
(The) **Teen Commandments**	Paul Anka, George Hamilton, and Johnny Nash	1959	#29
(The) **Three Stars**	Tommy Dee	1959	#11
(The) **Three Stars**	Ruby Wright	1959	#99
Big Bad John	Jimmy Dean	1961	#1
Old Rivers	Walter Brennan	1962	#5
P.T. 109	Jimmy Dean	1962	#8
Ten Commandments of Love	James MacArthur	1963	#94
(The) **Men in My Little Girl's Life**	Mike Douglas	1966	#6
Gallant Men	Senator Everett Dirksen	1966	#29
We Love You, Call Collect	Art Linkletter	1969	#42

Chart 8.3.   Popular Spoken Word Recordings of the 50s and 60s

was Grandpa, the porch-rockin', gol-darnin', consarnin' old codger with the wheezy voice. *Old Rivers* is the story of a close relationship between a dog and an old man. His "Old Rivers and me" recording placed in the top-five in 1962.

Jimmy Dean's 1962 recording *P.T. 109* was an account of president John F. Kennedy's 1943 heroism in World War II after his torpedo boat was destroyed. Even politicians like the gravely voiced United States Senator from Illinois, Everett McKinley Dirksen, released spoken word recordings. *Gallant Men,* an ultra patriotic salute to the United States Armed Forces, was a top-thirty hit in December of 1966.

Instrumental Hits

For a decade that favored vocalists, the 1950s still welcomed instrumental music. The range of styles included Anton Karas' zither and Les Paul's electric guitar. Keyboard artists included Julliard-trained pianist Roger Williams, honky tonk pianist Joe 'Fingers' Carr, and happy organist Dave 'Baby' Cortez.

As the vocalists began to dominate popular music, big bands began a significant reduction in the size of their rosters to survive economically in the post-war years. Bebop with its small combos and lack of traditional pop structure took off from mainstream swing in one direction, while rhythm 'n' blues and all its components took off in another direction leading inevitably to rock 'n' roll. Still, rather than isolate certain musical styles as 'out of the mainstream' the decade of the 50s seemed open to anything and everything—and that's just what it got (see chart 8.4).

Stan Kenton, with instrumental hits in the forties and fifties including *Laura* in 1951, was one of the first to add violins in his arrangements, blurring the distinction between a band and an orchestra. Les Baxter's fiddle-laden *Poor People of Paris (Jean's Song)* was a #1 hit in the mid-fifties.

Music from south of the boarder, Latin, tango, and mambo rhythms, became the latest-hot-thing in fifties instrumental pop music. Les Baxter's *April in Portugal* had a cha-cha rhythm and Cuban bandleader Perez Prado's exhilarating brass punctuated *Cherry Pink and Apple Blossom White.*

Popular Instrumental Recordings of the 50s

Title	Artist	Year Released	Highest chart rank
(The) Third Man Theme	Anton Karas	1950	#1
	Guy Lombardo	1950	#1
Laura	Stan Kenton & orchestra	1951	#12
Blue Tango	Leroy Anderson & orchestra	1951	#1
Delicado	Percy Faith	1952	#1
April in Portugal	Les Baxter & orchestra	1953	#2
(The) Song from 'Moulin Rouge'	Percy Faith with Felicia Sanders	1953	#1
(The) High and the Mighty	Les Baxter & orchestra	1954	#4
Melody of Love	Billy Vaughn	1955	#2
Cherry Pink & Apple Blossom White	Perez Prado & orchestra	1955	#1
Unchained Melody	Les Baxter	1955	#1
Autumn Leaves	Roger Williams	1955	#1
Lisbon Antigua	Nelson Riddle	1956	#1
(The) Poor People of Paris	Les Baxter & orchestra	1956	#1
Moonglow/ Theme from 'Picnic'	Morris Stoloff	1956	#1
Man With the Golden Arm	Richard Maltby	1956	#14
Portuguese Washerwomen	Joe 'Fingers' Carr	1956	#19
Around the World in 80 Days	Mantovani	1957	#12
So Rare	Jimmy Dorsey	1957	#2
Patricia	Perez Prado	1958	#1
Manhattan Spiritual	Reg Owen	1958	#10
(The) Happy Organ	Dave 'Baby' Cortez	1959	#1
Quiet Village	Martin Denny	1959	#4
(Theme from) A Summer Place	Percy Faith	1960	#1

Chart 8.4.   Popular Instrumental Recordings of the 50s

Martin Denny brought exotic sounds, offering unusual explorations of music from foreign lands. In his *Quiet Village,* birdcalls and resonant vibes placed sounds of the jungle into a jazzy palatable setting. Les Paul popularized a dense sound created by overdubbing his electric guitar and overdubbing the vocals from his wife, Mary Ford. Percy Faith, Nelson Riddle, and Billy Vaughn brought their talents as arrangers to instrumental hit recordings of their own.

Inclusive 50s EASY-POP

The variations in 50s EASY-POP songs show how inclusive the field was for music that could appeal to a wide broadcast audience. Listening to a typical popular AM radio station you would hear the popular singers and EASY-POP songs interspersed with novelty songs, instrumental hits, choral ensembles like the Norman Luboff Choir, the Harry Simeone Chorale, the Ray Conniff Singers, and Mitch Miller and his Gang, as well as the occasional 'spoken word' record. This was the time in broadcast history when radio stations were indeed mass media, appealing to a general audience, before the appearance of narrowcasting (labeling stations by music format: Adult Contemporary, Urban, Rock, Rhythmic, etc.) and segregating the audience by age.

The 1950s would be the last decade in which quiet musical arrangements could compete with their noisier counterparts for the attention of the masses. The sixties would change all that.

References from Chapter 8:

Menendez, Albert and Shirley Menendez. *Christmas Songs Made in America*. Nashville, Tennessee: Cumberland House Publishing, 1999.

Simon, William, editor. *The Reader's Digest Merry Christmas Songbook*. Pleasantville, New York: The Reader's Digest Association, 1981.

Whitburn, Joel. *Christmas in the Charts, 1920-2004*. Cincinnati, Ohio: Billboard Books, 2004.

Music arouses in us various emotions, but not the more terrible ones of horror, fear, rage, etc. It awakens rather the gentler feelings of tenderness and love...it likewise stirs up in us the sense of triumph.

Charles Darwin in *The Descent of Man* (1871)

Chapter 9

50 Fabulous, all-but-forgotten, EASY-POP Songs

Chapter 3 presented more than a hundred of the biggest hits of the 1950s. This chapter examines fifty, single-release, 45rpm records that should have been big hits but most people have never heard them. These EASY-POP songs are just as good, many think they are better, than the more popular recordings, but are comparatively unknown. Not to be excluded are the all-but-forgotten songs recorded on long-playing 33 $^1/_3$ rpm albums. They are described in the next chapter. This chapter uncovers 45rpm singles—fifty fantastic EASY-POP gems from the 1950s just waiting to be discovered.

Contemporary artists like Michael Buble, Harry Connick Jr., Michael Feinstein, Martina McBride, Mandy Patinkin, Linda Rondstat, Frank Stallone, and Rod Stewart often capture the feeling, sound, and style of the fifties songs in new recordings. It is a pleasure to hear today's singers bring a fresh recording and a new voice to EASY-POP songs. But, it is especially exciting and delightful to discover a great 50s EASY-POP song that is 'new-to-you.' These songs, that were actually recorded by a fifties singer in the fifties, are just waiting to be recognized.

Forgotten 45rpm Singles, recorded in the 1950s, that should-have-been Smash Hits

The pace of life was slower in the fifties: there seemed to be more time, music was easy to listen to, to daydream to, and to relax to. Life was easier—driving around town with the radio on, going to the local hangout, putting change into the jukebox, and listening to the latest hits—without a care in the world. The familiar as well as the forgotten EASY-POP music of the fifties reflects that period in time.

Why didn't these great recordings become chart-topping hits? Most likely it was because the song did not get much radio airplay and the potential audience did not get to hear it. *Wonderful! Wonderful!* was Johnny Mathis' first record and DJs had not yet heard of him. Jaye P. Morgans' *If You Don't Want My Love* was one of her last recordings and DJs thought her style was no longer fresh. Elvis Presley's *You're So Square* was overlooked because it was in the same film as the more obvious commercial hits *Teddy Bear* and the title song *Jailhouse Rock*.

The popularity of EASY-POP music peaked before its creative style peaked—rock 'n' roll was beginning to dominate the popularity charts. Perfected sound and outstanding arrangements of the late fifties EASY-POP era produced amazing recordings but they were not always popular successes. There are probably as many reasons for a recording's limited popularity as there are songs, sometimes it was just a matter of unfavorable timing of the record's release, sometimes a recording was relegated to the 'B' side of the 45rpm record where it got lost, maybe the A&R men were pushing something else, or another recording or event eclipsed it.

The underappreciated gems in this chapter were culled from collections of old 45s and researched in obscure publications. Recordings were discovered on new CD compilations, which include a complete discography of every recording from a particular vocalist. In the fifties, singers recorded huge catalogs of songs. During her recording career at Columbia records, Doris Day recorded more than 500 songs. Frank Sinatra recorded 400 at Capitol, and still more at Bluebird, Columbia, and Reprise—many estimate his total at more than 1300 recordings. Dean Martin, Rosemary Clooney, and Perry Como also recorded hundreds of songs. Only a very small percentage of these recordings became #1 hits.

Frank Sinatra and Tony Bennett are instantly recognizable around the world, but even these singers released EASY-POP records that weren't major hits. A handful of other popular male singers in the fifties, Nat King Cole, Perry Como, Sam Cooke, Vic Damone, Bobby Darin, Eddie Fisher, Buddy Holly, Dean Martin, Johnny Mathis, Elvis Presley, Johnnie Ray, and Andy Williams contributed to this list of all-but-forgotten, should-have-been-hits. The list also includes less well known singers that never made the top of the charts—Tommy Edwards, Jerry Keller, and Julius LaRosa—and a couple of outstanding recordings are from male singers that never even managed to become one-hit-wonders—Garry Miles, Garry Mills, Nick Nobel, and Don Rondo.

Doris Day was the most popular box-office movie star of the early fifties. Teresa Brewer, Joni James, Jaye P. Morgan, Kay Starr, and Patti Page had dozens of #1 hit songs in the fifties. These girl singers recorded scores of songs and on occasion an outstanding song failed to become a hit. Some of the girl singers are less well known—Pearl Bailey, Eydie Gorme, Eartha Kitt, Jane Morgan, Debbie Reynolds, June Valli, and Sarah Vaughan. They did release hit songs, but it is their less-well-known recordings that are described here. Many of the girl singers and their songs may be totally unfamiliar—Toni Arden, Gale Storm, Betty Johnson, Peggy King, and Margie Rayburn—but they did record fascinating songs that contributed to this list of all-but-forgotten, should-have-been-hits.

Duets flourished in the fifties. Brothers like the Kalin twins and sisters like Patience & Prudence and Rosemary & Betty Clooney released great records during the decade. In addition, almost every studio had their popular singers like Guy Mitchell & Mindy Carson and Tony Martin & Dinah Shore pair up to double the appeal of their releases. Many duets were successful, but some should-have-been-hit recordings never reached the top-ten.

Audiences loved the freshly pressed, starched, and smiling trios and quartets. Vocal groups who recorded all-but-forgotten songs were very popular—the Ames Brothers, the Chordettes, the Crew-Cuts, the Four Aces, the Four Lads, the Mills Brothers, and the McGuire Sisters. Less well-known groups like the Four Preps, the Poni-Tails, and the Teen Queens and virtual unknowns like the Play-Mates all recorded should-have-been-hits too. Fifty fantastic, all-but-forgotten, should-have-been-hit songs are shown in chart 9.1 on the next page.

Fifty Fabulous-but-Forgotten,
EASY-POP Songs from the Fifties

Chart 9.1.   Fifty Fabulous-but-Forgotten EASY-POP Songs from the Fifties
(Chart continues on the next page)

Fifty Fabulous-but-Forgotten
EASY-POP Songs from the Fifties (continued)

Chart 9.1.   Fifty Fabulous-but-Forgotten EASY-POP Songs from the Fifties

The next 25 pages detail information on fifty fantastic, all-but-forgotten, should-have-been-smash-hit songs. There is a description of each of the 50s EASY-POP recordings and the artist. Following that is a list of dozens of additional ALMOST-AS-GREAT recordings.

Criteria for choosing the should-have-been hits

Choosing the should-have-been hit songs for this book is subjective and there are undoubtedly oversights. Three criteria were used to select these fabulous-but-forgotten, should-have-been-hit songs: (1) The singer had to be easy-to-listen-to; (2) The arrangement had to be bright; and (3) the lyric had to be infectious.

The Quintessence of the Singer

An EASY-POP singer has to possess a mellifluous voice and display essential 50s qualities: light, fun, personable, easy-to-like.

The Uniqueness of the Sound

The musical arrangement had to typify the contagious, bright fifties sound and essential beat. Some of the sounds in this list are fresh and unique while others are more polished examples of classic fifties music. Unusual instruments, orchestral flourishes, and outstanding background singers support the vocalist on each of these selections.

The Quintessential Fifties Imagery and the Cleverness of the Lyric

Sing-along words to a song were important—the infectious lyrics had to be clever with easy-to-remember, simple rhymes that the audience could relate to. The records on this list contain lyrics that are typically fifties.

The following fifty recordings represent outstanding, quintessential fifties singers, songs, and sounds that are virtually unknown. Some may be vaguely familiar, some you might recall when you hear them, but some are guaranteed to be absolute gems that you've never heard before.

Anywhere I Wander recorded by Tony Bennett
with orchestra directed by Percy Faith,
background vocals by the Ray Charles Singers

Written by Frank Loesser
Recorded: August 26, 1951, on Columbia records #48153

(Length 2:57)

The glowing intensity of Tony Bennett's vocal artistry was never on better display than in this intriguing, without-you-my-heart-will-have-no-home, lyrical ballad. The Ray Charles Singers (not to be confused with Ray Charles, the great soul singer of the same name) open this record with a dramatic flourish. *Anywhere I Wander* was written for the 1952 film 'Hans Christian Andersen' and performed in the film by Danny Kaye. A recording of the song by Mel Torme appeared in the top-forty in 1952 and Julius LaRosa's version made the top-ten in 1953. Tony Bennett's convincing, stylish version made the song spring to life, but unfortunately, it did not place in the top-forty. He did have a remarkable string of #1 hits in the fifties including *Because of You, Cold, Cold Heart,* and *Rags to Riches*; he flooded show tunes like his hit recording of *Stranger in Paradise*, with warmth and spontaneity; but his expressive, top-flight single of the 50s *Anywhere I Wander* is rarely heard.

Down By The Station recorded by the Four Preps

Written by Bruce Belland and Glen Larson
Introduced December 28, 1959, on Capitol records #4312

(Length 2:45)

The clean-cut, milk-fed-looking Four Preps had huge hits with *26 Miles (Santa Catalina)* and *Big Man*, but in spite of their collegiate appearance and four-part vocal harmonies, one of their consummate recordings, *Down by the Station,* never made it into the top-ten. The recording, written by two members of the group, grabs with a unique guitar and bass sound at the start and expresses a young guy's carefree, 'clever-fella' attitude as he juggles his third girlfriend but she gets the last word telling him that if he wasn't true to his other two girlfriends he won't be true to her. On a more distinctive note, *Down by the Station* is undoubtedly the only 50s pop song to include the words 'malt-shop' and 'puffer-bellies' in the same song. Brian Wilson's harmony-driven production for the Beach Boys in the 1960s was a direct antecedent of the Four Preps' sound.

Gonna Get Along Without Ya Now
recorded by Patience & Prudence
with the Mark McIntyre Orchestra

Written by Milton Kellem
Introduced December 1, 1956, on Liberty records #55040

(Length 1:55)

Beguiling, young teenage sisters Patience and Prudence McIntyre had a top-five hit in the summer of 1956 with their first recording *Tonight You Belong To Me;* later in the same year they released the more adolescent *Gonna Get Along Without Ya Now.* The callow I-didn't-love-you-anyhow attitude in the lyric befits the sister's pre-adolescent harmony, and Liberty Records, Si Waronker, added overdubs to strengthen their ethereal vocals. Their father, orchestra leader Mark McIntyre's arrangement begins with the sisters' chanting "mm, mm, my honey; mm, mm my dear; gonna get along without ya now" and between verses, it incorporates a plucked violin bridge that suits the plucky young sisters who claim that they "got along without ya before I met ya" and they'll "get along without ya now" besides that, they're gonna find "someone twice as cute." So there!

Here Comes Summer recorded by Jerry Keller

Written by Jerry Paul Keller
Introduced June 29, 1959, on Kapp records #277

(Length 2:08)

Singer/songwriter Jerry Keller's *Here Comes Summer* is the epitome of a young guy's idea of summer vacation in the fifties with double-feature movies at drive-in theaters. His light, easy voice, like Frankie Avalon's and Pat Boone's, is perfect for this bright, upbeat, optimistic song. The finger-snapping arrangement with a "do-do, do-do" chorus and organ accompaniment suits the sing-along fantasies: "swimming every day," "summer's better than school," and "more time to hold my girl." *Here Comes Summer* was Jerry Keller's only recording to ever appear on Billboard's top 100 chart. It may have made his flat top curl but the refreshing and idealistic *Here Comes Summer* never made it into the top-ten. Jerry Keller was born in 1937 in Fort Smith, Arkansas, moved to Tulsa, Oklahoma, and attended the University of Tulsa. In addition to *Here Comes Summer*, he wrote *Almost There*, Andy Williams' 1964 hit featured in the film 'I'd Rather Be Rich.'

I Dreamed recorded by Betty Johnson
with Lew Douglas and his Orchestra

Written by Charles Grean and Marvin Moore
Introduced November 24, 1956, on Bally records #1020

(Length 2:04)

Betty Johnson, born in North Carolina in 1931, was a regular performer on the original NBC-TV 'Tonight Show' starring Jack Paar. *I Dreamed* was her biggest hit even though it barely edged into the top-ten in 1956. Her husband, musical conductor Charles Randolph Grean, and Marvin Moore wrote the song for her in an episode of the NBC TV daytime series 'Modern Romances.' Betty Johnson's wholesome personality suited this fluffy song about a young girl's dream of being a queen who abdicates her throne for her true love. It begins with a male chorus repeating "dream on little girl, dream on little girl" and as her dream progresses, the background singers, repeat the catchy refrain "Knights in armor, princes, kings, buccaneers, and wedding rings." The song ends with her upbeat belief that she would be the queen of the world and all of her dreams would come true if only the boy in her dreams would choose her. In 1954, she recorded an amusing, top-forty, holiday song, *I Want Eddie Fisher for Christmas*, and scored a modest hit in 1958 with another novelty song, *The Little Blue Man*.

I Understand recorded by June Valli
with Hugo Winterhalter's Orchestra and Chorus

Written by Pat Best
Introduced, June 12, 1954, on RCA Victor records #5740

(Length 2:24)

As church bells peel and the chorus chimes "bumm, bumm, bumm" a most understanding June Valli can't bear to watch her love walk away. Hugo Winterhalter's arrangement conjures up a church-like ambiance to accompany this desperate plea from a woman rejected, but not ready to give up on her man if he would change his mind and come back to her. With all it had going for it in 1954, *I Understand* did not find the popularity of her surprisingly similar 1953 recording *Crying In The Chapel*. In 1958, in still another church setting, June Valli's recording of *The Wedding* placed 43rd on the charts. June Valli's version of *I Understand* was a cover of the original recording by the R&B group the Four Tunes. The G-Clefs recorded *I Understand* in 1961 as did Freddie & the Dreamers in 1965.

I'll Take Romance recorded by Eydie Gorme
arranged & conducted by Don Costa

Written by Ben Oakland and Oscar Hammerstein II
Introduced April 13, 1957, on ABC-Paramount records #9780

(Length 2:22)

In spite of her television exposure and immense popularity, Eydie Gorme never had a top-ten hit in the 1950s—the only top-ten recording in her career was *Blame It On the Bossa Nova* in 1963. Although she gives her young, eager, and gay heart away in *I'll Take Romance*, it never even broke into the top-fifty. The scintillating, Don Costa arranged, recording gets off to a finger snapping start and her bright, warm voice sparkles from the first note. Her histrionic vocal range is impressive as she closes the record with "I'll...take...roma...a...a...a...a...a...nce." She combines her bubbly personality and youthful zest with an excellent vocal quality and secure intonation. Faring only slightly better was her 1956 recording, *Too Close for Comfort* from the Broadway musical 'Mr. Wonderful' also arranged by Don Costa. During the mid-fifties, Eydie Gorme appeared regularly on the original NBC-TV 'Tonight Show' with host Steve Allen.

I'm Available recorded by Margie Rayburn

Written by Dave Burgess
Introduced October 28, 1957, on Liberty records #55102

(Length 1:50)

The dual track recording technique that was popular throughout the fifties has Margie Rayburn, whose voice is somewhat reminiscent of Teresa Brewer's, singing with herself on her recording of *I'm Available (and willing—it's true)*. The arrangement opens with Margie Rayburn warbling the song's signature trill "dewey, do...we, dewey, do; dewey, do...we, dewey, do." Her clipped delivery gives the word 'willing' just one syllable 'w-ling' but then she extends 'you' into the three syllables with a high-pitched middle syllable, 'you^{-OO-}oo,' she also expands 'to' into 'to^{-OO-}oo,' and 'love' into 'luh^{-UH-}ove.' *I'm Available* was written and originally recorded by Dave Burgess of The Champs, an instrumental group who had a #1 hit in 1958 with *Tequila*. It was Margie Rayburn's only recording to be listed on Billboard's top 100 charts; it just edged into the top-ten in 1957. Margie Rayburn, born in 1924 in Madera, California, was a vocalist with Ray Anthony's Orchestra and she was a member of the vocal group, The Sunnysiders, who had a hit with *Hey, Mr. Banjo* in 1955.

If Only I Could Live My Life Again by Jane Morgan
with orchestra directed by Vic Schoen

Written by Louis Amade, Pierre Delanoe, Gilbert Becaud (French lyrics),
and Elly Leighton (English lyrics)
Introduced May 16, 1959, on Kapp records #K-253X

(Length 1:57)

With her caressing voice, versatile Jane Morgan's most popular song
Fascination made the top-ten in 1957. She had other hits in the late
fifties with *Two Different Worlds, The Day the Rains Came, With Open
Arms,* and *Happy Anniversary.* In her powerful recording of *If Only I
Could Live My Life Again,* she draws on a wealth of womanly
understanding to interpret the lyrics. With disarming sincerity she sings
about avoiding mistakes in her life and a desire to be more forgiving if
she were given another chance, but while she would make many changes
in her life, she would never change her love for her sweetheart. Elegant
Jane Morgan is often described as having moonlight in her voice and in
this recording the sophisticated, American-born, singer conveys her
acquired European polish. *If Only I Could Live My Life Again* never
made the top 100 in the United States, but was a top-twenty hit in
England.

If You Don't Want My Love recorded by Jaye P. Morgan
with Hugo Winterhalter's Orchestra and Chorus

Written by Albert Von Tilzer and George Brown
Introduced November 12, 1955, on RCA Victor records #6282

(Length 2:44)

Just like her million-selling first session recording *That's All I Want
From You,* her equally classic performance a year later in *If You Don't
Want My Love (I know one who will)* benefits from Hugo Winterhalter's
brilliant arrangement. In spite of its similarity, or maybe because of it, *If
You Don't Want My Love* never scored above #40 on the charts. Her
distinctive, husky, yet crystal clear voice and background singers
repeating "If you don't want my love" makes this a must-hear 50s song.
It was the 'B' side of her top-twenty hit *Pepper-Hot Baby.* In the early
fifties, RCA Victor was looking for a female singer to balance their
mostly male roster of Perry Como, Tony Martin, and Eddie Fisher.
Colorado native Jaye P. Morgan filled the bill. In addition to her solo
hits, she recorded duets with RCA stars Perry Como (*Two Lost Souls*)
and country singer Eddy Arnold (*Mutual Admiration Society*).

In the Cool, Cool, Cool of the Evening
recorded by Bing Crosby & Jane Wyman
with Matty Matlock's All Stars Orchestra
background vocals by The 4 Hits & A Miss

Written by Hoagy Carmichael and Johnny Mercer
Introduced August 4, 1951, on Decca records #27678

(Length 3:27)

The most popular crooner of all time, Bing Crosby, released two duets from his 1950s films. His duet with Grace Kelly, *True Love*, from the smash MGM musical film 'High Society' climbed to #3 and remained on the charts for six months in 1956-57. But earlier in the decade, his academy award winning duet, *In the Cool, Cool, Cool of the Evening*, with actress Jane Wyman, from the engaging 'Here Comes the Groom' produced and directed by Frank Capra, was not so successful. In spite of everything this hip, Academy-Award winning, shank-of-the-night, doins-are-right duet had going for it, it never made it into the top-ten. Film actress/singer Jane Wyman co-starred with Bing Crosby in two 50s comedies 'Here Comes the Groom' and 'Just for You.' She won an academy award in 1948 for 'Johnny Belinda' and was the first wife of fellow actor and U.S. President, Ronald Reagan.

Jamie Boy recorded by Kay Starr
with Hugo Winterhalter's Orchestra and Chorus

Written by Joe Shapiro and Lou Stallman
Introduced April 20, 1957, on RCA Victor records #6864

(Length 2:07)

Kay Starr's successful three-decade recording career began and ended at Capitol Records, but between 1955 and 1959, she recorded *Rock and Roll Waltz, My Heart Reminds Me,* and the exciting and dynamic *Jamie Boy* at RCA. *(My) Jamie Boy* is a uniquely constructed, fast paced recording with an energetic chorus chanting 'by-by-ou-bop' while Kay Starr's crystal clear voice asks Jamie Boy why he is walking all alone, unaware that she is longing for him. It was a fresh and beguiling song, but even with its propulsive arrangement, Kay Starr's *Jamie Boy (walking by the water)* did not make much of a splash—never breaking into the top-fifty. She did strike gold during the early fifties with *Bonaparte's Retreat, Hoop-Dee-Doo, If You Love Me (Really Love Me),* and her platinum slice of 50s pop, *Wheel of Fortune.*

Jilted recorded by Teresa Brewer
with orchestra conducted by Jack Pleis

Written by Robert Colby and Dick Manning
Introduced April 24, 1954, on Coral records #61152

(Length 2:10)

Typically Teresa Brewer—coquettish and bouncy—*Jilted,* parlays a very fifties expression into a very catchy song. On fast and breezy recordings like her big hit *Ricochet* in 1953, her *You'll Never Get Away* duet with Don Cornell, and here again in *Jilted* she displays her wide vocal range and simple, carefree, but controlled high pitch clips. The technique is employed most effectively in *Jilted* on her piercing snip of the word 'hot' in the phrase "even though our ^{HOT} romance has wilted." According to this jaunty recording, she's been jilted, but claims that two can play that game as well as one and now she's happy that he jilted her. It is every bit as good as her earlier #1 hits *Music, Music, Music,* recorded when she was barely 19 years old, *Till I Waltz Again with You,* and *Ricochet,* but the song did not break into the top-five for 'sweet old fashioned girl' Teresa Brewer; neither did two of her other lively, up-tempo recordings, *Bell-Bottom Blues* and *Silver Dollar.*

(The) Jones Boy recorded by the Mills Brothers
with orchestra directed by Sy Oliver

Written by Vic Mizzy and Mann Curtis
Introduced December 19, 1953, on Decca records #28945

(Length 2:53)

It's easy to associate the Mills Brothers with their 1940s recordings: *Paper Doll, You Always Hurt the One You Love, Till Then,* and *Someday (You'll Want Me to Want You).* But when Sy Oliver, the renowned arranger for Jimmie Lunceford and Tommy Dorsey, became the Mills Brothers' arranger in 1951, a rocking beat was injected into some of their songs and it is as timely today as it was when they created it. They had a huge hit in 1952 with *The Glow Worm* and followed it with *The Jones Boy (The buzzin' over the fence is, that he's goin' out of his senses).* It is very much a fifties song, arranged with a fifties beat and musical stabs. According to the lyrics, the whole town is talking about *The Jones Boy* who happens to be in love but this recording never made it into the top-ten on the charts. The Mills Brothers' Latin-tinged recording *Say "Si Si"* in 1953 did not break into the top-ten either.

Lay Down Your Arms recorded by the Chordettes

Written by Leon Land, Ake Gerhard (Swedish lyrics), and
Paddy Roberts (English lyrics)
Introduced September 29, 1956, on Cadence records #1299

(Length 2:26)

Between their top-ten recordings of *Mr. Sandman* in 1954 and the pop music classic *Lollypop* in 1958, the Chordettes, with their characteristic close, smooth harmony, and full round-like arrangements, recorded *Lay Down Your Arms (and Surrender to Mine)*. This march-at-the-double-down-lover's-lane recording included all the bounce, zest, and lively harmonizing that makes the Chordettes one of the most famous and renowned girl groups in fifties music history. However, this record with its clever soldier-boy theme and lively military-inspired arrangement, never managed to climb above sixteenth place in the charts. The original Swedish title of *Lay Down Your Arms* was *Ann-Caroline*. The Chordettes, made up of Janet Ertel, Carol Buschman, Lynn Evans, and Margie Needham, stood apart from other 'girl' barbershop quartets from the beginning in that they had a true bass singer—petit Janet Ertel—and a skilled arranger, Archie Bleyer, Janet Ertel's husband.

Learning to Love recorded by Peggy King
with Jimmy Carroll and his Orchestra

Written by John Harper
Introduced November 12, 1955, on Columbia records #4-40562

(Length 2:25)

The breathtaking pace and driving beat of *Learning to Love* was a departure from the traditional standards associated with Peggy King. The striking arrangement begins with a hollow-body electric jazz guitar setting the tone for the recording. *Learning to Love (Be Kind to Me)* should have been a smash hit. The juxtaposition of a very fifties lyric, the jazz/rock arrangement, and Peggy King's vibrant voice came together in this unique take-it-slow-it's-my-first-time record that, unfortunately, never even made it into the top-fifty. A slot on self-effacing comedian, George Gobel's television variety show earned her an Emmy nomination in 1955. He labeled her 'pretty, perky, Peggy King.' A popular Hunt's tomato sauce jingle led to a contract with Columbia, where she scored her biggest solo success, *Make Yourself Comfortable* early in 1955. Both Downbeat and Billboard magazines selected her as the Best New Singer of 1955-56.

Look for a Star recorded by Garry Mills
(also recorded by Garry Miles aka Buzz Cason)
with orchestra conducted by Muir Mathieson

Written by Mark Anthony (also known as Tony Hatch)
Introduced June 20, 1960 on Imperial records #5674

(Length 2:10)

The rippling arrangement in *Look for a Star* sets up Garry Mills' smooth and easy, almost non-descript, tenor vocal. Only the flourish at the end of each refrain "someone to love" where the word 'love' becomes the lilting, three syllable word 'luh-^{uh}-uhv' gives any personal touch to the lyrics. *Look for a Star (Where there's a friend waiting to guide you)* was featured in American International Pictures' suspense film 'Circus of Horrors' and sung as background music during a circus rope ballet. This fascinating record never made it into the top-twenty for original British artist Garry Mills. A second, nearly identical, version of *Look for a Star* by similarly named American, Garry Miles, and released on London records on the same date, reached 16th place. Garry Miles was a contrived name for singer/songwriter Buzz Cason who, in 1967, co-wrote the hit *Everlasting Love*. Both Garry Mills and Garry Miles were 'one-hit-wonders' never releasing another successful record.

Look Homeward Angel recorded by Johnnie Ray
with Ray Conniff and his Orchestra and Chorus

Written by Wally Gold
Introduced January 26, 1957, on Columbia records #40803

(Length 2:47)

Johnnie Ray's passionate, soulful vocal style with R&B influences was captured most faithfully in *Look Homeward Angel*. Trumpets and a chorus set the mood, Johnnie begins softly by asking an angel to kiss his lost love while she's dreaming, the song and the arrangement continue to build and the recording ends on an emotional, if-she-still-yearns-for-me-then-homeward-I-must-go, high. His similar but adolescent lost-love emotion-packed laments, *Just Walking in the Rain* and *Please Mr. Sun* were top-ten hits, but the more mature *Look Homeward Angel*, the 'B' side of *You Don't Owe Me a Thing*, never made it into the top-twenty. A later 1957 recording, *Build Your Love (on a Strong Foundation)*, a jaunty, rousing romp for Johnnie Ray failed to make the top-fifty. Partially deaf since childhood his first hit, the two-sided *Cry* and *The Little White Cloud That Cried* sold more than two million copies in 1951.

Love Me in the Daytime   recorded by Doris Day
with Frank DeVol and his Orchestra

Written by Bob Hilliard and Robert Allen
Recorded January 12, 1959, on Columbia records #4-41354

(Length 2:47)

Doris Day scored big hits with *A Guy is a Guy, Secret Love, Que Sera, Sera,* and *Everybody Loves a Lover.* But she also recorded several fabulous, flirty, carefree, light-hearted but less popular songs like *Kissin' My Honey, Oh What a Lover You'll Be, Anyway the Wind Blows,* and *Another Go 'Round.* The delightful and enthusiastic *Love Me in the Daytime* (that spent just a week on the popularity charts at position #100) is typical of the fresh, inviting shuffle rhythms so often associated with Doris Day and it is just plain fun to listen to. Her sincere approach, the attractive timbre in her voice, and the glee in her delivery can be heard in this playful I-can't-get-enough-of-you plea. Doris Day was always a very expressive singer who could act out a lyric without losing sight of the musical part of the song and it shows in *Love Me in the Daytime.*

Lovin' Spree   recorded by Eartha Kitt
with Henri Rene's Orchestra and Chorus

Written by Joan Javits and Phil Springer
Introduced February 13, 1954, on RCA Victor records #47-5610

(Length 2:57)

Eartha Kitt is probably best known for the come-hither purr which she so effortlessly employed in her signature hit recording of the French import *C'est Si Bon (It's So Good)* in 1953 and two years later in her tongue-in-cheek version of *Just An Old Fashioned Girl.* In 1954, Eartha Kitt released *(Goin' on a) Lovin' Spree,* an unusual country-flavored record featuring a Henri Rene arrangement replete with steel guitars backing her light vibrato-laden voice. It was the most typical fifties song she recorded, but her kiss-me-hard-kiss-me-strong *Lovin' Spree* never made it into the top-twenty. Her vast, eclectic repertoire included the calypso-styled *Somebody Bad Stole De Wedding Bell,* the frothy, fantastic, but forgotten *I Wantcha' Around,* the breathless, bitter monologue *The Heel,* and the Turkish folk song *Uska Dara,* but her biggest and most memorable hit, was the Christmas season perennial, her slyly salacious novelty song, *Santa Baby,* released in 1953.

Lucky Lips recorded by Gale Storm
with Billy Vaughn's Orchestra

Written by Jerry Leiber and Mike Stoller
Introduced March 16, 1957, on Dot records #15539

(Length 2:05)

Gale Storm's recordings for Dot Records are most often associated with her popular 'cover' recordings of rhythm and blues songs originally released by less well-known artists. Her hit *Why Do Fools Fall in Love?* was originally recorded by Frankie Lymon & Teenagers; *I Hear You Knockin'* was first recorded by Smiley Lewis; Otis Williams and the Charms introduced *Ivory Tower*; and *Dark Moon* was a cover of the Bonnie Guitar recording. Even this light-rock/slightly-country pop recording, *Lucky Lips (Are always kissin')* was originally recorded by R&B vocalist Ruth Brown. But Gale Storm brought her acting talent into the recording studio—you can hear the perky smile in her distinctive chirpy voice explaining that she's got more than other girls. A chorus repeats "lucky lips, lucky lips" and a strong beat moves the song along, but never enough to break into the top-fifty in the charts.

May You Always recorded by the McGuire Sisters
with orchestra directed by Dick Jacobs

Written by Larry Markes and Dick Charles
Introduced January 5, 1959, on Coral records #62059

(Length 2:56)

You can recognize a McGuire Sisters' song in an instant and their sentimentally wishful recording *May You Always (Walk in Sunshine)* is no exception. Their unaffectedly beguiling manner and the flawless harmony of their work was the ideal musical embodiment of the popular 'may you always be a dreamer' culture of the fifties. Producer Bob Thiele at Coral Records added perfect arrangements by Neal Hefti and outstanding instrumental talent with bandleader Dick Jacobs. One of their best recordings, the melancholy, yet gently upbeat *May You Always* failed to make it into the top-ten. Their number one hits include *Sincerely* (written by radio's rock DJ, Alan Freed), *Something's Gotta Give,* and *Sugartime,* but some of their other outstanding recordings including *It May Sound Silly*, *Muskrat Ramble*, and *Picnic* also failed to make it into the top-ten.

Morningside of the Mountain recorded by Tommy Edwards
with orchestra conducted by Leroy Holmes

Written by Dick Manning and Larry Stock
Original version introduced on July 28, 1951, on MGM records #10989
Second version introduced on March 2, 1959, on MGM records #12757

(Length 2:41)

Tommy Edwards, one of the few mainstream black recording artists in the fifties, embraced the mellow style of Johnny Mathis and Nat King Cole. *Morningside of the Mountain* was a tale of star-crossed lovers, separated by geography—She, on the morning side of the mountain; He, on the twilight side of the hill—they never met and never kissed. A soft and soothing voice, a lush arrangement, a light beat, a humming "ba-ba-ba" chorus, and a clever lyric was not enough to make a big hit. Tommy Edwards' original version of the song was released in 1951 and never made the top-twenty, he released it again in 1959 and again it didn't make the top-twenty. This popular singer, songwriter, and composer did hit #1 in 1958 with a new version of his 1951 recording *It's All in the Game*. His last chart recording was *It's Not The End of Everything* in 1960.

Mostly Martha recorded by the Crew-Cuts
with David Carroll's Orchestra

Written by Dorcas Cochran and Ralph Sterling
Introduced December 24, 1955, on Mercury records #70741

(Length 2:30)

In 1955, the underrated Crew-Cuts strayed from recording R&B covers to record *Mostly Martha*, a fifties set of lyrics grafted onto the classic aria *M'appari tutt' amor* from German composer Friedrich von Flotow's opera 'Martha.' In this unique, should-have-been-a-smash-hit song with a fifties beat and imagery—they can forget other girls, but will live to regret *Mostly Martha*. The orchestra gets off to a rousing start, the Crew-Cuts energetic vocal harmony is at its best, and the finger-snapping arrangement is innovative, but it didn't manage to break into the top-twenty. It was the 'B' side of *Angels in the Sky* that did reach #11 on the charts. Baritone, Rudy Maugeri, was the lead singer and musical arranger for the Toronto group that also included Johnnie Perkins, his brother Ray Perkins, and Pat Barrett. The Crew-Cuts remain best known for their 'cover' versions of doo-wop and R&B songs *Sh-Boom* and *Earth Angel*.

Mr. Wonderful recorded by Sarah Vaughan
with Hugo Peretti and his Orchestra

Written by Larry Holofcener, Jerry Bock, and George Weiss
Introduced February 11, 1956, on Mercury records #70777

(Length 2:44)

Swinging, sassy Sarah Vaughn resorts to no tricks to create popular hits like *Make Yourself Comfortable, Whatever Lola Wants*, and *Broken-Hearted Melody*. With her phenomenal voice and impeccable taste she brings a unique intimate sound to her recording of *Mr. Wonderful (That's You)*. The why-this-feeling, why-this-glow song from the Sammy Davis, Jr. Broadway musical 'Mr. Wonderful' never reached the top-ten for Sarah Vaughn, nor Peggy Lee, nor Teddi King who all recorded it in 1956. With her perfectly controlled vibrato and expressive abilities, 'The Divine One' is considered the epitome of the musician's singer and one of the most technically accomplished singers in the world. A jazz derived popular artist, Sarah Vaughn, dubbed 'Sass,' could infuse art into any song. Hugo Peretti's grand background on this recirding singularly suited her attitude and technique.

My Bonnie Lassie recorded by the Ames Brothers
with Hugo Winterhalter's Orchestra and Chorus

Written by Roy Bennett, Sid Tepper, and Marion McClurg
Introduced September 24, 1955 on RCA Victor records #47-6208

(Length 2:27)

The Ames Brothers' recordings *Rag Mop, Sentimental Me, Undecided, You, You, You, The Naughty Lady of Shady Lane*, and *Melodie D'Amour* were all top-five hits. Their Irish-flavored, drums-drumming, bagpipes-humming, *My Bonnie Lassie (Comin' to me)* was one of their more unusual recordings. It begins with the brothers humming the tune, then the song builds, and the group hits one of their strongest performances. This superb 1955 record, with its catchy lyric, international flavor, fifties arrangement, and up-tempo beat, never made the top-ten. The very next year, another exceptional recording from this close harmony vocal quartet, *It Only Hurts for a Little While* also failed to make it into the top-ten. Brothers Joe, Gene, Vic and Ed Urick formed the Ames Brothers in the late 1940s. Youngest brother, Ed Urick (retaining the name Ed Ames), became a solo star in the 1960s with his top-twenty hits *My Cup Runneth Over* and *Who Will Answer?*

My Little Angel recorded by the Four Lads
with Ray Ellis and his Orchestra

Written by Dazz Jordan and Gordon Charles
Recorded on February 29, 1956, on Columbia records #40674

(Length 3:05)

The Four Lads had huge top-ten hits in the fifties with *Skokiaan, Moments to Remember, No, Not Much!, Standing on the Corner, Who Needs You, Put a Light in the Window,* and *There's Only One of You,* but inexplicably one of their best recordings, *My Little Angel,* never made it into the top-twenty. Lead tenor Bernie Toorish, under the pseudonym Dazz Jordan, co-wrote this she-must-be-an-angel/there-is-heaven-in-her-eyes song for his wife, Angela Tabor. With its lush orchestral arrangement, fanfares of trumpets, and angelic singers in the background, *My Little Angel (will walk down the aisle as my bride),* had a bright, melodic, sentimental, and uncomplicated sound. The Four Lads had perfect pitch, a distinctive Canadian burr, and their sound, with an overlay of vibrato on the long notes, was delightful and crisp—classic fifties harmony.

Now That I'm In Love recorded by Patti Page
with orchestra conducted by Jack Rael

Written by K. C. Rogan (pseudonym for Johnny Burke)
Introduced May 16, 1953, on Mercury records #70127

(Length 2:20)

During her meteoric 1948-62 tenure at Mercury records, warm, honey-voiced Patti Page racked up no less than 77 hit records, with 15 of her singles going gold. She defined the decade of earnest, adult pop with her dreamy legato phrasing and her wide range of material. *All My Love, I Went to Your Wedding, Old Cape Cod,* and *The Doggie in the Window,* were number one hits. Patti Page's biggest hit, *The Tennessee Waltz,* was one of the best-selling singles of all time. However, one of her most exuberant songs *Now That I'm in Love (I don't seem able to pocket my pride)* barely made it into the top-twenty and remained on the charts for only two weeks in the spring of 1953. Her Oklahoma accent shines and she is irrepressible capturing all of the giddiness of new love in this catchy recording that starts with a rousing 'William Tell Overture' introduction. *Now That I'm In Love* is a phenomenal, infectious, easy-to-sing-along-with song from the most popular girl singer of the fifties.

On An Evening In Roma recorded by Dean Martin

English Lyrics by Nan Frederics, Italian Lyrics by Umberto Bertini,
Music by Alessandro Taccani
Introduced July 13, 1959, on Capitol records #4222

(Length 2:26)

In the 1950s, Americans were enamored with Italian songs—*Arrivederci Roma, Al Di La,* and *Domani* and with Italian singers—Vic Damone, Julius La Rosa, Al Martino, and Jerry Vale. But the best remembered Italian/American songs were recorded by affable Dean Martin. *That's Amore, Innamorata,* and *Return To Me (Ritorna-Me),* are better known than his last recording at Capitol records, *On an Evening in Roma (Como e' bella ce' la luna brille e' strette),* which never made it into the top-fifty. Dean sighs "I am only one, and that's one too few." Even if it was not as popular as some of his other releases, *On an Evening in Roma* is one of his finest "grinning and mandolining in sunny Italy" songs. Smooth, sly, and snappy, Dean Martin was one of the best selling recording artists of the fifties and sixties. Dozens of the popular, melodious, EASY-POP ballads of the decade were ideally suited to his loose, lazy, *Lay Some Happiness on Me,* charm.

Only Sixteen recorded by Sam Cooke

Written by Sam Cooke
Introduced June 8, 1959, on Keen records #2022

(Length 2:03)

Considered by many as the definitive soul singer, Sam Cook recorded dozens of pop songs in the 50s and 60s. His recording of *Only Sixteen* has youthful fifties imagery 'she is too young to fall in love—he is too young to know', a lively arrangement, and dynamic back-up singers. The joy and happiness in the song emanates from Sam Cooke whose gospel roots give his recordings the sense of release that you rarely hear outside of gospel music. Produced by the small Keen label, *Only Sixteen* placed a meager 28th on the record charts. His first #1 hit, *You Send Me,* in 1957, was written by his brother Charles 'L.C.' Cooke. After his move to RCA in 1960, he had hits with *Cupid, Chain Gang, Twistin' the Night Away,* and *Another Saturday Night.* He appreciated popular music, particularly the melodious, harmony-based sound of the Ink Spots whose influence can be heard in his recordings of *You Send Me* and *For Sentimental Reasons.*

Padre recorded by Toni Arden
with chorus and orchestra directed by Jack Pleis

Written by Alain Romans and Paul Francis Webster
Recorded on May 26, 1958, on Decca records #30628

(Length 3:05)

While there were dozens of lost-love songs throughout the fifties, very possibly the best recording in the genre was Toni Arden's first release at Decca records, *Padre*. Having lost her lover to another woman "with golden eyes and honeyed lies" a distraught Toni Arden, who now finds solace only in prayer, "wondering where love has flown, counting her beads alone," gives us a heart rending version of the break-up of her marriage. Her desperate question to the padre "What happened to our love?" never made it into the top-ten in the charts. *Padre* is much in the same vein as June Valli's *Crying in the Chapel*, Miss Toni Fisher's *The Big Hurt,* Patti Page's *I Went to Your Wedding*, Debbie Reynold's *Am I That Easy to Forget*, Johnnie Ray's *Cry*, Joni James' *Have You Heard*, Teresa Brewer's *A Tear Fell*, Eddie Fisher's *I'm Walking Behind You,* and Rosemary Clooney's *Half as Much*. Toni Arden is best known for her intensely dramatic version of *Kiss of Fire* in 1952.

Rollin' Stone recorded by the Fontane Sisters
with orchestra conducted by Billy Vaughn

Written by Robert Riley
Recorded on June 4, 1955, on Dot records #15370

(Length 2:16)

Like their #1 hit *Hearts of Stone* in 1954 and *Eddie My Love* in 1956, *Rollin' Stone* was one of several R&B 'cover recordings' that the Fontane Sisters released at Dot in the mid fifties. The mambo-rocking *Rollin' Stone* was originally recorded by the Marigolds with lead singer, Tennessee State Penitentiary inmate, Johnny Bragg and written by fellow prison inmate Robert Riley. In their version of *Rollin Stone*, the wholesome, unthreatening Fontane Sisters, warn the guy in the song that while he enjoys moving from one girl to another, he'll pay for being nothing more than a rolling stone one day when he's all alone. The Marigolds recorded the song in the early fifties and the Fontane Sisters released their single in 1955, just months after *Hearts of Stone*, but none of the versions made the top-ten. While the practice of 'cover' recordings remains controversial (see a full discussion in chapter 11) this rarely heard recording is an interesting example.

Same Old Saturday Night recorded by Frank Sinatra
with Nelson Riddle and his Orchestra

Written by Sammy Cahn and Frank Reardon
Introduced September 24, 1955, on Capitol records #3218

(Length 2:37)

Recorded the same year as Frank Sinatra's huge hits, *Learnin' the Blues, Love and Marriage*, and *(Love Is) The Tender Trap*, this swinging version of *Same Old Saturday Night* with it classic fifties lyrics did not break into the top-ten. Describing his Saturday night "in an empty row at a movie show," it featured the fantastic partnership of Frank Sinatra's style and Nelson Riddle's arrangement that became trademarks in Sinatra's groundbreaking 'concept' albums. Just a year later, *Hey Jealous Lover* was a top hit, but another of his light and easy masterpieces *(How Little It Matters) How Little We Know* didn't crack the top-ten either. From heartthrob to mature artist, 'The Chairman of the Board' worked hard to maintain the standards he set. Fifty years of recordings, his series of MGM musicals with Gene Kelley, his TV appearances, and live performances made 'Old Blue Eyes' the most important figure in popular music.

See You in September recorded by the Tempos
produced by Jack Gold with orchestra conducted by Billy Mure

Written by Sid Wayne and Sherman Edwards
Introduced June 29, 1959, on Climax records #102

(Length 2:08)

The Tempos are considered one-hit-wonders, and their biggest hit, the classic summer vacation goodbye, *See You in September*, never made it to the top-twenty. Originally, this sentimental end-of-the-school-year song was the 'B' side of *Bless You My Love*. The treatment was in the same vain as *Graduation Day, Memories are Made of This,* and *Magic Moments* and their sound is a bit like the Four Lads and the Crew-Cuts. In *See You in September* the guy says a three-month goodbye to his girlfriend until classes resume in the fall—he promises to be alone every night, but he worries that she might find a new love during the summer. The Tempos, with Jim Drake, also included lead singer Mike Lazo, fellow Duquesne University student, Gene Schachter, who met Mike Lazo while they were in the Army in Korea, and Pittsburg native Tom Monito. *See You in September* was also recorded by Shelley Fabares in 1962 and by the Happenings in 1966.

Somebody to Love recorded by Bobby Darin
with orchestra conducted by Richard Wess

Written by Bobby Darin
Introduced September 26, 1960, on Atco records #6179

(Length 2:13)

After *Splish Splash**, *Queen of the Hop*, *Dream Lover**, *Mack the Knife*, and *Beyond the Sea* zoomed to the top-ten in the late fifties, Bobby Darin's 1960 recording of *Somebody to Love** didn't fare nearly as well—landing only 45th place in the Billboard Top 100. It should have been a much bigger hit because it is a jaunty recording with an infectious arrangement, a lively chorus, a catchy fifties lyric, a snappy beat, and Bobby Darin at the top of his form. In *Somebody to Love*, he laments "travelin' so doggone much" that he doesn't have a steady girl. It was released as the 'B' side of *Artificial Flowers*, the tear-jerking story of the despair and death of 'little Annie' from the Broadway musical 'Tender-loin.' During his short, fifteen year recording career Bobby Darin's repertoire included popular standards, rock 'n' roll, folk, and lounge singing. He left behind a considerable quantity and diversity of recorded work.

* Songs recorded and written by Bobby Darin

Suddenly There's a Valley recorded by Gogi Grant
with orchestra conducted by Buddy Bregman

Written by Biff Jones and Chuck Meyer
Introduced October 1, 1955, on Era records #1003

(Length 2:55)

Gogi Grant's early recordings at RCA were unsuccessful, but a move to Era Records yielded better results. An angelic chorus introduces her first Era release and her voice soars to "kiss the falling rain" where "friend-ships never end" in the buoyant and majestic ballad, *Suddenly There's a Valley (Where Hope and Love Begin)*. Gogi Grant undertook a 28-city tour to promote this beautiful, timeless song that encourages us to try again…even when we feel we can't. In spite of her tireless promotional efforts, it only rose to #9 on the charts, it did however prompt several less successful cover versions by: Jo Stafford (#13); Julius La Rosa (#20); the Mills Brothers (#45); Patty Andrews (#69); and in England by Petula Clark. Gogi Grant is best known for her atypical, vaguely folk-flavored, hit recording of *The Wayward Wind*, which knocked Elvis Presley's *Heartbreak Hotel* off of the #1 spot in 1956.

Takes Two to Tango recorded by Pearl Bailey
with Don Redman's Orchestra featuring Taft Jordan on trumpet

Written by Al Hoffman and Dick Manning
Introduced September 27, 1952, on Coral Records #60817

(Length 2:59)

Pearl Bailey's uninhibited personality, inimitable style, and mischievous you-can-go-to-pot-on-your-own spirit, sparkle in her recording of *Takes Two to Tango*. The brassy arrangement—saxophones, trombones, and trumpets—matches the vocal style of Pearl Bailey's indomitable throaty voice. Her natural laughs, her gravelly "I mean to tell ya" and her "one more time" entreaty come across spectacularly in this one-of-a-kind recording. You just can't listen without catching her infectious "get the feeling of romance" spirit. *Takes Two to Tango* was her only recording to place in Billboard's top 100 but it never made it above 7th place. Movie and stage actress, crowd-pleasing performer, and vocalist, Pearl Bailey, the daughter of a Newport News, Virginia, minister, won a singing contest at Harlem's Apollo Theater in 1938 and a Tony award for the title role in 'Hello Dolly' in 1970.

Tell Us Where the Good Times Are recorded by
Guy Mitchell and Mindy Carson
with Mitch Miller and his Orchestra

Written by Bob Merrill
Introduced July 18, 1953, on Columbia records #39992

(Length 2:31)

The inviting soprano quality of Mindy Carson's voice led Columbia records to partner her with their popular baritone, Guy Mitchell, for a series of memorable duets. Guy Mitchell's biggest solo hits were *My Heart Cries for You, My Truly, Truly Fair,* and *Singing the Blues.* Mindy Carson solos included *My Foolish Heart* and *Wake the Town and Tell the People.* They're exuberance comes across as a young-and-in-our-prime fresh sounding duet. In this fast-paced song they make it clear that anywhere they roam and wander, they want to have one big time—*Tell Us Where the Good Times Are.* In spite of its driving harmonica and 'rat-ta-tat-tat' orchestra arrangement, this highly contagious recording, even with the magic of Columbia Records' Mitch Miller's production genius, couldn't catch a place in the top-twenty.

There Goes My Heart recorded by Joni James
arranged by Chuck Sagle   with orchestra conducted by Tony Aquaviva

Written by Abner Silver and Benny Davis
Introduced September 15, 1958, on MGM records #12706

(Length 2:32)

This plaintive, yet lilting, lament is full of orchestral crescendos as a broken-hearted Joni James sighs "There goes the one I love and here am I." The arrangement is topped off with 'ah, ah, ahs' from background singers completing the musical there-goes-the-boy-I-was-not-worthy-of mood. One of her best recordings, *There Goes My Heart*, displays a glimpse of Joni James' vocal range with her spectacular flourish on the last line "there goes my heart." Inexplicably, it barely made it into the top-twenty on the charts. Years earlier, bandleader Enric Madriguera had a 1934 hit version of *There Goes My Heart* and in the 50s Nat King Cole also recorded it. Joni James became an overnight success when her #1 hit song *Why Don't You Believe Me* was released in 1952 and stayed on top of the charts for six weeks. Other hits included *Have You Heard* that peaked at #4 in 1953 and *How Important Can It Be?* that reached #2 in 1955.

To the Ends of the Earth recorded by Nat King Cole
with Nelson Riddle and his Orchestra

Written by Joe Sherman and Noel Sherman
Introduced October 27, 1956, on Capitol Records #3551

(Length 2:20)

A rich, throaty voice and precise enunciation scored Nat King Cole more than one hundred successful pop single hit recordings over a twenty-year period, making him one of the top singers in recording history. His velvet sound was at its hickory-smoked best 'pursuing his love' in the beguiling *To the Ends of the Earth (just to be where you are)*, a haunting, thousand-goodbyes-won't-convince-me-you-are-gone, beguine. Nelson Riddle's classic arrangement includes subtle stabs, castinets, and a background male chorus. Unlike his #1 hits *(I Love You) For Sentimental Reasons, Nature Boy, Mona Lisa*, and *Too Young,* his recording of *To the Ends of the Earth*, the 'B' side of *Night Lights*, did not make it into the top-twenty, but even though the melody dies, the song lingers on. With his warmth, intimacy, and humor, Nat King Cole succeeded with dozens of ballads and novelties throughout the fifties.

We Could recorded by Nick Noble
produced by Snuff Garrett with orchestra and chorus

Written by Felice Bryant
Introduced September 15, 1957, on Liberty records #55488, LB-1465

(Length 2:32)

We Could (You and I) is a simple melody, with an unpretentious arrangement featuring a piano, a small group of backup musicians, and an unlisted female joining Nick Noble on the title line "we could—you and I." If there was ever a quintessential, optimistic fifties young love song, this attractive, effortless country-styled if-anyone-could-find-true-love-we-could ballad is it. Nick Noble's honest and gentle baritone voice vowing that 'he'd be happy anywhere as long as he's with his girl' is certainly an overlooked should-have-been-hit that never even made it onto the top 100. Seven years later Al Martino's version did managed to reach #41 on the charts. Nick Nobel was born Nicholas Valkan in Chicago on June 21, 1936. He had modest success with *The Bible Tells Me So* on Wing Records in 1955 and also recorded *To You My Love, A Fallen Star,* and *Moonlight Swim* for Mercury, but none made it into the top-twenty.

(I'm Always Hearing) Wedding Bells recorded by Eddie Fisher
with Hugo Winterhalter's Orchestra and Chorus

Written by Robert Mellin and Herbert Jarczyk
Introduced April 2, 1955, on RCA Victor records #6015

(Length 2:38)

Eddie Fisher had huge top-ten hits with *Any Time, Wish You Were Here, I'm Walking Behind You, Oh! My Pa-Pa, I Need You Now, Heart, Dungaree Doll,* and *Cindy Oh Cindy.* His appeal was in the incredible sweetness of his baritone voice; he didn't push to sell a song, he threw back his head and belted out a ballad—and he rarely belted better than in *Wedding Bells* (German title *Hochzeitsglocken),* the 'B' side of *A Man Chases a Girl.* The arrangement included chimes, background bells, a trumpet, an 'oo, oo, oo' chorus, and Eddie Fisher's full-throttle "I never thought I'd fall." In spite of everything going for it, this warmly vibrant Eddie Fisher song was only on the charts for a week. Always hearing *Wedding Bells* seems appropriate given his 'walking down the aisle' with Debbie Reynolds, then Elizabeth Taylor, and then Connie Stevens.

What Is Love? recorded by the Play-Mates
with orchestra conducted by Joe Reisman

Written by Lee Pockriss and Paul Vance
Introduced July 6, 1959, on Roulette records #4160

(Length 2:18)

While the Play-Mates are not well known, between 1958 and 1962 they released ten recordings that made the charts but only their novelty recording of *Beep Beep* made it into the top-five. They were one of the first artists to sign with Roulette Records. What is probably the trio's best classic fifties song *What is Love?* didn't make it above 15th place in the charts in the summer of 1959. Five-feet-of-heaven-in-a-pony-tail "swaying with a wiggle" as she walks, creates an unforgettable fifties image of sex and fashion. The Play-Mates three part harmony and a bright, foot-tapping arrangement featuring castanets and tambourines, produced an outstanding fifties sound. While the word playmates might suggest women, the Play-Mates were actually three young men from Waterbury, Connecticut. Donny Conn (born in 1930), Morey Carr (born in 1932), and Chic Hetti (born in 1930) created the nucleus of their act in the early 50s while they were students at the University of Connecticut, initially placing more emphasis on comedy than singing (they were originally known as the Nitwits).

When recorded by the Kalin Twins

Written by Jack Reardon and Paul Evans
Introduced June 23, 1958, on Decca records #30642

(Length 2:25)

Catchy right from the first note, *When* jumps off with clicking percussion and snapping fingers that introduce the two-part harmony and unique blend of the Kalin Twins, Herb and Hal. The arrangement includes a rich orchestra and chorus and their unexpected pauses between the repetitious first two words of each refrain "When (pause) when you smile" and "Well (pause) well I know" and again with "I (pause) I don't want" and "If (pause) if you will." *When* was the Kalin's first and only popular song. It never made it to the top of the charts but it did manage to climb up to 5th position in 1958. Born in 1939 and raised in Port Jervis, New York, the twins' success in school shows prompted them to go on the nightclub circuit and then Decca records discovered them in 1957. Their effect on the evolution of POP music was acknowledged when the Rolling Stones paid tribute to the Kalins' unique two-part harmony on one of their LPs.

Who'll Be My Judge recorded by Joan Weber
with orchestra and chorus conducted by Jimmy Carroll

Written by Hal Gordon and Guy Wood
Introduced February 3, 1957, on Columbia records #40898

(Length 2:35)

A fantastic yet seldom-heard recording, *Who'll Be My Judge*, should have been a smash hit, but Joan Weber was giving birth to a baby daughter at the time and was unable to promote her career. Joan Weber in *Who'll Be My Judge* (much like Joni James in her recording of *How Important Can It Be*) chastises her classmate critics. She wants to know who has the right to "cast the first stone" as she questions "whose life is pure?" and "whose conscience is clear?" She reminds her boyfriend that only angels never do wrong, and while his friends tell him to leave her, he shouldn't listen to them. Neither *Who'll Be My Judge* nor any of her dozen or so follow-up recordings could match the success of her single hit *Let Me Go Lover* and Mitch Miller, the head of A&R at Columbia Records did not renew her contract. Her recording of *Let Me Go Lover* was her only hit.

Wild Horses recorded by Perry Como
with Hugo Winterhalter's Orchestra and Chorus

Written by K. C. Rogan (pseudonym for Johnny Burke)
Introduced February 14, 1953, on RCA Victor records #5152

(Length 2:38)

Versatile Perry Como was at the peak of his popularity—his recordings of *Hoop-Dee-Doo, If, Don't Let the Stars Get in Your Eyes, No Other Love, Wanted, Hot Diggity, Round and Round,* and *Catch a Falling Star* were all #1 hits in the fifties. Perry Como's baritone voice and style are perfectly showcased in *Wild Horses*, adapted from Robert Schumann's *Wilder Reiter (Wild Horseman)*. In this outstanding recording, nothing, not even a pack of *Wild Horses* pulling her away in a wagon, could keep these lovers apart. However, the song failed to become a top hit in spite of a unique arrangement that included plucked and bowed violins and a background chorus of 'hi-yup, hi-yup, hi-yup.' The recording was a bit of a dramatic departure for Perry Como who was especially successful recording free-and-easy ballads. His unrivaled appeal in the fifties defined the style of music known as middle-of-the-road pop.

(The) *Wonder of You* recorded by Ray Peterson
with orchestra and chorus conducted by Shorty Rogers

Written by Baker Knight
Introduced May 18, 1959, on RCA Victor records #47-7513

(Length 2:34)

An 'ow...ow...ow'ing chorus repeats *The Wonder of You* and Ray Peterson questions why his girlfriend loves him when no one else understands him and everything he does is wrong. This song was originally written by Baker Knight for Perry Como. Eleven years later Elvis Presley would have a top-ten hit with his version. Ray Peterson had an unusual start in the music business—he sang to entertain other patients while was being treated for polio in a Texas hospital. He wasn't discovered until he moved to Los Angeles. Ray Peterson began his career recording cover songs. He did his version of *Fever* (a year before Peggy Lee) and a version of Perez Prado's *Patricia* before releasing his first charting song in 1959, *The Wonder of You*. Ray Peterson's biggest success came in early 1960 when he made the top-ten with the teen-death-tear-jerker, *Tell Laura I Love Her*. In late 1960, he started his own label, Dunes, and worked with producer Phil Spector on *Corinna, Corinna* that also hit the top-ten.

Wonderful! Wonderful! recorded by Johnny Mathis
with Ray Conniff's Orchestra and Chorus

Written by Ben Raleigh and Sherman Edwards
Introduced February 9, 1957, on Columbia records #40784

(Length 2:47)

Vibrant with warmth and alive with understanding, *Wonderful! Wonderful!* was Johnny Mathis' first release. His voice and style are instantly recognizable and unmistakable. Emphasis on long sustained notes and a heavy vibrato reveal the influence an opera coach had on his singing. This enduring recording of 'a world of wonderful things that have no meaning with out you' did not make the top-ten as *Chances Are, It's Not for Me To Say*, and *The Twelfth of Never* would, but a subtle arrangement with a subdued background chorus let Johnny Mathis' easy style and uncommon sensitivity shine. Columbia Records A&R executive Mitch Miller guided him through these early recordings. Johnny Mathis was one of the last and most popular traditional male vocalists who emerged before the rock-dominated sixties.

(In the Summertime) You Don't Want My Love
recorded by Andy Williams
with orchestra conducted by Archie Bleyer

Written by Roger Miller
Introduced in 1960, on Cadence records #1389

(Length 2:11)

Andy Williams' expansive voice, easy delivery, and impeccable styling are usually associated with melodic ballads like *Moon River, Days of Wine and Roses,* and *Canadian Sunset.* His fast-paced *You Don't Want My Love,* written by Nashville performer/writer Roger Miller, arranged with piano, drums, tambourine, saxophone, and a chorus singing 'in the summer time, when all the trees are green,' is one of his best up-tempo recordings and the most overlooked. Even though the trees were green, he was blue, perhaps because *You Don't Want My Love* never rose above 64th place in the charts, while his similar, upbeat recordings *I Like Your Kind of Love* and *Can't Get Used to Losing You* were top-ten hits. The languid and gentle Andy Williams was the most solid and longest-lasting EASY-POP/Middle-of-the-Road singer of the era and charmed audiences for decades.

You're So Square (but I Don't Care) recorded by Elvis Presley
from MGM's 1957 Elvis Presley/Judy Tyler film 'Jailhouse Rock'

Written by Jerry Leiber and Mike Stoller
Introduced in 1957, on RCA Victor Records #EPA-4114

(Length 1:54)

While Elvis Presley is instantly remembered as the King of Rock 'n' Roll, he did record several middle-of-the-road fifties #1 pop standards including *Love Me Tender, Loving You, (Let Me Be Your) Teddy Bear, (Now and Then There's) A Fool Such as I*, and *It's Now or Never*, (adapted from the Italian song *O Sole Mio*). In a most unusual situation for the King, this recording of *You're So Square*, a fifties pop song with a light rock 'n' roll bridge never even made it into the top one hundred! In *You're So Square*, Elvis claims that even though his girl doesn't know any new dance steps, he knows that his 'heart flips' for her. Maybe *You're So Square* was overlooked and rarely heard because two much more familiar songs *Jailhouse Rock* and *Treat Me Nice* also came from his third film. Elvis Presley also recorded dozens of gospel/spiritual songs during his career including *(There'll Be) Peace In The Valley*.

There are more 'almost-as-great' singles of the fifties just waiting to be uncovered (see chart 9.2). Many remain just below the radar, did not make a big splash in the 50s, and are virtually never heard today.

Almost-as-Great, All-but-Forgotten, Songs from the Fifties

Am I That Easy to Forget　　　Debbie Reynolds　1959
This admirable recording from Debbie Reynolds was a typical 50s love-lost song and very topical one, coming on the heels of Eddie Fisher's move from his first marriage with Debbie Reynolds to his second marriage with Elizabeth Taylor.

April in Portugal　　　Vic Damone　1953
Originally written for the Univ. of Coimbra in Portuguese East Africa, this seldom-heard vocal version opens big and features a lush, lilting arrangement that soars to a dramatic crescendo. Tony Marin also recorded *April in Portugal* in 1953.

Bimbombey & Ring-A-Ling-A-Lario　　Jimmie Rodgers 1958-59
These two, rarely heard, pop/country/folk songs were typical of recordings by this popular fifties performer with the high sweet voice.

Blue Star　　　Felicia Sanders　1955
This version of the theme from the TV series 'Medic' was her only hit single other than her vocal on Percy Faiths' instrumental hit *Song from 'Moulin Rouge.'*

Bon Voyage　　　Janice Harper　1957
With a powerful, emphatic style, reminiscent of Georgia Gibbs, Janice Harper's string-laden sob story of lost love never made it into the top-forty, and this was her biggest hit.

Born Too Late　　　the Poni-Tails　1958
The wispy Poni-Tails released three recordings in the late fifties but this female trio never succeeded in achieving a top-five hit. *Born Too Late* is their best-remembered release.

Chanson d'Amour　　　Art & Dottie Todd 1958
The only chart-making song from Art and Dottie Todd barely made it into the top-ten and a version recorded by the Fontane Sisters didn't even do that well.

Domani (Tomorrow)　　　Julius LaRosa　1955
This classic American/Italian recording exemplifies the dozens of popular fifties Italian songs and singers. It is one of Julius La Rosa's most endearing and enduring releases.

Eddie My Love　　　the Teen Queens　1956
R&B sisters Betty and Rosie Collins charted just this one recording and it never hit the top-ten; neither did versions by the Fontane Sisters nor the Chordettes.

Chart 9.2. Almost-as-Great, All-but-Forgotten, Songs from the Fifties
(Chart continues on the next page)

Almost-as-Great, All-but-Forgotten, Songs from the Fifties
(continued)

Goodbye to Rome (Arrivederci Roma)   Georgia Gibbs   1955
Usually associated with popular male singers, this is another great version of the perennial Italian hit, popularized in the Mario Lanza film 'Seven Hills of Rome.'

Hold 'Em Joe   Harry Belafonte   1954 and 1957
An outstanding calypso recording, from the Broadway show 'John Murray Anderson's Almanac' was released twice, by this popular 50s Jamaican singer.

(How Little It Matters) *How Little We Know*   Frank Sinatra   1956
This light, easy masterpiece didn't break into the top-ten. It was overshadowed by his swinging hit *Hey! Jealous Lover.* Both featured trademark Sinatra style and Nelson Riddle arrangement from their groundbreaking 'concept' albums.

I Wanna Go Where You Go   Eddie Fisher   1955
This powerful, driving song is often overlooked because of his more popular 1955 records *Heart* and *Dungaree Doll.* It was the 'B' side of the equally unsuccessful *Magic Fingers.*

I'll Remember Today   Patti Page   1957
The decade's most popular singer recorded this forgotten gem. The touching, melodramatic lost-love song was released between her hits *Old Cape Cod* and *Left Right Out of Your Heart.*

Joey   Betty Madigan   1954
It was only Joey that she remembers…Joey made her change her last name, in this delightful Betty Madigan recording backed by the Ray Charles Singers. Debbie Reynolds also recorded this all-but-forgotten song.

Let It Be Me   Jill Corey   1957
(Now and Forever) Let It Be Me is an expressive, mournful, without-your-love-what-would-life-be, song that first appeared on the CBS-TV program 'Climax.'

Miracle of Love   Eileen Rodgers   1956
The chorus begins 'bom,bom,bom,bom' in this arrangement for lovely but seldom heard Eileen Rodgers. In spite of a great arrangement with Ray Conniff and his orchestra it never hit the top-ten.

Mister Tap Toe   Doris Day   1953
This is another outstanding, exhilarating, fast-paced, bouncy, release from everyone's favorite girl-next-door. She is backed by the Norman Luboff Choir.

A Penny a Kiss   Dinah Shore & Tony Martin   1951
RCA Victor teamed two of its most popular recording stars to produce this interesting light, bright romantic romp.

Chart 9.2. Almost-as-Great, All-but-Forgotten, Songs from the Fifties
(Chart continues on the next page)

Almost-as-Great, All-but-Forgotten, Songs from the Fifties

(continued)

Sisters Rosemary & Betty Clooney 1954

Rosemary Clooney and Vera-Ellen introduced *Sisters* in the musical film 'White Christmas.' For the single, Rosemary teamed with her sister Betty and the Clooney style—fine timing and diction with intimacy—is evident in this duet even though it never broke into the top-twenty.

Summertime, Summertime Jamies 1958 and 1962

Brother and sister, Tom and Serena Jamison formed the Jamies with Jeannie Roy and Arthur Blair. They twice released this upbeat 'no time to work, just time to play, we'll go swimming every day...have a ball, a regular free-for-all,' song that Tom wrote, but neither release made it into the top-twenty.

This I Know Gisele MacKenzie 1957

Hit parade regular, Gisele MacKenzie recorded this dramatic ballad that is similar in theme to Jane Morgan's 1959 *If Only I Could Live My Life Again.*

Two Different Worlds Don Rondo 1956

This little-known baritone had the most successful version of this commanding ballad that was also recorded by Jane Morgan and by Dick Haymes.

Warm and Tender Johnny Mathis 1957

This jaunty, seldom-heard song was issued as the B-side of *It's Not for Me to Say*. Both tunes were written by Hal David and Burt Bacharach and featured in the film 'Lizzie.'

With All My Heart Jodie Sands 1957

Opening with Jodie Sands chirping 'la, la, la, la, la' and backed by a chorus singing the lyrics in Italian, *With All My Heart* from little known Philadelphia singer Jodie Sands did edge into the top-twenty but has certainly been forgotten.

You Don't Know Me Jerry Vale 1956

This touching song of unrequited love was the most successful single from the popular ballad singer, born Genero Vitaliano in the Bronx. But even his most successful record never made it into the top-ten.

Young and Warm and Wonderful Tony Bennett 1958

Tony Bennett's glowing intensity was on display in this easy-going love song. He has his own special way of making its quiet mood spring unforgettably to life, but unfortunately, this recording would not place in the top-twenty.

Chart 9.2. Almost-as-Great, All-but-Forgotten, Songs from the Fifties

References from Chapter 9:

Whitburn, Joel. *Top Pop Singles 1955-1986*. New York: Billboard Books, 1987.

Whitburn, Joel. *Pop Memories 1890-1954*. Menomonee Falls, Wisconsin: Record Research Inc., 1986.

The good life, as I conceive it, is a happy life. I do not mean that if you are good you will be happy—I mean that if you are happy you will be good.

Bertrand Russell (1872-1970)

Chapter 10

Fabulous-but-Overlooked
EASY-POP Songs on Albums

The million-selling records and top-ten hits associated with the 1950s were released as single records on 45rpm discs. More than a hundred of these classic EASY-POP hit songs were described in chapter 3. Another fifty should-have-been hit singles were described in chapter 9. In this chapter there are descriptions of fabulous-but-overlooked EASY-POP songs released, not on singles, but on 33 $\frac{1}{3}$ LP long-playing records. These compilations of a dozen songs on extended-play discs were called albums and they provided singers of the fifties the opportunity to sell a collection of songs rather than just one.

Teresa Brewer, Perry Como, Rosemary Clooney, Eddie Fisher, the McGuire Sisters, and Patti Page tended to record mostly 45rpm singles. Ella Fitzgerald, Judy Garland, Dean Martin, Jane Morgan, and Andy Williams favored 33 $\frac{1}{3}$ LPs, while Tony Bennett, Doris Day, Johnny Mathis, and Frank Sinatra were successful in both formats. Scores of great 50s songs were released only on LPs (see fabulous-but-overlooked EASY-POP songs from albums in chart 10.1). Some of the songs are unfamiliar while some are unexpected versions of familiar songs.

Fabulous-but-Overlooked EASY-POP Songs from Albums

Everything's Coming Up Roses   Kirby Stone Four   1959
Orchestra conducted by Jimmy Carroll   Written by Stephen Sondheim and Jule Styne
Following their 1958 hit *Baubles, Bangles, and Beads*, the inventive Kirby Stone Four, recorded their 3rd album in two years, 'The Kirby Stone Touch,' where they display their distinctive trademark 'GO' sound with this rousing tune from 'Gypsy.'"

Falling In Love With Love   Dinah Shore   1959
Orchestra conducted by Nelson Riddle   Written by Richard Rodgers and Lorenz Hart
Her first album after moving to swinging Capitol Records, 'Dinah, Yes Indeed,' featured her amazing version of *Falling in Love with Love*. Dinah Shore's warm, lilting voice moves soothingly over a surprising background of wild bongos and instrumental frenzy.

(The) Gypsy in My Soul   Doris Day   1956
With Paul Weston and his Music from Hollywood   Written by Moe Jaffe and Clay Boland
Some of Doris Day's finest performances appear on her LP 'Day By Day' where her appealing, personal style is most evident in the lively *Gypsy in My Soul*. The album also includes light, rhythmic versions of *Gone With the Wind*, *But Beautiful*, and *Day by Day*.

Hosanna   Harry Belafonte   1956
With Tony Scott and His Orchestra   Written by Irving Burgie (aka Lord Burgess) & William Attaway
This song was from 'Calypso,' the album that made Harry Belafonte's career. The West Indies album includes his two most successful songs *Day-O* and *Jamaica Farewell*, but it is the joyful house-building *Hosanna*, based on a Jamaican trade guilds song—a house built on a rock foundation will stand—that should have been a big Calypso hit for him.

I'm Shooting High   Eydie Gorme   1959
Arranged by Billy Byers, Produced by Don Costa   Written by Jimmy McHugh and Ted Koehler
Her fourth album for ABC-Paramount, 'Eydie Gorme...On Stage,' captures the vivacious and rollicking spirit of Eydie Gorme as she performs the rhythmic, but rarely heard *I'm Shooting High*.

It's Good To Be Alive   the Four Aces   1957
Orchestra directed by Jack Pleis   Written by Bob Merrill
The Four Aces are at their best, displaying a sheer joy of singing in *It's Good To Be Alive* from their Decca album 'Hits from Broadway, the Four Aces.' This underrated, upbeat song was introduced in the Broadway show 'New Girl in Town' starring Gwen Verdon.

Just for Once   Pat Suzuki   1959
Arranged and conducted by George Siravo   Written by Albert Hague and Dorothy Fields
Capitalizing on her success in the Broadway show 'Flower Drum Song,' the RCA album 'Pat Suzuki's Broadway '59' featured songs from seven late-fifties Broadway musicals. The snappy and flirtatious *Just for Once* was from 'Redhead.'

Love is a Simple Thing   Debbie Reynolds   1959
Arranged and conducted by Jerry Fielding   Written by June Carroll and Arthur Siegel
Her first album from Dot Records, 'Debbie,' features the actress singing one of her best recordings, the fresh and sincere, but undiscovered, *Love is a Simple Thing*. Her honesty and believability also come across in another song on the album, *Hooray For Love*.

Chart 10.1. Fabulous-but-Overlooked EASY-POP Songs from Albums

(Chart continues on the next page)

Fabulous-but-Overlooked EASY-POP Songs from Albums
(continued)

Love is like Champagne   Jane Morgan   1959
Orchestra directed by Vic Schoen   Written by Jean Constantin, Carl Sigman, Norbert Glanzberg
There are bubbles in her voice when she conveys the joy of discovering that *Love is like Champagne* in this fantastic song from '**Jane Morgan Time**' that also includes her hopeful hit *With Open Arms* and the tenderness of her best-selling *Happy Anniversary*.

Lullaby of Broadway   Tony Bennett   1957
Arranged by Ralph Sharon   Written by Al Dubin and Harry Warren
Only his third LP, '**The Beat of My Heart**' was his first 'concept' album. In it he gives full-voiced emotion to an imaginative percussion arrangement of this popular standard. The LP also includes *Let's Face the Music and Dance* and *Just One of Those Things*.

Married I Can Always Get   Beverly Mahr   1956
Arranged and conducted by Gordon Jenkins   Written by Gordon Jenkins
This lighthearted look at romance is from '**The Complete Manhattan Tower**' suite. Jeri Southern and Teddi King recorded singles of *Married I Can Always Get*, but it was never performed better than it is here by Beverly Mahr (Mrs. Gordon Jenkins).

Mountain Greenery   Ella Fitzgerald   1956
Arranged by Buddy Bregman   Written by Richard Rodgers and Lorenz Hart
Following her extremely popular album of Cole Porter songs, Ella Fitzgerald released the second in her 'Song Book' series, the 2-LP set, '**Ella Fitzgerald Sings the Rodgers & Hart Song Book**' with her medium-tempo *Mountain Greenery*, she is in peak form.

(All of a Sudden) My Heart Sings   Polly Bergen   1958
Orchestra conducted by Luther Anderson   Written by Harold Rome, Jean Blanvillain, Henri Herpin
Following her riveting dramatic performance as torch singer Helen Morgan on TV, Polly Bergen's fourth album '**My Heart Sings**' explores the livelier side of love with her stunning performance of the ascending and descending scales in *My Heart Sings*.

Things Are Swingin'   Peggy Lee   1959
Orchestra conducted by Jack Marshall   Written by Peggy Lee and Jack Marshall
All of the songs in her album '**Things Are Swingin'**' are pure and rich. Peggy Lee is at her most fervent and really shines with the up-tempo pace of the title song, her own composition, *Things Are Swinging*. She moves it along at a happy, sassy pace.

You Make Me Feel So Young   Frank Sinatra   1956
Orchestra conducted by Nelson Riddle   Written by Mack Gordon and Josef Myrow
Frank Sinatra returns to up-tempo material in his greatest swing album '**Songs for Swinging Lovers**' singing *You Make Me Feel So Young* with authority and joy. Other Nelson Riddle arrangements on this concept album include *Pennies from Heaven* and *I've Got You Under My Skin*.

Zing Went The Strings of My Heart   Judy Garland   1958
Orchestra conducted by Nelson Riddle   Written by James F. Hanley
Judy Garland conveys her stamina, virtuosity, and heart in all of her recordings. She gives one of her best performances singing *Zing went the Strings of My Heart* on her LP '**Judy in Love**' with Nelson Riddle's thrilling strings and brass to accompany her.

Chart 10.1. Fabulous-but-Overlooked EASY-POP Songs from Albums

The Evolution of the LP (Long-Playing Album) in the fifties

Until the 1950s, home sales of records were confined to a single standard format: the 10-inch diameter, nearly half-inch thick, shellac-coated, 78rpm (revolutions per minute) record. Original music was recorded in a studio on blank wax masters. The recordings were captured in one continuous session and could not be corrected or edited. The 78s were played on a 'Victrola' that had been introduced in 1906. The end of the 1940s, however, marked the end of a single-standard record format. For the next twenty years, two incompatible formats—the $33\frac{1}{3}$ rpm LP and the 45rpm single—would vie for dominance.

The brief playing time (less than 5 minutes) on the 78rpm record was a serious shortcoming for the recording industry. Record buyers wanted recordings of classical music without the need to break the flow of the compositions every few minutes to change records. Ted Wallerstein, who began his career at RCA, but moved to Columbia Records in 1938, envisioned a long-playing disc capable of containing 28 minutes of content (deemed an acceptable length for classical pieces) on each side of the record.

The research lab at Columbia Records achieved his goal in 1948 with the introduction of an unbreakable, vinylite (plastic) disc with microgrooves that rotated at a relatively slow $33\frac{1}{3}$ revolutions per minute—less than half the speed of the standard 78rpm discs. Radio stations had been using $33\frac{1}{3}$ rpm as the standard speed on their large radio transcription discs for years.

By 1950, Philco, a major radio and phonograph manufacturer had developed a lightweight stylus, needed to track the microgrooves in the long-playing discs, and they began producing record players for the new $33\frac{1}{3}$ records. Columbia made the long-playing technology available, at no charge, to all record companies as they attempted to establish the $33\frac{1}{3}$ LP as the new standard format to replace the older 78rpm records. In a popular advertising promotion, Dr. Peter Goldmark, head of CBS laboratories, was photographed with a 7-foot-high stack of 78rpm records on side of him and a small number of $33\frac{1}{3}$ LP records in his hands both containing the same amount of music. (Schicke, 1974, p.28)

The $33\frac{1}{3}$ LPs, containing eight to twelve songs on a single disc, opened the door for the groundbreaking 'concept' albums recorded by Frank Sinatra and the captivating 'Songbooks' by Ella Fitzgerald. While the $33\frac{1}{3}$ LPs did not become the single standard that Columbia had envisioned, the format was very profitable for the recording companies enticing buyers to purchase an album of a dozen songs instead of just one song on a single. The practice of marketing individual songs only as part of an album package continued into the twenty-first century.

The Evolution of the 45 (45rpm Single) in the fifties

To compete with Columbia Record's new $33 \frac{1}{3}$ LP discs, and replace old 78rmp phonograph records, a third format, the 45rpm single record was introduced by RCA Victor, initiating a virtual war-of-the-speeds between rivals RCA/NBC and Columbia/CBS. The 45rpm record was a small 7" format with a 1 ½" hole in the center. The inexpensive 45 (usually selling for $1.00, while the $33 \frac{1}{3}$ LP sold for $4.00) was unbreakable, light-weight, and lent itself to the recording of a single, well-promoted, prospective hit song on the 'A' side and a filler song on the 'B' side. The large center hole permitted easy creation of automatic-record-changing in the players. The record player was also small, inexpensive, and portable. The 45s became the primary format for releasing EASY-POP singles during the fifties and it was an ideal playback format for the 'Juke Box.' The ranking of hit songs on the popularity charts was determined by the sales of these 45s, the frequency of their airplay on the radio, and the number of times they were played on juke boxes.

Albums Released in a Variety of Formats

In 1950, Columbia Records, the company that developed the $33 \frac{1}{3}$ rpm format, released their albums on 10" discs, playing at $33 \frac{1}{3}$ rpm. Typically these albums contained 8 songs. RCA Victor, the company that developed the 45rpm format tended to release its 'albums' as boxed sets of 7" records playing at 45rpm with 2 songs on each disc. Decca and Capitol began to release multi-song albums on both formats: the single $33 \frac{1}{3}$ rpm disc and also as boxed sets of 45s (6 songs on three 45s or 8 songs on four 45s). By 1953, RCA Victor and Columbia realized that both formats had a following so they joined the other major recording companies and released albums on both formats. In 1955, the size of the $33 \frac{1}{3}$ rpm disc grew from 10" to 12" and the typical number of songs on albums increased from eight to twelve. While boxed sets of extended-play 45s continued for a few more years, by 1957 the $33 \frac{1}{3}$ rpm album on a 12" disc became the standard and that format dominated record album sales until the arrival of the digital CD in the 1980s.

Record Players Accommodate a Variety of Formats

It was never possible to play a $33\frac{1}{3}$rpm format record, with its small ¼" center hole on the inexpensive, portable 45rpm record players from RCA Victor with its 1½" thick center column. It was possible however to play 45rpm singles on $33\frac{1}{3}$rpm record players. Buyers could purchase small plastic inserts to snap-in to the large 1½" center holes in the 45s to reduce the size of the center hole to ¼"—then play the record on a player designed for $33\frac{1}{3}$rpm LPs. Of course you would have to be able to adjust the speed between $33\frac{1}{3}$rpm and 45rpm to accommodate each format.

As the fifties progressed it was common for buyers to purchase combination record players that could play 78, 45, and $33\frac{1}{3}$ rpm format records. The automatic record changers could hold a stack of 7 or 8 discs playing several hours of recorded music.

Original Broadway Cast and Soundtrack Albums

In addition to classical music and 'concept' albums, the $33\frac{1}{3}$ LPs invited recordings of entire scores from Broadway shows featuring the cast recreating their original live performances. One of the first original cast albums, from 'Oklahoma,' released in 1949, was so successful for Decca Records that dozens of original cast albums followed. Columbia Records had an even bigger hit later that year with the original cast album from 'South Pacific' that starred Mary Martin and Ezio Pinza.

The original Broadway cast album from 'Guys and Dolls' was another best-selling album for Decca Records in 1950, the album from 'The King and I' was a huge success in 1951, and Columbia Records released the best selling original cast album of the decade, 'My Fair Lady' starring Julie Andrews and Rex Harrison, in 1957. The ten best-selling original cast albums are shown in chart 7.11 in chapter 7. Some fantastic, hard-to-find EASY-POP songs, hide in these 'Original Cast' albums (see ten surprising songs and singers from musical theater in chart 10.2).

There were great songs from Hollywood musical films and the resulting 'Soundtrack' albums were another source of popular selling $33\frac{1}{3}$ LPs. The ten best-selling soundtrack albums are shown in chart 7.9 in chapter 7. Some overlooked EASY-POP songs are from popular films and some are from less-than-successful films (see ten phenomenal-but-unfamiliar songs from movies in chart 10.3).

Ten Surprising Songs and Singers
from Musical Theater

All the Time   Tony Randall   1958
Character actor and Broadway star Tony Randall introduced this seldom-heard, everlasting-love song in the musical 'Oh, Captain.' The recording by Johnny Mathis was the eighth top-twenty hit for him.

Everybody's Got a Home but Me   Judy Tyler   1955
Judy Tyler introduced this touching song in 'Pipe Dream.' Eddie Fisher's version was one of his best singles but it was not a big hit for him.

I Enjoy Being a Girl   Pat Suzuki   1958
'Miss Pony Tail,' American-born Pat Suzuki, describes herself in this engaging performance from 'Flower Drum Song.'

If'n   Gordon Polk & Virginia Gibson   1956
Ethel Merman was the star of 'Happy Hunting' but youngsters Virginia Gibson and Gordon Polk have an infectious great time imagining *If'n (I were to love you)*.

Just in Time   Judy Holiday & Sydney Chaplin   1956
This light and breezy up-beat duet was introduced by comedienne Judy Holiday and Broadway leading man Sydney Chaplin in 'Bells Are Ringing.'

Love in a Home   Edith 'Edie' Adams 1956
As Daisy Mae in 'Li'l Abner' Edie Adams sings this warm, touching, forgotten gem. Her duet with Peter Palmer, *Namely You*, was another outstanding number.

Luck Be A Lady   Robert Alda   1951
Robert Alda, father of actor Alan Alda, sings this propulsive song from the musical fable 'Guys and Dolls,' based on the story by Damon Runyon.

Steam Heat   Carol Haney   1954
Carol Haney was unknown to Broadway audiences when she co-starred in 'The Pajama Game' introducing the radiator clicking and hissing song *Steam Heat*. Patti Page had a top-ten hit with her version.

Take Me Along   Jackie Gleason & Walter Pidgeon 1959
Moving onto the Broadway stage from his acclaimed TV variety series, Jackie Gleason performs the roguish title song from 'Take Me Along.'

Too Close for Comfort   Sammy Davis, Jr.   1956
The Broadway show 'Mr. Wonderful' showcased the talents of this popular nightclub entertainer as he tapped and sang *Too Close for Comfort*. Sammy Davis, Jr. didn't have a top-forty hit with the song, but Eydie Gorme did.

Chart 10.2. Ten Surprising Songs and Singers from Musical Theater

On Frank Sinatra's film soundtrack albums you can rediscover *That Old Black Magic* from 'Meet Danny Wilson,' *The Lady is a Tramp* from 'Pal Joey,' and *All The Way* from 'The Joker is Wild.' Surprisingly, never available as singles, Judy Garland's *Get Happy* from 'Summer Stock' and Marilyn Monroe's *Diamonds Are a Girl's Best Friend* from 'Gentlemen Prefer Blonds' were available only on the soundtrack albums.

Vocal specialist Marni Nixon can only be heard on soundtrack albums. She dubbed songs for Deborah Kerr in 'The King and I,' Natalie Wood in 'West Side Story,' and Audrey Hepburn in 'My Fair Lady.' Gogi Grant provided the singing voice for Ann Blyth in 'The Helen Morgan Story,' Trudy Erwin sang for Lana Turner in 'The Merry Widow,' and Sidney Poitier's vocals were dubbed by Robert McFerrin in 'Porgy and Bess.' Betty Noyes dubbed for Debbie Reynolds in *You Are My Lucky Star* at the finale of 'Singing in the Rain' and Rex Dennis dubbed the vocals for Russ Tamblyn on *Hallelujah* at the beginning of 'Hit the Deck' while Clark Burroughs dubbed his vocals on *Hallelujah* at the end of the film. You can discover all of these hidden-behind-the-scenes vocalists on soundtrack albums.

The Evolution of the Cassette Tape in the Sixties

Competing with the 78, 45, and 33 $^1/_3$ grooved discs was the introduction of music on magnetic tape. In 1947, the 3M Company began selling magnetic tape to broadcast and record companies and adoption of the technology in the recording studio was immediate. Producers could record extended musical works without interruption and mistakes could be cut out of a tape and corrections inserted. In the sixties multi-track technology and layered recordings became common in the recording studio.

Audiocassettes and quadraphonic 4-track and 8-track tape cartridges were introduced to US consumers in 1964 and it was clear that magnetic tape had inherent benefits over records—there was no surface hiss and no needle scratches. The introduction of inexpensive audiocassettes delivered recorded music not only into the home, but also to car dashboards, and portable pocket players like the Sony Walkman in 1979. Audiotape seemed poised to dominate recorded music until the digital CD arrived and revolutionized the distribution industry.

Ten Phenomenal-but-Unfamiliar Songs from Movies

April in Paris   Doris Day   1952
One of Doris Day's best songs is from one of her weakest films, '**April in Paris**.' It also featured her lively production number *I'm Gonna Ring the Bell Tonight.*

Breezin' Along with the Breeze   Lucille Ball & Desi Arnez 1954
This is the bright and peppy Lucy & Desi honeymoon duet from their hit comedy film '**The Long, Long Trailer**.'

Heat Wave   Marilyn Monroe   1954
The sensual *Heat Wave* and the suggestive *After You Get What You Want, You Don't Want It* were both from '**There's No Business Like Show Business**.' Ironically, Dolores Gray performed Marilyn Monroe's songs on the soundtrack album, due to contractual obligations.

Here's What I'm Here For   Judy Garland   1954
Judy Garland displays just the right lightness in *Here's What I'm Here For*, sometimes cut from shorter versions of her triumphant film '**A Star Is Born**.'

Lonesome Polecat   Russ Tamblyn and ensemble 1954
The brothers swing axes to punctuate *Lonesome Polecat* from MGM's rousing '**Seven Brides for Seven Brothers**.' The McGuire Sisters and Freddy Martin also recorded the song.

(The)Night They Invented Champagne Leslie Caron   1958
Leslie Caron is joined by Louis Jourdan and Hermione Gingold in this sparkling highlight from Learner and Lowe's enchanting '**Gigi**.'

No Two People   Danny Kaye & Jeanmaire 1952
From the Samuel Goldwyn classic extravaganza '**Hans Christian Anderson**.'

Someday Soon   Eddie Fisher   1956
With the lilt in his voice, Eddie Fisher belts out *Someday Soon* in his first film, '**Bundle of Joy**,' opposite his wife, Debbie Reynolds.

True Love   Bing Crosby & Grace Kelly 1956
Aided by a concertina and a fair wind, Bing Crosby sings *True Love* to a rapt Grace Kelly in '**High Society**,' the film that also includes Frank Sinatra's rarely heard *Mind If I Make Love to You* and *You're Sensational.*

You, My Love   Frank Sinatra   1955
An engaging, happy, but shy performance from the film '**Young At Heart**.'

Chart 10.3. Ten Phenomenal-but-Unfamiliar Songs from Movies

The Evolution of the CD (Compact Disc) in the eighties

In 1979, Philips presented the prototype of the compact disc that it had developed with Sony. On the digital CD, the music was converted into binary digits and engraved in microscopically small pits in the disc's surface. The CD player does not have a stylus; instead a laser beam (which does not wear out, but does detect fingerprints, scratches, dirt, and chips) reads the information stored on the disc. While the stylus on record players tracks grooves from the outside edge toward the inside, the CD laser beam tracks the disc from the inside to the outside.

The quality of the digital recording technique was far superior to the analog technology used on records and audiocassettes. The new CDs were introduced in the United States in 1983 and by 1988 more compact discs were sold than LPs. (Gronow, 1998, p.191) The following year record companies started phasing out LP record production. By the early nineties, audiocassette sales declined as well.

Recording formats during the twentieth century evolved from mechanical, to magnetic, to digital—from cylinders to CDs via: 78rpm records, 33 $^1/_3$ rpm LP albums, 45rpm singles, and cassette audiotapes. The 21st century delivers new digital music with on-line services like iTunes. By 2006, more digital tracks were sold in the US than CDs. (Leeds, 2006, p.C5)

References from Chapter 10:

Bordman, Gerald. *American Musical Theater*. New York: Oxford University Press, 1992.

Gronow, Pekka and Saunio, Ilpo (translated by Christopher Moseley). *An International History of the Recording Industry*. London: Cassell, 1998.

Hirschhorn, Clive. *The Hollywood Musical*. New York: Crown Publishers Inc., 1981.

Leeds, Jeff. "Squeezing Money From the Music." *The New York Times*, December 11, 2006, pp. C1-C5.

Schicke, Charles A. *Revolution in Sound*. Boston: Little, Brown and Company, 1974.

Whitburn, Joel. *Pop Hits, Singles & Albums 1940-1954*. New York: Billboard Books, 2002.

Whitburn, Joel. *Top Pop Albums 1955-1996*. New York: Billboard Books, 1996.

It is not the critic who counts, not the one who points out how the strong stumbled or where the doer of deeds could have done better.

The credit belongs to the one who is actually in the arena; whose face is marred by dust and sweat and blood; who strives valiantly; who errs and comes short again and again; who knows the great enthusiasms, the great devotions, and spends himself in a worthy cause; who, at the best, knows in the end the triumph of high achievement; and who, at the worst, if he fails, at least fails while daring greatly, so that his place shall never be with those cold and timid souls who know neither victory nor defeat.

Theodore Roosevelt, address at the Sorbonne, Paris (April 23, 1910)

Chapter 11

Politically Incorrect Songs, Cover Recordings, Payola, and Death Songs

Several controversial issues that surround fifties POP music continue to be debated today. With the benefit of five decades of hindsight, this chapter will examine four areas that are often subjected to criticism: (1) song lyrics that were acceptable in the fifties but would be considered politically incorrect today; (2) the practice of media-friendly white singers releasing 'cover' versions of R&B recordings that eclipsed the original versions by predominately black artists; (3) the 'payola' bribes record companies offered to promote certain recordings; and (4) songs of the late fifties that glamorized death and suicide.

Politically Incorrect Songs

We think of the 21st century as a very liberated time contrasted to the more repressive fifties, but there are recordings from the fifties that are censored today. An outstanding example is Doris Day's upbeat, flirtatious recording of the 1959 song simply titled '*No.*' Released by Columbia records with a lively arrangement and conducted by Frank deVol, the simple, impish song is sung by one of the decade's most popular girl singers. Written by Lee Prockriss and Paul J. Vance, the lyrics were considered rather innocuous at the time but would be considered decidedly politically incorrect today. In the song a male chorus sings "give me a kiss" and "I want to hug you" while a wholesome Doris Day responds with a firm "No." But when the boy in the song wants to leave her and find some other girlfriend, Doris Day responds "Don't you know that a girl means YES when she says NO." In the fifties this mixed-message to guys was 'girls are coy—they might say "NO"—but would welcome convincing' but by the end of the century the message was exactly the opposite 'when a girl says "NO" you can be arrested if you persist.'

Other politically incorrect songs during the fifties include the insensitivity of Arthur Godfrey's *She's Too Fat for Me*, Joni James' lack of feminist values singing that she is not 'worthy' of her boyfriend in *There Goes My Heart**, and Frankie Laine's references to, and treatment of, his Asian girlfriend in *Rose, Rose I Love You*. Although these songs were popular in the fifties, these recordings are rarely played today.

Politically incorrect songs did not begin nor end in the fifties. Early in the century, Fanny Brice introduced the poignant torch song, *My Man,* in the 'Ziegfeld Follies of 1921.' Written by Channing Pollock and Maurice Yvain, the vanquished woman returns 'on her knees' to the man who mistreats her and 'beats her too.' Cole Porter's *Love for Sale* glamorized youth prostitution. Written in 1931 for the Broadway musical 'The New Yorkers' it was considered too wicked for radio broadcasting.

Lyrics reinforcing a male-behavior-demeaning-women paradigm didn't end with the 50s either. In her 1962 hit recording *Johnny Get Angry* written by Sherman Edwards and Hal David, Joannie Sommers pleaded with her boyfriend to 'get angry' so that she would know that he cared for her. She wanted him to be brave and act more like a 'cave man.'

The Crystals, in their 1962 recording *He Hit Me (It Felt Like a Kiss),* written by Gerry Goffin and Carole King, made it clear that abuse from a boyfriend can not only be acceptable, it might be desirable. This recording produced by Phil Spector, paints a disturbing role for women as victims of male dominance.

---

*Before anyone draws the conclusion that only women in the fifties could consider themselves not 'worthy' of their boyfriends, it should be noted that *There Goes My Heart*, like many POP recordings during the fifties, was recorded by both genders. In the Nat King Cole version, he was not 'worthy' of his girlfriend.

Societal values evolve over time and popular music reflects and affects, mirrors and shapes those values at any specific point in time. While we do not rewrite our history like the revisionists in George Orwell's novel '1984' many people find it disquieting to listen to music with 'offensive' lyrics that are out of touch with present day values. At least the recordings were not burned like the books in Ray Bradbury's novel 'Fahrenheit 451' and they give us an insight into attitudes of the past.

Cover Songs

The decade of the fifties saw a transition in popular music. During the forties there were three distinctive types of recordings—'pop,' 'race,' and 'hillbilly'—and the success of each of these types of recordings was measured by its own popularity chart. Rhythm & blues recordings and country & western songs did not enter into mainstream popular music until the mid-fifties, and the timing coincided with the birth of rock 'n' roll.

'Pop' music records were usually released by one of the six major labels: Capitol, Columbia, Decca, MGM, Mercury, and RCA Victor. The large majority of popular vocalists were under contract to one of these major recording companies or their subsidiaries (see chart 11.1). 'Race' and 'hillbilly' records were usually the province of one of the specialty recording companies. These independent labels were scattered all over the country: CHESS in Chicago, KING in Cincinnati, PEACOCK in Houston, SAVOY in Newark, MODERN in Los Angeles, SPECIALITY in Hollywood, and the largest, ATLANTIC in New York. In the fifties, 'race' music became known as 'rhythm & blues,' and the success of its recordings was measured on the R&B chart. 'Hillbilly' music became 'country & western' and was measured on the C&W chart.

Rhythm and blues artists had difficulty getting their records played on white-dominated radio. Instead, mainstream artists recorded their own versions of R&B hits. The term 'cover recordings' referred to the record company practice of utilizing a popular singer to record a version of a song that was very similar to an original recording from a less-well-known singer, released by a small independent record label.

Black musicians found themselves isolated from the dominant recording companies and thus separated from the majority of the record-buying public. Worse yet, when a black artist developed an original, potentially

Record Company Labels and Recording Vocalists in the 50s
(Listed Alphabetically by Label)

ABC-PARAMOUNT RECORDS A&R chief: Buck Ram, Arranger: Don Costa:
Paul Anka, Eydie Gorme, Poni-Tails

ATCO RECORDS (Subsidiary of Atlantic Records): Bobby Darin

ATLANTIC RECORDS: Ruth Brown, Ray Charles, Aretha Franklin

BRUNSWICK RECORDS (Subsidiary of Decca Records): Crickets

CADENCE RECORDS Music Director: Archie Bleyer:
Everly Brothers, Chordettes, Julius LaRosa (until 1955), Andy Williams

CAPITOL RECORDS Music Directors: Les Baxter, Billy May, and Nelson Riddle:
Nat King Cole, Four Preps, Judy Garland, Peggy Lee (before 1952 & after 1957),
Dean Martin, Al Martino, Les Paul and Mary Ford,
Frank Sinatra (after 1953), Kay Starr (until 1955)

CHANCELLOR RECORDS: Frankie Avalon

COLUMBIA RECORDS Musical Director and A&R chief: Mitch Miller:
Tony Bennett, Don Cherry (after 1954), Rosemary Clooney, Vic Damone (after 1955),
Doris Day, Four Lads, Johnny Horton, Kitty Kallen (1958-1960),
Frankie Laine (after 1951), Johnny Mathis, Guy Mitchell, Johnnie Ray,
Dinah Shore (until 1950), Frank Sinatra (until 1953), Jo Stafford,
Sarah Vaughan (until 1954), Joan Weber

CORAL RECORDS (Decca Subsidiary) A&R Director: Dick Jacobs, Producer: Bob Thiele:
Ames Brothers (until 1953), Teresa Brewer, Karen Chandler, Dorothy Collins,
Don Cornell, Buddy Holly, McGuire Sisters, Debbie Reynolds

CUB RECORDS: Impalas

DECCA RECORDS Music Director: Gordon Jenkins:
Don Cherry (until 1954), Bing Crosby, Ella Fitzgerald, Four Aces,
Bill Haley and his Comets, Al Hibbler, Kitty Kallen (1953-1956),
Peggy Lee (1952-1957), Mills Brothers (until 1957), Caterina Valente

DERBY RECORDS: Jaye P. Morgan (until 1954)

DORE RECORDS: Teddy Bears

Chart 11.1. Record Company Labels and Recording Vocalists in the 50s
(Chart continues on the next page)

Record Company Labels and Recording Vocalists in the 50s
(continued)

DOT RECORDS Producer: Billy Vaughn: Pat Boone,
Fontane Sisters (after 1954), Tab Hunter, Mills Brothers (after 1957), Gale Storm

ERA RECORDS: Gogi Grant

FRATERNITY RECORDS: Cathy Carr

GROOVE RECORDS (Subsidiary of RCA Victor): Mickey and Sylvia

IMPERIAL RECORDS Producer: Dave Bartholomew: Ricky Nelson (after 1957)

JUBILEE RECORDS: Della Reese (1957-1958)

KAPP RECORDS: Jane Morgan

KEEN RECORDS: Sam Cooke

LIBERTY RECORDS Producer: Al Bennett: Patience & Prudence

MERCURY RECORDS A&R Directors: Art Talmadge and Clyde Otis:
The Crewcuts, Vic Damone (until 1955), Gaylords, Georgia Gibbs, Kitty Kallen (until
1952), Patti Page, The Platters, June Valli (after 1958), Sarah Vaughan (after 1954)

MGM RECORDS:
Tommy Edwards, Connie Francis, Frankie Laine (until 1951), Joni James

RCA VICTOR RECORDS A&R Directors: NY-Steve Sholes; Nashville-Chet Atkins
Music Director: Hugo Winterhalter: The Ames Brothers (after 1953), Eddy Arnold,
Harry Belafonte, The Browns, Perry Como, Eddie Fisher,
Fontane Sisters (until 1954), Eartha Kitt, Julius LaRosa (after 1956),
Jaye P. Morgan (after 1954), Elvis Presley (after 1955), Della Reese (after 1959),
Dinah Shore (after 1950), Kay Starr (1955-1960), June Valli (until 1957)

ROULETTE RECORDS Producers: Hugo and Luigi: Jimmie Rodgers

RPM RECORDS: Teen Queens

SIGNET RECORDS: Miss Toni Fisher

SUN RECORDS Producer: Sam Phillips: Elvis Presley (until 1955)

VERVE RECORDS: Ricky Nelson (until 1957)

Chart 11.1. Record Company Labels and Recording Vocalists in the 50s

successful tune through a small independent recording outfit, white artists, including Pat Boone, the Crew-Cuts, Gale Storm, and the Fontane Sisters, hurriedly supplied the white-record-purchasing-audience with an acceptable 'cover' version of the same tune. Popular fifties singers, Perry Como, Teresa Brewer, Eddie Fisher, and the McGuire Sisters, all recorded 'safe' sanitized cover recordings of material from black and R&B artists. The major record companies would use their influence to promote their cover versions to the exclusion of the work of the original performers.

The major record labels started recording covers in the early 1950s to deal with the threat of 'cross-over' songs from the rhythm and blues and country artists. The major labels didn't want the specialized country, R&B, and black musicians to threaten the dominance the major studios enjoyed in the mainstream POP music market. Sometimes the covers of the original songs kept the same lyrics but re-orchestrated the music with arrangements that would burr off the rough edges and turn the raw, driving beat and the fast tempo of the originals into the familiar, mellow, and non-threatening style of white popular music. Covers of R&B songs might include the feelings of guitars and drums, but not emphasize them. Independent recording companies, Dot and Cadence, were formed in the fifties and specialized in producing cover recordings.

Recording different versions of popular songs is an established practice—*St. Louis Blues* is reputed to be the world's most-recorded song and there are dozens of versions of *Stardust, Night and Day,* and *April in Paris.* Cover versions were an extension of this and have been around as long as records have been made. There are examples of R&B artists recording 'country' and 'pop' songs and there were certainly instances of country singers recording 'pop' and 'R&B,' but the practice of established white singers recording covers of R&B records by black artists was especially frequent during the 1950s. Sociologist B. Lee Cooper, in his book 'Popular Music Perspectives' asserts that this cover phenomenon occurred frequently enough to confirm the suspicion that prejudice, plagiarism, and financial exploitation were central factors in American recording industry practices between 1953 and 1956. (Cooper, 1991, p.140)

Perry Como covered Gene and Eunice's *Ko Ko Mo* while the Crew Cuts covered the Chords' *Sh-Boom* and the Penguins' *Earth Angel.* The list of covers is long and most of the covers were the hit versions. Pat Boone covered Fats Domino's *Ain't That a Shame* as well as Little Richard's *Long Tall Sally* and *Tutti' Frutti.* June Valli had a hit with her cover of the Four Tunes' recording of *I Understand Just How You Feel* in 1954 (see chart 11.2).

Promotion man, Mickey Addy, at Dot Records in Gallatin, Tennessee, had a reputation for, and made a lot of money producing, cover recordings. Crooner Pat Boone, screen star Tab Hunter, and TV star Gale Storm performed with Billy Vaughn and his Orchestra often imitating an R&B record note for note, with a bit of cleaning and tightening and dressing it with saxes in rippling thirds. Mickey Addy also revived old songs and two of them, *Love Letters in the Sand* and *Melody of Love,* are in the all-time top ten of the fifties decade. (Whitcomb, 1974, p.222) Pat Boone had a number one hit with *Love Letters in the Sand* in 1957 but it had been a top ten hit for Ted Black twenty-five years earlier. The song was loosely based on *The Spanish Cavalier* written in 1881. Billy Vaughn's 1955 instrumental hit *Melody of Love* was written in 1903.

Lavern Baker, whose *Tweedle Dee* was covered by Georgia Gibbs right down to the crucial arrangement, tried to get a law passed which gave copyright protection to arrangements—but her attempt was unsuccessful. In fairness it must be said that sometimes the cover versions sounded very different than the R&B original. Bill Haley's *Shake Rattle and Roll* cover record was very different from Joe Turner's original. Haley's record was a hybrid and his was the hit.

Johnny Ace originally recorded *Pledging My Love*, but before it reached the top of the R&B charts, Johnny Ace had lost his life in a failed game of Russian roulette. Teresa Brewer recorded this beautiful song and it became a top-twenty hit for her. Most often the cover artist was white and the original artist was black but that was not always the case. Eddie Fisher had a hit with his cover of the Tarriers' version of *Cindy, Oh Cindy* in 1956. Tab Hunter covered Sonny James' *Young Love* and Gale Storm covered Bonnie Guitar's *Dark Moon*.

Why did the 'covers' sell? Was it race prejudice, better distribution, or public taste? In many ways, the original was a rougher gem and the cover a more polished stone. Today, rock purists prefer the raw, rough, gritty original versions. Fans of fifties EASY-POP often prefer the softer, more professional 'covers.' The singers on the 'covers' almost always provided a recognizable sparkle in their voice, a more trained sound in their delivery, and the accompaniment was softer and more mellow.

Cover Recordings during the mid 50s
(listed alphabetically by song title)

Song	Record label		Performer	Year recorded	Highest chart position
Ain't That A Shame	DOT	cover by	Pat Boone	1955	#1
	IMPERIAL	original by	Fats Domino	1955	#10
Bo Weevil	CORAL	cover by	Teresa Brewer	1956	#17
	IMPERIAL	original by	Fats Domino	1956	#35
Butterfly	CADENCE	cover by	Andy Williams	1957	#1
	CAMEO	original by	Charlie Grace	1957	#1
Cindy, Oh Cindy	RCA	cover by	Eddie Fisher	1956	#10
	GLORY	original by	Vince Martin & the Tarriers	1956	#9
Crying in the Chapel	RCA	cover by	June Valli	1953	#4
	JUBILEE	cover by	the Orioles	1953	#11
	VALLEY	original by	Darrell Glenn	1953	n/a
Dance with Me Henry **The Wallflower** **Work with Me Annie**	DOT	cover by	Georgia Gibbs	1955	#1
	MODERN	original by	Etta James	1954	n/a
	FEDERAL	original by	Hank Ballard & the Midnighters	1954	n/a
Dark Moon	DOT	cover by	Gale Storm	1957	#4
	DOT	original by	Bonnie Guitar	1957	#6
Earth Angel	MERCURY	cover by	the Crew-Cuts	1955	#3
	SOUND	cover by	Gloria Mann	1955	#18
	DOOTONE	original by	the Penguins	1955	#8
Eddie My Love	DOT	cover by	the Fontane Sisters	1956	#11
	CADENCE	cover by	the Chordettes	1956	#14
	RPM	original by	the Teen Queens	1956	#14
Empty Arms	CORAL	cover by	Teresa Brewer	1957	#13
	ATLANTIC	original by	Ivory Joe Hunter	1956	#43
Goodnight, Sweetheart, Goodnight	CORAL	cover by	the McGuire Sisters	1954	#7
	RCA	cover by	Sunny Gale	1954	#26
	VEE-JAY	original by	the Spaniels	1954	#24
Hearts of Stone	DOT	cover by	the Fontane Sisters	1954	#1
	DE LUXE	original by	Otis Williams & the Charms	1954	#15

Chart 11.2. Cover Recordings during the mid 50s

(Chart continues on the next page)

Cover Recordings during the mid 50s (continued)

Song	Record label		Performer	Year recorded	Highest chart position
I Hear You Knockin'	DOT	cover by	Gale Storm	1955	#2
(But You Can't Come In)	IMPERIAL	cover by	Fats Domino	1961	#67
	IMPERIAL	original by	Smiley Lewis	1955	n/a
I Understand	RCA	cover by	June Valli	1954	#6
(Just How You Feel)	JUBILEE	original by	the Four Tunes	1954	#8
I'm in Love Again	DOT	cover by	the Fontane Sisters	1956	#38
	IMPERIAL	original by	Fats Domino	1956	#3
I'm Walkin'	VERVE	cover by	Ricky Nelson	1957	#17
	IMPERIAL	original by	Fats Domino	1957	#4
Ivory Tower	FRATERNITY	cover by	Cathy Carr	1956	#2
	DOT	cover by	Gale Storm	1956	#6
	DE LUXE	original by	Otis Williams & the Charms	1956	#11
Just Walking in the Rain	COLUMBIA	cover by	Johnnie Ray	1956	#2
	SUN	original by	the Prisonaires	1953	n/a
Ko Ko Mo	RCA	cover by	Perry Como	1955	#2
(I Love You So)	MERCURY	cover by	the Crew-Cuts	1955	#6
	COMBO	original by	Gene & Eunice	1954	n/a
Little Darlin'	MERCURY	cover by	the Diamonds	1957	#2
	EXCELLO	original by	the Gladiolas	1957	#41
Long Tall Sally	DOT	cover by	Pat Boone	1956	#8
	SPECIALTY	original by	Little Richard	1956	#6
Lucky Lips	DOT	cover by	Gale Storm	1957	#77
	ATLANTIC	original by	Ruth Brown	1957	#25
Pledging My Love	CORAL	cover by	Teresa Brewer	1955	#3
	DUKE	original by	Johnny Ace	1955	#17
Rollin' Stone	DOT	cover by	the Fontane Sisters	1955	#13
	EXCELLO	original by	the Marigolds	1955	n/a

Chart 11.2. Cover Recordings during the mid 50s

(Chart continues on the next page)

Cover Recordings during the mid 50s (continued)

Song	Record label		Performer	Year recorded	Highest chart position
Seventeen	DOT	cover by	the Fontane Sisters	1955	#3
	MERCURY	cover by	Rusty Draper	1955	#18
	KING	original by	Boyd Bennett & his Rockets	1956	#5
Sh—Boom	MERCURY	cover by	the Crew-Cuts	1954	#1
	CAT	original by	the Chords	1954	#5
Shake Rattle & Roll	DECCA	cover by	Bill Haley & his Comets	1954	#7
	ATLANTIC	original by	Joe Turner	1954	#22
Silhouettes	MERCURY	cover by	the Diamonds	1957	#10
	ABC-PARAMOUNT	cover by	Steve Gibson	1957	#63
	CAMEO	original by	the Rays	1957	#3
Sincerely	CORAL	cover by	the McGuire Sisters	1955	#1
	CHESS	original by	the Moonglows	1954	#20
A Tear Fell	CORAL	cover by	Teresa Brewer	1956	#5
	ATLANTIC	original by	Ivory Joe Hunter	1956	n/a
Tutti' Frutti	DOT	cover by	Pat Boone	1956	#12
	SPECIALTY	original by	Little Richard	1956	#17
Tweedle Dee	MERCURY	cover by	Georgia Gibbs	1955	#2
	ATLANTIC	original by	LaVern Baker	1955	#14
Two Hearts, Two Kisses	DOT	cover by	Pat Boone	1955	#16
	COLUMBIA	cover by	Doris Day	1955	n/a
	DE LUXE	original by	Otis Williams & the Charms	1955	n/a
Why Do Fools Fall in Love	DOT	cover by	Gale Storm	1956	#9
	MERCURY	cover by	the Diamonds	1956	#12
	DECCA	cover by	Gloria Mann	1956	#59
	GEE	original by	Frankie Lymon & the Teenagers	1956	#6
Young Love	DOT	cover by	Tab Hunter	1957	#1
	MERCURY	cover by	the Crew-Cuts	1957	#17
	CAPITOL	original by	Sonny James	1957	#1
	RCA	earlier by	co-writer Ric Cartey	1956	n/a

Chart 11.2. Cover Recordings during the mid 50s

Elvis Presley encounters 'Covers' on the movie screen

The shady business of 'cover' recordings was the central plot line of Elvis Presley's third film *Jailhouse Rock* in 1957. In it he plays an ex-convict who forms a record company with his co-star Judy Tyler. His first recordings at his new company are 'covered' word-for-word by an established vocalist and the 'cover' even copies his unique arrangement. The 'cover' is a big hit and it threatens his career and his new recording company. Ultimately his music and his company prevail, he does get the girl, and there is a happy ending to the movie; in real life though, Judy Tyler, the Broadway singer/actress who played his girlfriend, died tragically in an automobile accident shortly after the film's completion. This was one of the few Elvis Presley movies that had a serious plot, but there were of course frequent intervals to let the music rock and the pelvis roll. Adolescents of all ages gave it a frenzied welcome. Two of Elvis Presley's biggest hit songs, *Jailhouse Rock* and *Treat Me Nice* were from this profitable movie, along with less commercial numbers *Young and Beautiful, I Wanna Be Free, You're So Square (Baby I Don't Care)*, and *Don't Leave Me Now*.

EASY-POP singers record versions of Show Tunes

It was common practice in the fifties for popular singers, contracted to the major recording companies, to record songs that original artists introduced on the stage, but no one refers to these pop versions of show tunes as 'cover' recordings. The stage singer recorded the song on the 'original cast' album, but it was the familiar pop singer who usually scored the big hit single. Broadway superstar Ethel Merman never had a top-twenty POP hit even though many of the songs she introduced became classic standards.

Popular Broadway leading man John Raitt introduced the song *Hey There* in 'Pajama Game,' but it was Rosemary Clooney's record that became a #1 hit; Richard Kiley introduced *Stranger in Paradise* in 'Kismet,' while Tony Bennett scored one of his biggest hit records with his version; Larry Kurt introduced *Maria* in 'West Side Story,' but Johnny Mathis had the popular recording; and Jerry Orbach introduced *Try To Remember* in 'The Fantastics,' but Ed Ames had the popular record. In 'Guys and Dolls' Robert Alda introduced *Luck Be A Lady*, but Frank Sinatra recorded it; and in the same show Vivian Blain introduced *A Bushel and a Peck*, but Perry Como had the big hit (see chapter 7 for a more complete list of pop singers and show tunes). Two of Broadways' brightest singing stars, Julie Andrews and Mary Martin, never had a popular hit recording.

Payola

Pay-for-play gifts of cash, shares of copyright, or cases of liquor from publishers became known in the music business as 'payola.' One enterprising form of reward was to give a promoter a financial share in a song that had no hit potential. The song would then be recorded and released on the 'B' side of a 45 with a sure-fire hit on the 'A' side. Copyright owners of the songs on both sides of a record earn the same royalties.

Bribery was never as rampant as it was in the mid-fifties. Influential radio disc jockeys with their large listening audiences became the prime targets of promoters working for record companies and distributors. Many deejays increased their modest income by demanding money in exchange for plugging selected records on the air. Competition for the limited number of time slots threw record promotion men into a frenzy. Stakes were higher than ever.

The situation reached its climax at the infamous national disc jockey convention in Miami Beach in the spring of 1959. Publishers engaged in a wild competition to win the favors of disc jockeys by plying them with sumptuous meals, expensive liquor, and high-priced prostitutes. Time Magazine reported the juicier aspects of the convention under the headline 'Booze, Broads, and Payola.' Within months, government committees were holding hearings and the scandal produced a stringent federal antipayola law. (Schicke, 1974, p.139)

Death songs

Toward the end of the fifties and the beginning of the sixties a short-lived death theme appeared in several popular songs (see chart 11.3). Within the popular teenage 'coffin' song arena, automobile accidents and airline crashes constitute events that entail the unexpected loss of life. Death interrupts anticipated continuity. The studies of these ballads explore youthful experiences with either accidental death or suicide. Sociologist R. Serge Denisoff, a perceptive music analyst, alleged in 1983 that the popularity of love-lost-through-death songs was due to rapid cultural and political change at the end of the decade.

Popular 'Death' Songs Recorded in the 50s and early 60s

Song	Singer	Year released
I'd Rather Die Young	the Hilltoppers	1953
Endless Sleep	Jody Reynolds	1958
El Paso	Marty Robbins	1959
Running Bear	Johnny Preston	1959
Teen Angel	Mark Dinning	1960
Tell Laura I Love Her	Ray Peterson	1960
Ebony Eyes	the Everly Brothers	1961
Moody River	Pat Boone	1961
Leah	Roy Orbison	1962
Patches	Dicky Lee	1962
Last Kiss	J. Frank Wilson	1964
Terry	Twinkle	1965

Chart 11.3. Popular 'Death' Songs Recorded in the 50s and early 60s

Songs which recount self-inflicted death are numerous, melancholy, and somewhat mysterious. Most often, an act of suicide is described by a forlorn lover, by a remaining relative, or by a sad and confused friend. (Cooper, 1991, p.85) Lovers mourn the loss of mates in *Endless Sleep*, an Indian couple produce a watery Romeo and Juliet death scene in *Running Bear,* and after *Patches* commits suicide her forsaken lover, in spite of his parents disapproval, joins her the next night.

It is especially ironic that while there were popular fifties and sixties songs that glamorized death, tragic deaths actually took the lives of several popular singing stars. Sam Cooke died in an altercation with a woman guest and the night manager at a seedy motel where he was shot to death while allegedly trying to attack the manager. Jimmie Rodgers suffered severe head injuries in a controversial incident involving a Los Angeles police officer. Fifties singer/actor Sal Mineo, who co-starred with James Dean in 'Rebel Without a Cause' was stabbed to death. Country music's greatest legend, Hank Williams died in 1953 as a result of drinking and drug use, Johnny Ace died backstage at a show in 1954 in a game of Russian roulette, and singer/actress Judy Tyler, who played Elvis Presley's girlfriend in 'Jailhouse Rock', died in an automobile accident shortly after the film's completion. The most shocking event at the end of the decade was the plane crash that killed Buddy Holly, singer Ritchie Valens, and rock 'n' roll singer the 'Big Bopper' in 1959. Tommy Dee, Carol Kay, and the Teen-Aires eulogized the event in their top-ten song *Three Stars*.

The adversities in the fifties, the controversy over 'covers' in the recording industry, and the scandal of 'payola' in broadcasting, pale in comparison to the radical impact and world-wide turmoil that rock 'n' roll would deliver. The trustful and enthusiastic fifties disappeared as more skeptical and cynical decades dawned. Popular music encouraged intensity not subtlety and lyrics turned harsh rather than mellow. Flowing against the tide of rock 'n' roll, however, EASY-POP music continued to evolve as a new decade arrived. Chapter 12 looks at fifties-style EASY-POP songs recorded in the 60s and beyond.

References from Chapter 11:

Cooper, B. Lee. *Popular Music Perspectives: Ideas, Themes, and Patterns in Contemporary Lyrics*. Bowling Green, Ohio: Bowling Green State University Popular Press, 1991.

Denisoff, R. Surge. "Death Songs and Teenage Roles" in *Sing a Song of Social Significance* (Bowling Green, Ohio: Bowling Green State University Press, 1972), pp. 171-176.

Denisoff, R. Surge. " 'Teen Angel': Resistance, Rebellion, and Death—Revisited": *Journal of Popular Culture*, XVI (Spring 1983), pp. 116-122.

Gillett, Charlie. *The Sound of the City – The Rise of Rock 'n' Roll*. New York: Dell Publishing, 1970.

Schicke, Charles A., *Revolution in Sound – A Biography of the Recording Industry*. Boston: Little, Brown and Company, 1974.

Whitcomb, Ian. *After the Ball*. London: Allen Lane the Penguin Press, 1972.

Some would say that myth does nothing but feed fantasies and distort reality, but the crucial point about myth is that it provides a greater reality.

Timothy Scheurer in *Born in the U.S.A.* (1991)

Chapter 12

Fifties-style EASY-POP in the 60s and Beyond

Fifties EASY-POP recordings didn't disappear on the last day of 1959. Even though rock 'n' roll was dominating the musical scene, songs with upbeat vocalists, infectious arrangements, and bright lyrics continued to be recorded. In the sixties, new talents Anita Bryant, Connie Francis, Dionne Warwick, Bobby Darin, Bobby Vinton, Paul Anka, Frankie Avalon, and Al Martino, joined fifties pop singers Johnny Mathis, Andy Williams, and Dean Martin in recording fifties-style EASY-POP songs. The Supremes and the Temptations brought the Motown sound, while the Beach Boys brought a California surf sound as pop music evolved (see chart 12.1).

The reigning superstars of the fifties scored big hits in the sixties. Tony Bennett continued to perform and recorded his signature song *I Left My Heart in San Francisco* in 1962. Patti Page had one of her most successful recordings with *Hush, Hush, Sweet Charlotte* in 1965. Frank Sinatra had a big hit recording with *Strangers in the Night* in 1966.

Pop megastar Cher emerged in the sixties and Ray Charles recorded his first #1 song, *I Can't Stop Loving You,* in 1962. Dionne Warwick and Jack Jones surfaced in the sixties and Barbara Streisand had her first hit with *People* from her Broadway show 'Funny Girl' in 1964.

245

The Early Sixties

In 1960, the fresh, unpretentious, and melodic musical 'Bye, Bye Birdie' premiered on Broadway and it was made into a very successful film two years later. In addition to kidding the flourishing rock 'n' roll rage and wriggling superstar, Elvis Presley, it is ironic that the show introduced a very typical fifties song, *One Boy*, that made the charts for Joanie Sommers. Other sixties records included The Tokens' *The Lion Sleeps Tonight*, Ray Charles' *I Can't Stop Loving You* (both were #1 hits in 1961), and the 4 Seasons' *Sherry* that zoomed to #1 in 1962.

Two popular films produced in the early sixties, 'Where the Boys Are' in 1961 and 'Follow the Boys' in 1963, were stories about youngsters seeking fun and romance; they both featured pop singer Connie Francis, and both were liberally interspersed with typically 50s style EASY-POP songs. In 1965, the youth film 'Ski Party' introduced Leslie Gore's top twenty hit, *Sunshine, Lollipops and Rainbows,* another 50s style song.

The early sixties (before the arrival of the Beatles) saw big hits for rock 'n' roll stars. Chubby Checker's *The Twist*, Bobby Lewis' *Tossin' And Turnin',* Del Shannon's *Runaway,* and of course, several Elvis Presley recordings placed #1 on the charts. According to pop music researcher Joel Whitburn's point system for ranking the popularity of recording artists, the twenty most popular performers of the sixties were:

#1 Elvis Presley	#8 The 4 Seasons	#15 Jackie Wilson
#2 The Beatles	#9 Marvin Gaye	#16 Roy Orbison
#3 Brenda Lee	#10 The Supremes	#17 Brook Benton
#4 Ray Charles	#11 Bobby Vinton	#18 Sam Cooke
#5 Connie Francis	#12 Chubby Checker	#19 Dionne Warwick
#6 The Beach Boys	#13 The Miracles	#20 Rolling Stones
#7 James Brown	#14 The Temptations	(Whitburn, 1987. p.724)

The sixties brought a major change in radio listening habits. Popular music broadcast on AM radio stations hit its peak in the fifties. In 1961, stereo FM radio brought a higher quality to music broadcasting. At the same time marketing analyst, Gordon McLendon, developed the concept of format radio—identifying a station with just one particular music genre—and with that commercial radio gave birth to the narrowcasting style that began to segment the radio audience by musical taste. Today all radio stations have specialized into Adult Rock, Urban, Alternative, Country, Christian, Jazz, or some other identifiable form of musical taste.

Fifties-style EASY-POP Songs Recorded in the early Sixties

Title	Artist	Year released	Highest chart rank
Puppy Love	Paul Anka	1960	#2
Paper Roses	Anita Bryant	1960	#5
I Can't Stop Loving You	Ray Charles	1962	#1
Venus in Blue Jeans	Jimmy Clanton	1962	#7
Chain Gang & *Cupid*	Sam Cooke	1960 & 1961	#2 & 17
Beyond the Sea & *Things*	Bobby Darin	1960 & 1962	#6 & 3
Goodbye Cruel World	James Darren	1961	#3
Save the Last Dance for Me	The Drifters	1960	#1
Angel on My Shoulder	Shelby Flint	1960	#22
Big Girls Don't Cry & *Sherry*	4 Seasons with Frankie Valli	1962	#1
Everybody's Somebody's Fool	Connie Francis	1960	#1
Pineapple Princess	Annette Funicello	1960	#11
North to Alaska	Johnny Horton	1960	#4
She Cried	Jay and the Americans	1962	#5
Go Away Little Girl	Steve Lawrence	1962	#1
I'm Sorry & *I Want to Be Wanted*	Brenda Lee	1960	#1
Come Back Silly Girl	The Lettermen	1962	#17
Please Mr. Postman	The Marvellettes	1961	#1
Teenage Idol	Ricky Nelson	1962	#5
I Love How You Love Me	The Paris Sisters	1961	#5
She's Not You & *Follow That Dream*	Elvis Presley	1962	#5 & 15
Anything That's Part of You	Elvis Presley	1962	#31
One Boy	Joanie Sommers	1960	#54
Sixteen Reasons	Connie Stevens	1960	#3
My Coloring Book	Sandy Stewart	1962	#20
Sad Movies Make Me Cry	Sue Thompson	1961	#5
The Lion Sleeps Tonight (Wimoweh)	The Tokens	1961	#1
Take Good Care of My Baby	Bobby Vee	1961	#1
Roses Are Red (My Love)	Bobby Vinton	1962	#1

Chart 12.1. Fifties-style EASY-POP Songs Recorded in the early 1960s

The Mid Sixties

The mid-sixties will always be associated with the British invasion of the popular music scene. It began in 1964 with the Beatles arrival in the United States from Liverpool, England. Their recording of *I Want To Hold Your Hand* hit #1 on the US charts in January and stayed there for seven weeks. But while the Beatles were changing music, fifties-style songs were still being recorded by the Murmaids, Leslie Gore, Dean Martin, and Nat King Cole (see chart 12.2). The Beatles' *I Want to Hold Your Hand* and the Supremes' *Baby Love* both placed #1 in 1964.

Two popular television series, 'Shindig' on ABC and 'Hullabaloo' on NBC, brought popular music to prime time in the mid-sixties. 'Shindig' regularly featured Bobby Sherman, the Righteous Brothers, Darlene Love, and Glen Campbell. The premiere telecast in 1964 starred Sam Cooke. One 1964 show, produced in England, featured the Beatles and the fall 1965 premiere included the Rolling Stones, the Kinks, the Byrds, and the Everly Brothers.

'Hullabaloo' had a different guest host each week including Paul Anka, Jack Jones, Frankie Avalon, and Annette Funicello. The Supremes, the Ronettes, and Sonny and Cher were some of the performers. The youth-oriented program often included a black & white filmed feature hosted by Beatles manager, Brian Epstein. That segment introduced new British acts like Gerry and the Pacemakers, Marianne Faithful, Herman's Hermits, and the Moody Blues.

The husband and wife songwriting team, Jeff Barry and Ellie Greenwich, were prolific in the sixties. *Da Doo Ron Ron, Not Too Young to Get Married, Be My Baby*, and *Then He Kissed Me,* were some of their hits.

Movies scored big with audiences in the sixties with 'Psycho,' 'Lawrence of Arabia,' and 'Cleopatra.' In addition to the dramatic hits there were a handful of successful musicals—the 1961 film 'West Side Story,' 1962's 'The Music Man,' and 1964's 'Mary Poppins' and 'My Fair Lady.' Memorable songs also came from less well-known films. The New Christy Minstrels sang *Today, Company of Cowards*, and *This Old Riverboat* in the 1964 light-hearted western comedy 'Advance To the Rear' starring Glenn Ford. Judy Garland sang her favorite song *Little Drops of Rain* in the 1962 animated musical film 'Gay Purr-ee.' The song was written by Harold Arlen with lyrics by Yip Harburg—the same team that wrote her signature *Over the Rainbow* twenty years earlier.

Fifties-style EASY-POP Songs Recorded in the mid Sixties

Title	Artist	Year released	Highest chart rank
Downtown	Petula Clark	1964	#1
Those Lazy Hazy Crazy Days of Summer	Nat King Cole	1963	#6
Another Saturday Night	Sam Cooke	1963	#10
Then He Kissed Me	Crystals	1963	#6
Let the Little Girl Limbo	Doris Day	1963	n/a
Chapel of Love	The Dixie Cups	1964	#5
The Shoop, Shoop Song (It's in His Kiss)	Betty Everett	1964	#6
Walk Like a Man	4 Seasons with Frankie Valli	1963	#1
It's My Party	Leslie Gore	1963	#1
Blame It on the Bossa Nova	Eydie Gorme	1963	#7
Only in America	Jay and the Americans	1963	#25
I Will Follow Him	Little Peggy March	1963	#1
Wait Till My Bobby Gets Home	Darlene Love	1963	#26
Everybody Loves Somebody Sometime	Dean Martin	1964	#1
I Love You Because	Al Martino	1963	#3
Popsicles and Icicles	The Murmaids	1963	#3
Green, Green	The New Christy Minstrels	1963	#14
Oh, Pretty Woman	Roy Orbison	1964	#1
Pretty Boy Lonely	Patti Page	1963	#98
Puff the Magic Dragon	Peter, Paul & Mary	1963	#2
Love Me With All Your Heart	The Ray Charles Singers	1964	#3
Navy Blue	Diane Renay	1964	#6
The Wedding	Julie Rogers	1964	#10
Don't Let the Rain Come Down	The Serendipity Singers	1964	#6
Wishin' and Hopin'	Dusty Springfield	1964	#6
Baby Love	The Supremes	1964	#1
My Guy	Mary Wells	1964	#1
Can't Get Used to Losing You	Andy Williams	1964	#1
White on White	Danny Williams	1964	#9

Chart 12.2.   Fifties-style EASY-POP Songs Recorded in the mid 1960s

The Late Sixties

New performers were beginning careers that would make them legends in the music world. Late sixties hit recordings included the Rolling Stones' (*I Can't Get No*) *Satisfaction* and Sonny & Cher's *I Got You Babe* in 1965, Simon & Garfunkel's *The Sounds of Silence* and the Beach Boys' *Good Vibrations* in 1966, Aretha Franklin's *Respect* in 1967, the Beatles' *Hey Jude* and Marvin Gaye's *I Heard It Through the Grapevine* in 1968, and the 5th Dimension's *Aquarius* in 1969.

In addition to new rock music, fifties-style recordings were still being released in the late sixties (see chart 12.3). New performers, Petula Clark, Shelby Flint, the Vogues, and Neil Diamond joined more traditional vocalists, Frank Sinatra, Ed Ames, and Patti Page with top hits.

Two genres of network television series dominated the ratings in the sixties—westerns and lowbrow comedies. The TV western 'Gunsmoke' on CBS was the most popular series during the early sixties and NBC's 'Bonanza' was the most popular series of the late sixties. CBS' situation comedies 'The Beverly Hillbillies' and 'Gomer Pyle' were also top rated during the decade along with NBC's long running western 'Wagon Train.' There were two outstanding TV events in 1965: CBS presented Barbara Streisand's first TV special 'My Name is Barbara' in April and NBC countered with Frank Sinatra's one-man show 'A Man and His Music' in November. Other major TV firsts that are essential viewing today include: the first showing of Dr. Seuss' 'How the Grinch Stole Christmas' children's treat in 1966 and professional football's first Super Bowl that aired in 1967.

While dramatic films like 'Doctor Zhivago' and 'The Graduate' scored big at the box office, several major musical movies were also popular. The 1965 film 'The Sound of Music' with Julie Andrews was one of the highest grossing films of all time. The late sixties also saw the release of Barbara Streisand's 'Funny Girl' and 'Hello Dolly.' Films were becoming more permissive in the sixties and with Hollywood's new indulgence came a new rating system for films. The 'G,' 'PG,' 'R,' and 'X' ratings were established by the motion picture industry in 1968 to advise parents of the appropriateness of the content of films for viewing by youngsters.

Fifties-style EASY-POP Songs Recorded in the late Sixties

Title	Artist	Year released	Highest chart rank
My Cup Runneth Over	Ed Ames	1967	#8
Cherish & Windy	The Association	1966 & 1967	#1
Wichita Lineman	Glen Campbell	1968	#3
It Must Be Him	Vikki Carr	1967	#3
Hold Me, Thrill Me, Kiss Me	Mel Carter	1965	#8
Just a Drop of Rain	Don Cherry	1969	n/a
My Love	Petula Clark	1965	#1
Yesterday, When I Was Young	Roy Clark	1969	#19
Sweet Caroline	Neil Diamond	1969	#4
Up-Up and Away	The 5th Dimension	1967	#7
Cast Your Fate to the Wind	Shelby Flint	1966	#61
Working My Way Back to You	4 Seasons with Frankie Valli	1966	#9
Honey	Bobby Goldsboro	1968	#1
59th Street Bridge Song (Feelin' Groovy)	Harpers Bizarre	1967	#13
The Race is On	Jack Jones	1965	#15
You Gave Me a Mountain	Frankie Laine	1969	#24
What's New Pussycat?	Tom Jones	1965	#3
Take Me Back	Little Anthony & the Imperials	1965	#16
Hush, Hush, Sweet Charlotte	Patti Page	1965	#8
Angel of the Morning	Marrilee Rush	1968	#7
La, La, La (If I Had You)	Bobby Sherman	1969	#9
Strangers in the Night	Frank Sinatra	1966	#1
You Don't Have to Say You Love Me	Dusty Springfield	1966	#4
You Can't Hurry Love	The Supremes	1966	#1
Hooked on a Feeling	B.J. Thomas	1968	#5
Where Were You When I Needed You	Jerry Vale	1965	#99
Five O'Clock World & You're the One	The Vogues	1965	#4
Turn Around, Look at Me	The Vogues	1968	#7
I Say a Little Prayer	Dionne Warwick	1967	#4

Chart 12.3. Fifties-style EASY-POP Songs Recorded in the late 1960s

The Seventies

Nostalgia for the 1950s became big business in the 1970s. The film 'American Graffiti' with its fifties-style soundtrack was released in 1973. It starred Richard Dreyfus, Ron Howard, Cindy Williams, and Harrison Ford. George Lucas, who would later astound the world with the 'Star Wars' films, directed the instant classic.

In 1974, ABC-TV brought the 50s era back to network television. 'Happy Days,' a version of teenage life in the mid-1950s, started modestly and built in popularity throughout the seventies. Ron Howard played innocent teenager Richie Cunningham and Henry Winkler play hip, cool, dropout, Fonzie, on the series that ran for ten years. The spin-off series, 'Lavern & Shirley,' also set in the era, was slapstick comedy starring Penny Marshall and Cindy Williams that ran on ABC from 1976 until 1983. The theme songs from both of these series were hits in the mid seventies.

While the Bee Gees and ABBA brought a cool disco sound to seventies popular music, new pop singers Barry Manilow, Bette Midler, Helen Reddy, and Linda Ronstadt joined returning rock performers including Elvis Presley (until his death in 1977) on the popularity charts. Tony Bennett continued to perform in the seventies and Frank Sinatra had another big hit recording with the theme from *New York, New York* in 1980 (see chart 12.4). The twenty most popular performers of the seventies were:

#1 Elton John	#8 Neil Diamond	#15 John Denver
#2 Paul McCartney	#9 The Jacksons	#16 Earth, Wind & Fire
#3 Chicago	#10 Stevie Wonder	#17 Aretha Franklin
#4 The Carpenters	#11 Olivia Newton-John	#18 Helen Reddy
#5 James Brown	#12 Diana Ross	#19 Barry Manilow
#6 Elvis Presley	#13 Gladys Knight & the Pips	#20 Marvin Gaye
#7 The Bee Gees	#14 Three Dog Night	

(Whitburn, 1987. p.724)

The fifties were remembered on Broadway in 1972 when 'Grease' premiered with Barry Bostwick as greaser Danny, Carole Demas, as innocent Sandy, and Adrienne Barbeau as Rizzo who originated the show-stopping popular song, *Look at Me I'm Sandra Dee*. A successful film version was released in 1975 starring John Travolta, Olivia Newton-John,

Fifties-style EASY-POP Songs
Recorded in the Seventies and Eighties

Title	Artist	Year released	Highest chart rank
I Have a Dream	ABBA	1979	n/a
Feelings	Morris Albert	1975	#6
(You're) Having My Baby	Paul Anka	1974	#1
Rhinestone Cowboy	Glen Campbell	1975	#1
Close to You & *Top of the World*	The Carpenters	1970 & 1973	#1
Gypsys, Tramps, and Thieves	Cher	1971	#1
It's Impossible	Perry Como	1970	#10
The Candy Man	Sammy Davis, Jr.	1972	#1
Love Grows (Where My Rosemary Goes)	Edison Lighthouse	1970	#5
The Happiest Girl in the Whole USA	Donna Fargo	1972	#11
December, 1963 (Oh, What a Night)	4 Seasons with Frankie Valli	1975	#1
Gone	Joey Heatherton	1972	#24
Brandy	Looking Glass	1972	#1
Looks Like We Made It	Barry Manilow	1977	#1
You Needed Me	Anne Murray	1978	#1
I Can See Clearly Now	Johnny Nash	1972	#1
Garden Party	Ricky Nelson	1972	#6
Daddy Don't You Walk So Fast	Wayne Newton	1972	#4
I Honestly Love You & *Physical*	Olivia Newton-John	1974 & 1981	#1
Happy Days	Pratt & McClain	1976	#5
The Wonder of You	Elvis Presley	1970	#9
I Am Woman	Helen Reddy	1972	#1
Somewhere Out There	Linda Ronstadt & James Ingram	1986	#2
Touch Me in the Morning	Diana Ross	1973	#1
Theme from New York, New York	Frank Sinatra	1980	#32
Everything is Beautiful	Ray Stevens	1970	#1
The Way We Were	Barbra Streisand	1973	#1
(Where Do I Begin) Love Story	Andy Williams	1971	#9

Chart 12.4. Fifties-style EASY-POP Songs Recorded in the 1970s and 80s

and Stockard Channing. John Travolta and Olivia Newton-John had a number #1 hit with *You're the One that I Want* and a #5 hit with *Summer Nights* both singles released from the 'Grease' movie soundtrack.

Changing Times and Changing Music

As the twentieth century ended, the fun and innocence that typified the EASY-POP music of the fifties evaporated as the pace of society and popular music accelerated. The media celebrates speed and a frenetic pace as a virtue and rarely encourages reflection and satisfaction. Performers are more hyperactive and intense. Computers, cell phones, and instant messaging make us impatient. Some days, when it seems that there is little time for relaxation, appreciation, and happiness, it makes the subtle imagery and the EASY-POP music of the halcyon fifties seem alluring.

A Fifties EASY-POP Music Story

In 1952, Breese, Illinois, was a small coal mining and farming town of 2,500 people in Clinton County, 25 miles east of the Mississippi River and St. Louis, Missouri. Robert Berndsen was a 45-year-old coal miner and father of two sons and four daughters. He was sitting in his rocking chair in their front room listening to his favorite AM radio station KWK with his teen-age daughter Rita Ann. KWK was a popular St. Louis radio station that played the most requested adult POP hit songs of the day. On this day, they were listening to the radio together to hear the same song, the Doris Day hit, *A Guy is a Guy*. It was the favorite song for both of them.

What are the odds today that a father and his teenager would choose the same recording as their favorite song or even spend their time listening to the same radio station? That is the fifty-year-old memory of my father-in-law and his daughter, my wife, that provided me with the inspiration for this book.

References from Chapter 12:
Whitburn, Joel. *Top Pop Singles 1955-1986.* New York: Billboard Books, 1987.

It must be remembered that there is nothing more difficult to plan, more doubtful of success, nor more dangerous to manage than the creation of a new system. For the initiator has the enmity of all who would profit by the preservation of the old institutions and merely lukewarm defenders in those who would gain by the new ones.

Machiavelli's *The Prince* (1513)

References

Barnes, Ken. *Twenty Years of Pop*. Kenneth Mason Publications Ltd: London, 1973.

Bloom, Ken. *The American Songbook: The Singers, The Songwriters, and The Songs*. New York: Black Dog & Leventhal Publishers, 2005.

Bogdanov, Vladimir, Chris Woodstra, and Stephen Thomas Erlewine. *All Music Guide: The Definitive Guide to Popular Music*. Fourth Edition. Backbeat Books, 2001.

Bordman, Gerald. *American Musical Theater*. Second Edition. New York: Oxford University Press, 1992.

Brooks, Elston. *I've Heard Those Songs Before: The Weekly Top Ten Tunes*. New York: Quill, 1981

Brooks, Tim and Earle Marsh. *The Complete Directory to Prime Time Network and Cable TV Shows*. New York: Ballantine Books, 1995.

Clark, Donald. *Penguin Encyclopedia of Popular Music*. London: Viking Penguin Group, 1989

Cooper, B. Lee. *Popular Music Perspectives: Ideas, Themes, and Patterns in Contemporary Lyrics*. Bowling Green, Ohio: Bowling Green State University Popular Press, 1991.

Croteau, David and William Hoynes. *The Business of Media*. Thousand Oaks, California: Pine Forge Press, 2001

Denisoff, R. Surge. "Death Songs and Teenage Roles" in *Sing a Song of Social Significance* (Bowling Green, Ohio: Bowling Green State University Press, 1972), pp. 171-176.

Denisoff, R. Surge. "Teen Angel: Resistance, Rebellion, and Death—Revisited," *Journal of Popular Culture,* XVI (Spring 1983), pp. 116-122.

Dorough, Prince. *Popular Music Culture in America.* New York: Ardsley House Publishers, Inc., 1992.

Ewen, David. *The Life and Death of Tin Pan Alley.* New York: Funk and Wagnalls, 1964.

Gammond, Peter. *The Oxford Companion to Popular Music.* New York: Oxford University Press, 1991.

Gammond, Peter and Peter Clayton. *Dictionary of Popular Music.* New York: Philosophical Library, Inc, 1961.

Gillett, Charlie. *The Sound of the City – The Rise of Rock 'n' Roll.* New York: Dell Publishing, 1970.

Gordon, Lois and Alan Gordon. *The Columbia Chronicles of American Life 1910-1992.* New York: Columbia University Press, 1995.

Gronow, Pekka and Ilpo Saunio (translated by Christopher Moseley). *An International History of the Recording Industry.* London: Cassell, 1998.

Halberstam, David. *The Fifties.* New York: Random House Publishing Group, 1993.

Hamm, Charles. *Yesterdays: Popular Song in America.* New York: Norton, 1979.

Harris, James F. *Philosophy at 33 $^1/_3$ rpm – Themes of Classic Rock Music.* Chicago: Open Court Publishing, 1993.

Hirschhorn, Clive. *The Hollywood Musical.* New York: Crown Publishers Inc., 1981.

Iger, Arthur, L. *Music of the Golden Age, 1900-1950 and Beyond – A Guide to Popular Composers and Lyricists.* Westport, Conn: Greenwood Press, 1998.

Jacobs, Dick and Harriet Jacobs. *Who Wrote That Song.* Cincinnati, OH: Writer's Digest, 1994

Larkin, Colin. *The Virgin Encyclopedia of 50s Music.* London: Virgin Books Ltd, 2002.

Leeds, Jeff. "Squeezing Money From the Music." *The New York Times*, December 11, 2006, pp. C1-C5.

Lissauer, Robert. *Lissauer's Encyclopedia of Popular Music in America*. New York: Paragon House, 1991.

Marsh, Dave and Steve Propes. *Merry Christmas, Baby: Holiday Music from Bing to Sting*. New York: Little, Brown and Company, 1993.

Mattfeld, Julius. *Variety Music Cavalcade*. Englewood Cliffs, NJ: Prentice Hall, 1971.

McNeil, Alex. *Total Television*. New York: Viking Penguin Inc., 1984.

Menendez, Albert and Shirley Menendez. *Christmas Songs Made in America*. Nashville, Tennessee: Cumberland House Publishing, 1999.

O'Neil, Thomas. *The Emmys*. New York: Berkley Publishing Group, 1998.

Otfinoski, Steve. *The Golden Age of Novelty Songs*. New York: Billboard Books, 2000.

Princeton Language Institute. *21st Century Dictionary of Quotations*. New York: Dell Publishing Company, 1993.

Sackett, Susan. *The Hollywood Reporter Book of Box Office Hits*. New York: Billboard Books, 1990.

Scheurer, Timothy. *Born in the U.S.A. The Myth of America in Popular Music from Colonial Times to the Present*. Jackson, MS: University Press of Mississippi, 1991.

Schicke, Charles A. *Revolution in Sound – A Biography of the Recording Industry*. Boston: Little, Brown and Company, 1974.

Shapiro, Nat. *An Encyclopedia of Quotations About Music*. Garden City, New York: Doubleday and Company, 1978.

Simon, William, editor. *The Reader's Digest Merry Christmas Songbook*. Pleasantville, New York: The Reader's Digest Association, 1981.

Tyler, Don. *Hit Parade*. New York: Quill, 1985.

Whitburn, Joel. *Billboard Book of Top 40 Hits*. Seventh Edition. New York: Billboard Books, 2000.

Whitburn, Joel. *Christmas in the Charts, 1920-2004*. Cincinnati, Ohio: Billboard Books, 2004.

Whitburn, Joel. *Top Pop Albums 1955-1996*. New York: Billboard Books, 1996.

Whitburn, Joel. *Top Pop Singles 1955-1986*. New York: Billboard Books, 1987.

Whitburn, Joel. *Pop Hits, Singles & Albums 1940-1954*. New York: Billboard Books, 2002.

Whitburn, Joel. *Pop Memories 1890-1954*. Menomonee Falls, Wisconsin: Record Research Inc., 1986.

Whitcomb, Ian. *After the Ball*. London: Allen Lane the Penguin Press, 1972.

Wiley, Mason, and Damien Bona. *Inside Oscar*. New York: Ballantine Books, 1987.

Web sites:

http://www.deadoraliveinfo.com

http://www.musicals101.com

http://home.earthlink.net/~jaymar41/ietitle.html
        (World of Marion-Net E-zines: The Interlude Era)

http://www.vghf.org (Vocal group hall of fame website)

Technology is moving us forward to our past, back toward a time when images and sounds were the dominant forms of human communication. We are visual beings. Our perceptions of the world are overwhelmingly visual. We think and dream in pictures. We replay and re-create life visually in our heads. Even when we read, we transform the words into mental pictures.

Robert Lindstrom, *Presentations* Magazine (June 2000)

Index of EASY-POP Recording Artists

The years immediately preceding the emergence of rock 'n' roll were dominated by the Tin Pan Alley – Hollywood - Broadway Style.

Charles Hamm in *Yesterdays* (1979)

Index of EASY-POP Songs recorded in the 50s

(also includes fifties-style EASY-POP songs recorded in the 1940s, 1960s, and 1970s noted with asterisks)

* song recorded in the 1940s.
** song recorded in the 1960s.
***song recorded in the 1970s.

Statistics are no substitute for judgment.

Henry Clay

Index

for additional information visit   www. 50sMusic.com
or contact the author at   Daniel.Niemeyer@Colorado.edu

Lightning Source UK Ltd.
Milton Keynes UK
27 January 2010

149183UK00001B/267/P